Scarecrow Studies in Young Adult Literature
Series Editor: Patty Campbell

Scarecrow Studies in Young Adult Literature is intended to continue the body of critical writing established in Twayne's Young Adult Authors Series and to expand it beyond single-author studies to explorations of genres, multicultural writing, and controversial issues in young adult (YA) reading. Many of the contributing authors of the series are among the leading scholars and critics of adolescent literature, and some are YA novelists themselves.

The series is shaped by its editor, Patty Campbell, who is a renowned authority in the field, with a thirty-year background as critic, lecturer, librarian, and teacher of YA literature. Patty Campbell was the 2001 winner of the ALAN Award, given by the Assembly on Literature for Adolescents of the National Council of Teachers of English for distinguished contribution to YA literature. In 1989 she was the winner of the American Library Association's Grolier Award for distinguished service to young adults and reading.

1. *What's So Scary about R. L. Stine?* by Patrick Jones, 1998.
2. *Ann Rinaldi: Historian and Storyteller*, by Jeanne M. McGlinn, 2000.
3. *Norma Fox Mazer: A Writer's World*, by Arthea J. S. Reed, 2000.
4. *Exploding the Myths: The Truth about Teens and Reading*, by Marc Aronson, 2001.
5. *The Agony and the Eggplant: Daniel Pinkwater's Heroic Struggles in the Name of YA Literature*, by Walter Hogan, 2001.
6. *Caroline Cooney: Faith and Fiction*, by Pamela Sissi Carroll, 2001.
7. *Declarations of Independence: Empowered Girls in Young Adult Literature, 1990–2001*, by Joanne Brown and Nancy St. Clair, 2002.
8. *Lost Masterworks of Young Adult Literature*, by Connie S. Zitlow, 2002.
9. *Beyond the Pale: New Essays for a New Era*, by Marc Aronson, 2003.
10. *Orson Scott Card: Writer of the Terrible Choice*, by Edith S. Tyson, 2003.
11. *Jacqueline Woodson: "The Real Thing,"* by Lois Thomas Stover, 2003.
12. *Virginia Euwer Wolff: Capturing the Music of Young Voices*, by Suzanne Elizabeth Reid, 2003.
13. *More Than a Game: Sports Literature for Young Adults*, Chris Crowe, 2004.

Richard Peck

The Past Is Paramount

Donald R. Gallo
Wendy J. Glenn

Scarecrow Studies in Young Adult Literature, No. 29

The Scarecrow Press, Inc.
Lanham, Maryland • Toronto • Plymouth, UK
2009

SCARECROW PRESS, INC.

Published in the United States of America
by Scarecrow Press, Inc.
A wholly owned subsidiary of
The Rowman & Littlefield Publishing Group, Inc.
4501 Forbes Boulevard, Suite 200, Lanham, Maryland 20706
www.scarecrowpress.com

Estover Road
Plymouth PL6 7PY
United Kingdom

Copyright © 2009 by Donald R. Gallo and Wendy J. Glenn

Portions of this book are based on an earlier work by Donald Gallo, *Presenting Richard Peck*, Twayne Publishers, 1989.

British Library Cataloguing in Publication Information Available

Library of Congress Cataloging-in-Publication Data

Gallo, Donald R.
  Richard Peck : the past is paramount / Donald R. Gallo, Wendy J. Glenn.
    p.   cm.—(Scarecrow studies in young adult literature ; no. 29)
  Includes bibliographical references and index.
  ISBN-13: 978-0-8108-5848-0 (alk. paper)
  ISBN-10: 0-8108-5848-7 (alk. paper)
    1. Peck, Richard, 1934–Criticism and interpretation.   2. Young adult
  literature, American–History and criticism.   I. Glenn, Wendy J., 1970–
  II. Title.
  PS3566.E2526Z683   2009
  818'.5409–dc22   2008036524

To our children and grandchildren.
May books inspire you to re-envision the world.

Contents

viii   *Contents*

Preface

$\mathcal{A}$t the time *Presenting Richard Peck* was published in 1989, followed by the updated paperback version in 1993, Richard Peck was considered one of the nation's most famous writers of novels for young people. Not long after that book was published, Peck's talents earned him even greater awards—including a Newbery Medal and the Margaret A. Edwards Award. Those, along with more than a dozen new books and other writings, made that text an antique. Just as well-constructed antiques retain and sometimes exceed their original value, most of the information in *Presenting Richard Peck* remains true and valid today. But the focus of Peck's work has shifted in the fifteen years since the publication of *Bel-Air Bambi and the Mall Rats*, and so much more has been written by and about Richard Peck that a new critical analysis begged to be written.

When series editor Patty Campbell asked me, as the author of the original Peck book, to write a new one about this distinguished author, I could not refuse. But I also knew I was committed to too many other projects to spend the time on the research such a book requires. So I suggested that we find someone to coauthor this book—someone experienced and knowledgeable about Richard Peck's writings. Someone, moreover, who would be willing to do the heavy lifting on the project while I supervised, made suggestions, provided bits and pieces, and edited as we went along. Dr. Wendy Glenn, from the University of Connecticut, was the perfect choice for the job.

After an exchange of ideas regarding our vision for the book and some initial planning around how to proceed, Wendy and I each read everything that Richard Peck had published since 1993 or that had been written about him. Then, using what I had written in the *Presenting* book, Wendy inserted new material and made revisions of the old material, chapter by chapter. I then made additional revisions in the original material as well as in Wendy's additions. As we progressed, I exchanged e-mails with Richard Peck, questioning him about a variety of details to ensure the accuracy of our information. After that, Wendy made a few minor adjustments, and I tweaked it a bit more, and she tweaked, and I tweaked . . . until we both finally said, "Enough!" and moved on. Then, when the resulting manuscript was far too long, we took turns deleting superfluous examples, less significant information, and unnecessary words chapter by chapter.

Whether a line or a paragraph or an entire chapter was written mostly by me or by Wendy Glenn, we tried to edit each other's work to the extent that readers will hear one voice and see one style throughout the text. More importantly, we hope our united voice clearly conveys the messages of the book and illuminates the voice of the book's illustrious subject, the charming, witty, nostalgic, insightful Richard Peck.

—Don Gallo

Acknowledgments

$\mathcal{W}$e can't imagine writing a book like this without the cooperation of the book's subject. And Richard Peck couldn't have been more helpful. While he was at first reticent about his involvement in the volume that preceded this one, he ultimately shared his time, perspectives, and wisdom with grace and good humor, chatting amiably and candidly on two different occasions for a total of more than eleven hours, then responding to numerous letters and phone calls, including one lasting nearly an hour and a half. He also provided copies of hard-to-obtain reviews of his books, two new short stories, the British edition of one of his adult novels, and a previously unpublished poem, then graciously read and critiqued preliminary drafts of three chapters of the manuscript.

When we approached him for information for this book, Richard Peck didn't hesitate for a second, immediately answering our questions via e-mail on several occasions. We are extremely grateful for his generosity. We are also thankful to Richard Peck for granting permission for us to reproduce excerpts from "The Geese" and other lines of poetry in this book.

In addition to the subject of this book, we wish to acknowledge the help of Suzanne Murphy, Paula Heller, and Teresa Roberts from the publicity office of what many years ago was Dell Publishing Company for access to files of reviews of and articles about Richard Peck's earlier novels; staff members in the public libraries of Hartford, West Hartford, Willington, and Simsbury, Connecticut, as well as the Curriculum Lab and the Inter-Library Loan department at Central Connecticut State University and the University of Connecticut Libraries for help in locating obscure sources; Linda Benson for providing hard-to-find *VOYA* reviews of some of Peck's books; Amanda Friedman and Thomas Mariani for their indexing efforts; the providers of numerous Internet sites from which we obtained invaluable information; Louann Reid for her critiques and valuable suggestions on drafts of the earlier edition of this book; and Patty Campbell for her guidance and conscientious editing of the final manuscript.

PERMISSIONS

Sign in bicycle store window excerpted from *Father Figure* © 1978 by Richard Peck. Published by Viking Juvenile. All rights reserved. Used with permission of Sheldon Fogelman Agency, Inc.

Poems from Grandma's trunk excerpted from *A Long Way from Chicago* © 1998 by Richard Peck. Published by Dial Books for Young Readers, a division of Penguin Young Readers Group. All rights reserved. Used with permission of Sheldon Fogelman Agency, Inc.

Poetic lines about boys excerpted from *A Long Way from Chicago* © 1998 by Richard Peck. Published by Dial Books for Young Readers, a division of Penguin Young Readers Group. All rights reserved. Used with permission of Sheldon Fogelman Agency, Inc.

Library rules excerpted from *Here Lies the Librarian* © 2006 by Richard Peck. Published by Dial Books for Young Readers, a division of Penguin Young Readers Group. All rights reserved. Used with permission of Sheldon Fogelman Agency, Inc.

Lines on tombstone excerpted from *Here Lies the Librarian* © 2006 by Richard Peck. Published by Dial Books for Young Readers, a division of Penguin Young Readers Group. All rights reserved. Used with permission of Sheldon Fogelman Agency, Inc.

Sign over schoolhouse door excerpted from *A Year Down Yonder* © 2000 by Richard Peck. Published by Dial Books for Young Readers, a division of Penguin Young Readers Group. All rights reserved. Used with permission of Sheldon Fogelman Agency, Inc.

The Person

$\mathcal{R}$ichard Peck—one of the most well-known and highly respected writers of young adult fiction—is a paradox. He reveres the study of Latin yet writes novels and stories that are unencumbered by difficult vocabulary. As an author, he labors alone yet travels thousands of miles each year to talk with members of his teenage audience. Although he left the teaching profession in 1971, he still sees himself as an educator, speaking regularly to teachers and librarians and teaching a course in young adult literature at Lousiana State University. While he jealously guards his personal privacy, he constantly delves into the feelings and lives of teenagers for insights he can use in his books. He is angry about many things, yet even his most serious novels contain humor. Although his speeches and essays reveal extreme criticism of contemporary teenagers as a group, he is unusually supportive of today's adolescents, striving to enrich their lives through his books and public presentations.

Tall, trim, always neatly dressed, Richard Peck is an intense, tightly wound individual dedicated to his craft. In appearance and behavior, he is a gentleman in the fullest sense of the word: gracious, honorable, independent, and charming. He is also a master of the one-liner, as you will see throughout this book, for no one else can describe his often jaundiced views of schools, books, parents, teenagers, and the world better than he in witty, insightful, sometimes well-rehearsed statements.

CONTRIBUTIONS TO THE FIELD

Richard Peck entered the field of young adult books at the beginning of the modern era, shortly after the publication of S. E. Hinton's *The Out-*

siders, Robert Lipsyte's *The Contender*, and Paul Zindel's *The Pigman*. Since his first published novel, Richard Peck has grown along with the field of young adult books to become one of its top authors, while his writing and speaking have been key influences in sustaining and advancing that field. When the Young Adult Services Division of the American Library Association (ALA) published its list of the Best of the Best Books 1970–1982, only two of the seventy-five authors had more than two books on that list: Richard Peck and Ursula K. LeGuin had three titles each.[1] Two of his novels appear on ALA's Best Books for Young Adults 1966–1986 list,[2] and one remains on the 1966–1992 list, even with a change in procedure that limits the number of times any one author is likely to be named.[3] In a 1988 survey of leaders in the Assembly on Literature for Adolescents of the National Council of Teachers of English (ALAN) to determine the hundred most important authors of novels for teenagers, Richard Peck received more votes than anyone except S. E. Hinton and Paul Zindel.[4] And that was before his most highly honored books (e.g., *A Year Down Yonder* and *The River between Us*) were published.

All told, fourteen of his thirty novels have been named ALA Best Books for Young Adults; all but two books he has written for young adults since 1995 have made their way onto this list. And between 1996 and 2006, eight of Richard Peck's ten works of young adult fiction have received the highest ratings for quality (5Q on a scale of 1 to 5) from reviewers in *Voice of Youth Advocates (VOYA)*. While *A Year Down Yonder* received only a 4Q rating, the novel later won that year's Newbery Medal, an honor awarded annually by the ALA for the most distinguished American children's book of the year.

The ultimate honor was bestowed jointly by *School Library Journal* and the ALA in June 1990 when members named Richard Peck the recipient of their Margaret A. Edwards Award. This distinction, awarded previously only to S. E. Hinton, is given in recognition of authors "whose book or books have provided young adults with a window through which they can view the world and which will help them to grow and understand themselves and their role in society." Later that year, Peck received the ALAN Award for his outstanding contributions to literature for young adults. The following year, he received the 1991 Medallion from the University of Southern Mississippi, which "honors an author who has made an outstanding contribution to the field of literature.'' In 2001, Peck became the first children's book author to receive the National Humanities Medal and was honored by President George W. Bush for his contribution to literature for young people that "stresses the importance of taking responsibility for one's actions." Most recently, *The River between Us* earned the 2004 Scott O'Dell Award for Historical Fiction, and *The Teacher's Funeral* earned the 2005 Christopher Medal, an award that honors creative works that "affirm the highest values of the human spirit." (See Appendix A for a list of Peck's honors and prizes.)

Although his writing has brought him material comfort and considerable recognition, Richard Peck writes because he feels driven to do so. He sees today's teenagers as lost in a focusless world, manipulated by peer pressure, mesmerized by shallow television programs and mind-numbing video games, unsupervised by parents too busy or too afraid to take charge, at sea in schools with wishy-washy curricula and undemanding administrators. Peck reaches out to those few students who read independently, hoping his messages will be heard once readers are attracted by the entertainment value of his novels. "Writing remains the act of reaching out in the dark, hoping for a hand to hold," he states.[5]

As part of his goal of writing books that feature characters who can serve as companions as well as role models for teenagers, Peck says, "I write for these people whose own parents haven't seen them for days."[6] He doesn't write for students who are leaders of the student council or the captains of athletic teams; instead he aims his books, as he puts it, at students on the edge of the crowd, young people who are capable of acting independently. Most of his lead characters, as well as the young people he believes he writes for, are not team players; "they're lonely, long-distance runners,"[7] characters who tend to be "self-reliant, semi-loner[s], standing at the edge of the action—observing it with a keen ironic eye,"[8] as they gather strength to launch themselves once the novel ends.[9] And, although he has written novels that fit into a variety of topical categories, one theme dominates them all: "YOU WILL NEVER BEGIN TO GROW UP UNTIL YOU START TO ACT AND THINK INDEPENDENTLY OF YOUR PEERS."[10] Each of Peck's young protagonists embarks on a journey "to learn something nobody can learn at home, or at the feet of a peer group leader." This journey "changes its meaning in midstream, like life, so the young characters are changed forever. If there is no change, there is no story."

Peck differs from most of his colleagues in terms of the age at which he began his writing career. Gordon Korman was only fourteen when his first novel was published. S. E. Hinton started publishing her novels as a teenager, as did Amelia Atwater-Rhodes. M. E. Kerr began writing right out of college, although she did not write for young adults until much later in her career. In contrast, Richard Peck did not write a line of fiction until he was thirty-seven years old. "I wonder what would have happened if I had gotten started earlier," he ponders. "I don't begrudge the time getting ready, because I think I needed it."[11] The preparation paid off, for Richard Peck has never written a novel that has failed to sell or attract attention.

Peck differs from his writing colleagues in other ways, too. While many authors spend most of their days writing, Peck spends many days each year traveling to schools and libraries to talk with young people, their teachers, and librarians. He has also written and published in a wider variety of literary forms than most young adult authors; in addition to writing poems, essays, reviews, nonfiction texts, and newspaper pieces, he has published four successful adult novels and a picture book for children and compiled and edited three poetry anthologies, a short story collection, and two essay collections.

When asked what makes his books better than others available to teenagers today, Peck at first deflects the question, reluctant to compare his work with others. But when asked, "What is your greatest strength as a young adult author?" his answer comes quickly and easily: "The use of research. Not library research. But sitting at home, imagining what it might be like, then going out and seeking what it *is* like," to put into the book "something that will make the reader write back and say, 'How did you know we wore that, or said that, or did that?'"

"On a good day, a very good day," he adds, "I receive a letter from some young reader in a town where I've never been, asking, 'How do you know me? Do you live around here?' I try to."[12]

Critics have been consistent in their praise of Peck's witty and realistic dialogue, as well as his adept plotting and empathy for teenagers' problems. In reviewing *The Dreadful Future of Blossom Culp*, for example, Marilou Sorenson observes: "His descriptions are vivid and succinct, and he spoofs the 'now' generation with their own slang. . . . And the dialogue is sharp and poignant."[13] A *Kirkus* reviewer writing about *Princess*

Ashley lauds Peck for "deftly captur[ing] the evolving concerns of 15-
and 16-year-olds—their speech, anxieties, and shifting relationships with
parents and peers."[14] His "beautifully crafted language, subtle humor and
insight into the teenagers' world" as well as his "finely honed style" are
extolled in a review of *Remembering the Good Times*.[15] And writing of
Princess Ashley in *Voice of Youth Advocates*, Evie Wilson notes the "timely
issues, characters of depth and feeling, and life-like scenarios which stun
the reader with the power of their reality."[16] In his more recently published historical novels, Peck has been praised for his ability to bring the
past into the present, to create characters and stories that bridge the gap
between then and now and allow today's readers to learn from elders
who inhabit worlds both removed from and reminiscent of their own.
In her review of *A Long Way from Chicago*, Hazel Rochman, for example,
notes: "The viewpoint is adult—elderly Joe is looking back now at the
changes he saw in those seven years—but many young people will recognize the irreverent, contrary voices of their own family legends across
generations."[17] In her review of *Here Lies the Librarian*, Connie Tyrrell
Burns calls Peck a "master of capturing voice" and praises his ability to
"aptly convey the nuances of rural life in the early years of the last century while weaving in early feminism, the history of the automobile, and
the message to be oneself."[18]

This is a writer of consistently good books for young people. What
factors have shaped him and influenced his style, focused his attention,
and earned his praise or evoked his condemnation?

FAMILY ROOTS

Although he makes his home in New York City, Richard Peck's roots
are in central Illinois, a place whose influence is evident in many of his
novels and his attitude about what's important in life. Born on 5 April
1934, he grew up in a white frame house on Dennis Avenue next to
Fairview Park in Decatur until he went away to college at the age of
eighteen. Peck characterizes Decatur as "a smug, stratified, endlessly various town that thought it was a city."[19] It was a town "where the Puritan
ethic had gone to die," he says, "a town in a time when teenagers were
considered guilty until proven innocent, which is fair enough."[20]

Located between what they called Little Egypt of southern Illinois and the big city of Chicago to the north, the residents, Peck claims, "came to the logical conclusion that we were the center of the earth."²¹ This midwestern town would later provide Peck with the setting for several of his novels. In *Representing Super Doll* and *Dreamland Lake*, it is called Dunthorpe, with Fairview Park becoming Dreamland Park. In the Blossom Culp novels, Decatur as it was in the early 1900s is called Bluff City. Although he has stepped away from his own hometown in his more recent novels, many of his tales continue to reflect the Midwest of his past: *A Long Way from Chicago* and *A Year Down Yonder* are set in his father's hometown, *The River between Us* in a small town in Illinois, and *The Teacher's Funeral* and *Here Lies the Librarian* in rural Indiana.

Unlike many children today who come from single-parent families or homes where they receive little attention or supervision from adults, Peck was surrounded by a loving, caring extended family, including his maternal grandmother, Flossie Mae Gray, and her four sisters, Pearl, Lura, Maude, and Ozena, all with roots in the rich farmland of the Midwest. His great-grandfather, William Gray, was an Irish immigrant who acquired a farm in western Illinois in 1852 that he passed down to his son, John, who farmed it until 1964. That prosperous Walnut Grove Farm, Peck recalls fondly, contained "a fine, high house with long, deep porches standing in a vast lawn of enormous trees and mounded flower beds. The views ran to the level line of the horizon. . . . The weedless garden rows ran straight as a die from the fence line, burdened with bounty."²² This same house provided the setting for his children's book *Monster Night at Grandma's House*.

His mother, Virginia Gray, had trained as a dietician and made an art of home cooking. From his growing-up years during World War II, Peck recalls his father bringing home the products of his hunting and fishing trips: pheasants, catfish, and croppie. Live chickens from his grandparents' farm were dispatched in the backyard as needed, an act Peck re-created vividly in the opening scene of *Representing Super Doll*. When meat was rationed, calves and hogs that had been raised on the farms of the Pecks' rural relatives provided ample reserves for Richard's family.

Wayne M. Peck, Richard's father, was raised on an Illinois farm. During Wayne Peck's teenage years, he dropped out of school and hopped freight trains to the Dakotas, where he joined in the wheat harvest, a dream shared by Russell Culver, the antsy fifteen-year-old protagonist in *The Teacher's Funeral*. When the First World War raged in Europe, Peck's father went off to fight in France, returning partially disabled with a shattered left shoulder. Back home, he was displeased to find that life had changed, and so he often reminisced about his youth. Peck strives to preserve some of his father's tales in *On the Wings of Heroes*, a story of a boy living during World War II as the son of a father wounded in World War I. According to Peck, "this is as nearly autobiographical as I've ever come, consciously, and I wanted to get something of my dad down on paper while I could. And so if ever a person I knew personally translated into any of my books, here he is." From his father, then, Richard Peck "learned nostalgia as an art form." As a result of these stories, young Richard came to believe that "if you didn't grow up on a farm, you wouldn't have had a childhood." And so Richard Peck, growing up in town, believed that he had been "born after the party was over." Peck allowed himself to reimagine and experience vicariously, at least, the rural childhood of his dreams by creating thirteen-year-old Rosie Beckett (*Fair Weather*), an Illinois farm girl granted adventure on her journey to the Chicago's World Fair.

Unable to farm, Wayne Peck settled in town, where he ran a Phillips 66 gas station during Richard's youth, the same town in Pliatt County, Illinois, that Grandma Dowdel (of *A Long Way from Chicago* and *A Year Down Yonder* fame) calls home. Her house in the novel is the same house in which Peck's own grandmother lived. While Peck never specifically names Grandma's town, he does name all of the towns around it, real places readers can find on a map. Despite the move to town, Peck's father remained true to his country roots. Instead of wearing a white shirt and driving to work in a Plymouth sedan each day as Richard remembers other fathers doing, his father wore coveralls and roared away on a Harley-Davidson motorcycle.

At his father's gas station, twelve-year-old boys rolled their newspapers, and from them, Richard learned vocabulary beyond his years. He was also privy to the conversations of older men. The gas station, Peck notes, was "like a club where elderly men—old truckers and farmers and railroaders—hung out, telling tales." Their stories were honed "with years of retelling and flavored . . . with tobacco juice."[23] At the Walnut Grove Farm, Richard listened in on stories of his grandparents' and great-aunts' Victorian pasts—"voices from the previous century."[24] At home, he heard the stories of his aunts and uncles, especially of Aunt Rozella, who lived with them for the first fifteen years of Richard's life. From all these people, Richard Peck says he learned style. And the phrasing of his great-aunts later provided him with the voice of Blossom Culp and Grandma Dowdel, a character readers often assume is a re-creation of Peck's grandmother. In response, Peck argues, "When you're a writer, you can give yourself the grandmother you WISH you had."

The most colorful of his relatives was his great-uncle Miles, an octogenarian carpenter "who terrorized the town in a Model A Ford fitted out with a carpentry box where the rumble seat had been." Peck remembers his rogue relative as "the worst snob in a town full of them."[25] He had "married often but not seriously" and had "a keen nose for scandal and inconvenient memories of other people's pasts." Peck explains, "he was as free as I hoped adults could be. Grownups dreaded him; I sopped up his every word."[26] In addition to local history—"for the past and present were a single tapestry in his [great-uncle's] mind"[27]—Richard learned a good deal of creative language from this foulmouthed rascal and later brought him back to life as a major character in *The Ghost Belonged to Me*. He appears, too, in *Fair Weather* as the riotous grandfather leading his grandchildren from one fantastic element of the fair to the next.[28] Dressed in a white suit and carrying a cane, he reminds readers of Peck's other favorite grown-up inspiration, Mark Twain. Thus the voices and stories of these living characters remained in Richard Peck's memory until they began to appear years later as models for fictional characters in his novels. "When you write to young readers, you need the wisdom of those people at the other end of life," Peck believes. "I came to writing with an entire crew of seasoned elders on my side."[29] He also came to writing, and to life in general, with a code of behavior that included "not airing your dirty laundry, living with your reputation, trying to give something in the community, and generally keeping your nose clean."[30]

SCHOOL DAYS

Richard Peck entered kindergarten on the day Hitler's army invaded Poland in 1939. Before he was enrolled in Dennis Grade School, he was already primed for a later literary life, having acquired a love for books in the lap of his mother. Peck maintains, "I fell easy prey to teachers and librarians. . . . My teachers, first and last, betrayed no interest in my ideas." What was important to his teachers, Peck remembers, was "the format of grammar, and later Latin. The symmetry of sentences, the shapes of paragraphs. The sense of words, and their sounds."[31]

The war, Peck notes, suited him quite well. It gave adults plenty to talk about at home, things they didn't all agree on. From those disagreements, Peck says he learned viewpoint, a novelist's stock in trade. In school, discipline became more militaristic. Fascinating new words—such as *blitzkrieg* and *kamikaze*—came to light, and names of foreign places were identified on maps of the world, all of which appealed to young Richard's desire to move beyond the safe streets of Decatur. The real world was out there somewhere; the exciting things were happening someplace else. Decatur wasn't the center of the universe.

An only child until third grade, Richard acquired a sister, Cheryl. Peck says, "I was the typical older kid; she was the typical younger. I conformed; she questioned. I recorded; she rebelled."[32] Richard never rebelled. Recalling his years at Woodrow Wilson Junior High School as a time when students respected and obeyed teachers without question, Richard never went to school without his homework completed. "I did homework out of fear, not goodness," he says. "From junior high on, I thought that the only safe way to a scholarship was a string of As on the report card."

Through his after-school paper route, he learned responsibility. And from Miss Van Dyke—"a small, fierce woman in a black dress"—he learned proper social behavior in her Fortnightly Dancing Class.[33] Peck concludes: "I touched all these bases because from early times I really thought you had a lot of dues to pay before they'd let you into adulthood. For middle-class kids, it was very much that kind of era, but I think I believed it more than most."

In Stephen Decatur High School, with the secret goal of becoming a writer, Richard studied hard, aiming for membership in the National Honor Society and a scholarship so that he could attend a private college. In retrospect, Peck believes that his schooling laid the groundwork for a novelist: "history, Latin, and geography: something to say, how to say it, and somewhere to set the story."[34]

But one serious problem existed for Peck: there were no role models. Young Richard noticed that all of the writers he and his fellow students studied in school were dead, and none had come from central

Illinois. How then could he, Richard, ever hope to be a writer? Then one day during his junior year, his English teacher, Miss Gorham, announced that the sister of Vachel Lindsay, a poet from Illinois, would read his poetry at nearby Millikin University. "I went that night to see what a poet's sister looked like," Peck recalls. Not only did he hear Olive Lindsay Wakefield recite her brother's cadenced poetry, but he also later visited the Lindsay family home where the lonely old sister lived before the house became a museum.[35]

During Richard's high school years, he was invited to visit a distant relative in New York City during the summer of his sixteenth year. Longing to explore other places, "I raked yards and shoveled snow for a chair-car ticket on the Pennsylvania Railroad and was on my way," he remembers. It was a breakthrough experience for him. As he tells it: "It came as quite a relief to me that the outside world was really there and somewhat better than the movies. I began to explore the streets of New York and plumb the depths of the subway system all the way to Coney Island. It occurred to me that this was the place I'd been homesick for all along, this place and London."[36] Fifteen more years would pass before Richard Peck made his way back to New York.

Managing to earn good grades, Richard was inducted into the National Honor Society, proud of his academic success as he entered his senior year. But between Richard and college stood the notorious Miss Franklin; at Stephen Decatur High School, if you were college bound, you took senior English from her. Peck recalls that, on the first day of his senior year, she assured the class, with dramatic emphasis, that she had the power to get them into the colleges of their choice—or keep them out.[37] And he believed her.

Accustomed to receiving As on his English compositions, Richard was surprised to find no grade on the first paper he wrote for Miss Franklin. Instead she had written: "NEVER EXPRESS YOURSELF AGAIN ON MY TIME. FIND A MORE INTERESTING TOPIC." Peck explains what happened next:

> Well, I was seventeen. I didn't know what a more interesting topic than me would be. I actually went to the woman and asked, "What would a more interesting topic be?"
>
> "Almost anything," she replied.
>
> That led me to the library, a place I'd successfully avoided up until

then, in search of subject matter that wasn't me. All these years later, I'm still searching for it. Miss F. taught us that writing isn't self-expression. Writing is communication, and you'd better have your reader far better in mind than yourself. Miss F. didn't teach Creative Writing, of course. She knew the danger of inspiration coming before grammar. She knew that without the framework for sharing, ideas are nothing.

I wasn't slated to write a line of fiction until I was thirty-seven years old, but it was Miss F. who made it possible. In the boot camp atmosphere of her classroom she taught us that the only real writing is rewriting. She taught us that deadlines are meant to be met, not extended. She taught us how to gather material more interesting than ourselves and to pin it on a page.[38]

Those things made all the difference in the world for Richard Peck.

THE COLLEGE EXPERIENCE

Encouraged and supported by his parents and the Rector Scholarship, Richard entered DePauw University in Greencastle, Indiana, during the fall of 1952. He, like many young men at that time, was also motivated by the threat of military service: unless they had a college deferment and remained in the upper half of their college class, all able males over the age of eighteen were likely to be drafted and find themselves in Korea. Discouraged by people who said how difficult it was to make a living writing, and encouraged by the models that his teachers provided, Peck concluded that teaching was the profession that would bring him closest to the written word.[39] So he continued to work hard, planning to be a teacher, even though he really wanted to be a writer.

Richard's junior year of college proved to be his most important one, for he spent it in England. Having always dreamed of distant places, he sailed across the Atlantic "with a tin steamer trunk full of Pat Boone clothes"[40] in the fall of 1954 aboard the *Ile de France*, one of the most distinguished liners of the time. He had raised the money by working as a dishwasher at George Williams College Camp on Lake Geneva, Wisconsin, the previous summer. The *Ile de France*, he explains, was "an ocean going Art Deco fantasy flowing with red wine even in Third Class. But I was drunk enough on the adventure of it all. The ship pitched through the gray waves while we passengers danced the nights away on slanting floors under swaying chandeliers."[41] It's an adventure he repeated from 1986 until 1994 when he worked as a lecturer and teacher of a creative writing seminar on the ships of the Royal Cruiseship Line, a job that took him around the world in the winter of 1991–1992.

In England, he studied both literature and British history at Exeter University in a picturesque medieval town surrounded by rolling farmland punctuated by thatch-roofed houses. At Mardon Hall, Richard acquired three scholarly friends: Henry Woolf, the university's most intelligent student; David Wheatley, who had grown up in Africa and India during the fading days of the British Empire; and Arthur Dark, the son of a retired sailor from Plymouth. He later met and was looked after by the Jones family, who provided him with a second home in the town of Barnstaple near Lorna Doone's Exmoor.[42] In addition to acquiring a taste for tweeds, losing some of his American midwestern accent, and overcoming his previous fear of speaking before a group, Richard Peck was able to explore a country that was later to be the setting for part of three of his young adult novels and two adult novels.

He returned home to focus on education courses during his senior year at DePauw, finding his worldview much expanded in contrast to that of his peers who, Peck claims, "were still talking about the same things they were talking about when I left."[43]

MILITARY SERVICE

Soon after graduation, Peck found himself in the army, which sent him back to Europe. Although he expected the worst, he admits that his two years in the military taught him twice as much as two years in college.[44] At a post just outside Ansbach, West Germany, Peck learned that "if you can type, spell, and improvise in midsentence, you can work in a clean, dry office near a warm stove" instead of being "knee-deep in a moist foxhole staring through barbed wire at an East German soldier who's staring back at you."[45] So he became a company clerk, whose competence with words led him into an unexpected field: ghostwriting sermons for the post's chaplains—"all denominations," Peck is quick to add. Having established himself as a ghostwriter, he was soon enlisted as chaplain's assistant and posted to Stuttgart. Today's army recruiters promise to train enlistees in practical skills such as computer programming or engine repair; in West Germany in the mid-1950s, the army promised Richard Peck nothing but gave him a lot more: it allowed him to hone his writing skills and learn to write for deadlines. In addition, Peck says he probably heard more confessions from his fellow soldiers than the chaplains did.[46] The problems he heard about still turn up in the novels he writes.

During his stint in the army and later while in graduate school, Peck continued to explore the Europe he had first encountered in his junior year abroad. He "hitch-hiked to Rome, slept in trains from Turin to Bruges, and discovered London, inch by literary inch," which led him to the belief that he has passed along to teenagers ever since: "Anyone just about to leave adolescence needs to cut himself out of the pack and be on his own." In addition, Peck was learning another valuable lesson: how to be alone—"the only way a writer can work, whenever he begins to do it in earnest," he says.[47]

GRADUATE SCHOOL EDUCATION

After his release from the army, Richard Peck enrolled in graduate school at Southern Illinois University at Carbondale, where he served as a teaching assistant. His assignment—the first of his teaching career—was to teach writing to freshmen. Expecting to find a group of adolescents who just a few weeks before had been high school seniors, Peck found himself facing a worried group of mature adults in an evening class. "I was never again to know students this vulnerable or this punctual."[48] From that class, he learned the importance of reassuring students that their experiences were valid. And the effort he put into his teaching kept him too busy to think about being a writer.[49]

For his master's thesis, Peck chose to examine Sinclair Lewis's use of European characters and settings to illuminate American life. "It's about what was happening to me when I was coming of age in Europe"—a perfect match between student and subject.

He continued to teach at Southern Illinois as an instructor in English after receiving his master's degree, doing additional graduate work at Washington University in St. Louis. But in the fall of 1961, he returned to his original plan and began teaching English in a public high school, Glenbrook North High School in the affluent Chicago suburb of Northbrook, Illinois. He was not happy with what he found.

A TEACHER (AND WRITER)

Unlike himself as a teenager, Peck found his students to be overindulged, self-centered, unchallenged, and rootless. They "were strongly armored with adolescent façades, peer-group allegiance, hair spray, and family money. . . . Every parent expected college entrance for his child. If there was an alternative, it was unthinkable."[50] His opinion of suburban teens has not changed to this day. But those adolescents, it turns out, provided Richard Peck with his first glimpse of the audience for whom he would eventually write best-selling novels. Glenbrook North High School itself later provided the setting for his tenth novel for young adults, *Close Enough to Touch*. But Richard Peck wasn't ready to be a writer yet. The New York publishing world was still two steps away.

After two years in Northbrook, he found employment as a textbook editor for Scott, Foresman and Company in Chicago. During his two years there, he and a college fraternity friend, Norman Strasma, wrote a lively guide to Chicago nightlife called *Old Town, A Complete Guide: Strolling, Shopping, Supping, Sipping*, which they published themselves in 1965. Although Peck dismisses it as a book of little consequence, it was his first significant published work.

NEW YORK, NEW YORK

Peck's long-standing dream of living in New York City came to fruition when he applied for and received a job teaching English and education courses at Hunter College and its laboratory school, Hunter College High School, in 1965. It was a school for academically gifted girls, located on New York City's Park Avenue. He was thirty-two years old.

Peck writes: "On the way to the first class my knees wobbled a little as they hadn't done for years. I wondered what I had to offer young geniuses flourishing in the rich cultural concrete of this world capital." It was a time of urban renewal of blighted city neighborhoods and of protests in the streets against American involvement in Vietnam. At Hunter, "there was talk of consciousness-raising in the faculty lounge. And among the students there had been Proust before puberty." Although the acceptance of paperbacks in the classroom had expanded the possibilities of the literature program, the faculty had just thrown out *To Kill a Mock-*

ingbird because of its "white bourgeois values." In spite of this being the city of his dreams, the school "seemed too narrow a universe for me," Peck concluded.[51]

But one chance experience changed everything for the young man from rural Illinois. It was, he says, "the one scene out of my life that was a movie." At the first faculty meeting of the year, an experienced colleague, Ned Hoopes, invited Peck to "do a book" with him and gave Peck the choice of material. Within a year after arriving in the East, Richard Peck had broken into the New York publishing world with *Edge of Awareness: Twenty-Five Contemporary Essays.* "I got $730 for it, which was almost two months' pay then," he recalls. The book has since sold millions of copies.

That first publishing experience did several things for Richard Peck. "It let me know that I was living in the same town with publishers, which I had never done before." It also enabled him to meet people in the publishing business, the most important of whom was George M. Nicholson, then a young editor, who later became a leading figure in the business of publishing books for children and young adults. Except for his three adult books, Richard Peck published all of his books under Nicholson's guidance through 1992. The relationship was mutually advantageous from the start: publishers were just beginning to expand their paperback lines and to look for ideas and materials that would help classroom teachers break away from the standard textbook anthologies; Richard Peck was a classroom teacher. "I learned that a teacher knew some things that publishers didn't. Well, I thought publishers knew everything! They asked: 'Would this work in the classroom?' and I said, 'This worked for me, and this is how I used it.' And they'd say, 'Well, fine.'" Because of the success of *Edge of Awareness*, the publishers commissioned Peck to compile a collection of contemporary poems for high school classes.

Meanwhile, the frustrations Peck had experienced in teaching students in suburban Illinois were even more extreme when he attempted to teach "gifted" New York City teenagers who, in Peck's judgment, felt they had nothing to learn. Nevertheless, he was an inventive, inspired teacher, doing everything he could to get students involved. Nancy Gallt, a former student who later became employed by a major publisher of books for young adults, remembers Peck as "a very good teacher" who was knowledgeable, committed, well prepared, and very funny though sometimes sarcastic. Although she recalls him as being somewhat formal (he called everyone "Miss—"), her most vivid memory of her eighth-grade English class is of Richard Peck standing on a desk to recite Mark Antony's fiery funeral oration from *Julius Caesar*. While Peck believed his students were indifferent to education, his students felt they just were interested in different things than he was. As Nancy explains, "He put a premium on quality literature when people were doing free-floating things." Moreover, it was a time when much was going on outside school. Organized protests were in style at the time, and students often were drawn to important issues beyond the classroom walls.[52] Traditional education in the classroom suffered, Peck believed, saying, "My teaching ground to a halt in this school. The place descended in those years from smugness to chaos, maybe not unlike many others but with melodramatic New York flourishes. Everything became optional, spearheaded by peace marches which spelled the effective end of attendance requirements. I was legally responsible for students I'd never met. Who in liberal New York dared keep a student from following her conscience and the crowd?"[53]

Peck found a small outlet for his frustrations in writing two poems about students, the first of which was published in *Saturday Review* in 1969. Entitled "Nancy," it characterizes a wealthy, smug, but vulnerable female student challenging the teacher, who, in spite of repeated attacks about the irrelevance of his teaching, remains sympathetic. The second poem, "Early Admission," written in 1971 but never published, is in the form of a letter recommending a student "To the College of Your Choice."

During these years, he also composed a series of writing activities that were published as part of the *Open Court Correlated Language Arts Program* textbook in 1967.

Receiving tenure at Hunter but longing to have a more effective voice in the educational world, Peck applied for and was granted a one-year Harold L. Clapp Fellowship, which gave him the title of assistant director of the Council for Basic Education in Washington, D.C. Expecting it to be a year off, Peck packed his bags. "I thought: I'll go to Washington; I can sit down; I won't have to do lesson plans."

The Council for Basic Education was then a small, privately funded organization that monitored and evaluateed educational innovations, focusing on English education. As Peck puts it:

They decided to give a fellowship to a working classroom teacher who could write. . . . When I got there they said: "The year is yours. If you want to sit around and read educational materials, you may do so. If you want to work up a project, you can do that. If you want to help us with our publications and our monthly newsletter, come on in and do that." And that's what I wanted to do: I wanted to write. . . .

I could write an article and take it into the next room; the editor was sitting in there and he'd say, "Yes, yes, no, no, change that . . ." and I began to see how to write a newsletter.

By the time he returned to the classroom in New York City, he was convinced that he needed to try to be a writer. He taught at Hunter for one more semester and turned in his grade book on 24 May 1971. "You always remember the day you turned in your tenure," he says.

Because of his contacts with publishers, Peck had already published other works in addition to his first essay anthology before he left teaching. The poetry anthology he had been compiling was published in 1970 as *Sounds and Silences: Poetry for Now*. In that collection, among the work of other contemporary poets, he included one of his own poems, "The Geese." In 1971, his second poetry anthology, *Mindscapes*, was published. In it, he included two more of his own poems, "Mission Uncontrolled" and "Jump Shot." "Jump Shot," about basketball, and "TKO," about boxing, were printed that same year in an anthology titled *Sports Poems*, edited by R. R. Knudson and P. K. Ebert. Another of his poems, "Street Trio," was published in the *Saturday Review* that same year, and two articles about education appeared in magazines addressed to parents: "Can Students Evaluate Their Education?" and "We Can Save Our Schools." He had not yet tried to write fiction, though he says with a straight face that his first fictional work was his attendance book at Hunter.

Had he taught other kinds of students in a different kind of school, Richard Peck might never have become a novelist. "If I had been teaching in the Middle West where my friends were," he says, "I would have ridden out the storm. Had I stayed in the Midwest, I also wouldn't have made personal contact with the publishers . . . and I wouldn't have known what's up." His teaching career had been filled with disappointments. He saw school curricula deteriorating, standards collapsing. Parents at home had lost or given up control of their children.

Peck recalls one girl who believed she was too gifted to type, another who felt she was so talented that she didn't need to do library research. Teenagers, he concluded, had established "a country of themselves."

But he has never been bitter, has always tried to look beyond the symptoms and the problems. "I tried to see through their defenses to themselves, huddled inside," he says.[54] But it was useless. He was never able to teach as he remembered being taught. And in the end, he says, "It seemed to me that teaching had begun to turn into something that looked weirdly like psychiatric social work—a field in which I was not trained or interested."[55]

Although Richard Peck felt he had not taught his students very much, he knew his students had provided him with almost all of the material he needed to get started as a young adult novelist. First, he had an insider's view of how teenagers behaved, dressed, talked, and interacted as well as what they valued. Second, he had learned what young people like and want in a book. As Peck tells it, "They taught me that a novel must entertain first before it can be anything else. I learned that there is no such thing as a 'grade reading level'; a young person's 'reading level' and attention span will rise and fall according to his degree of interest. I learned that if you do not have a happy ending for the young, you had better do some fast talking."[56]

Peck also knew he wasn't writing for all students. He explains: "As a teacher, I'd already learned that you can only teach those who are willing to be taught. I'd learned too, that the best, most independent, most promising students were the thoughtful, quiet ones—students who will reach for a book in search of themselves—who often get overlooked in our crisis-oriented society and the schools that mirror it."[57] And so he carried his typewriter into the garden of his Brooklyn home and began "writing a novel to some of the young people . . . left behind in the classroom."[58]

It was a courageous act. Most contemporary young adult novelists began writing fiction while they still had financial support from other jobs or working spouses. But Richard Peck was unmarried and, at the age of thirty-seven, gave up his teaching income along with his group medical insurance and retirement plan, determined to make it as a writer on his own. Even more risky was the fact that he had no experience writing fiction. He told one interviewer: "When I was doing that first book, I never went out of the house for fear of spending money."[59] But it was, he says, the only time in his life that he didn't worry about the future. "I didn't dare. I just thought about now. I didn't even worry about what I was going to do to make a living if this didn't work." In his autobiography, *Anonymously Yours*, he explains: "In those first quiet months, I learned that the only way you can write is by the light of the bridges burning behind you."[60]

A WRITER (AND TEACHER)

Many authors, whether writing fiction for adults or young adults, write from their personal experiences—especially in their first novel. Richard Peck maintains that he never consciously wrote anything autobiographical until his recent *On the Wings of Heroes*. "My past is my own," he states. "I grew up in an age now grown mythic, an age of debating teams and draft cards and diagrammed sentences and dance programs. It's an old story, and my readers don't believe it."[61] When young readers ask if any of his characters are drawn from his own life, Peck responds, "I don't think you'd want to read a story about a boy who did as much homework as I did."[62] He adds, "I was always more interested in other people's lives than in mine, right from the beginning." So, for his ideas and inspiration, he depends on the ideas and experiences of others, especially those of kids.

Peck finished writing his first novel, based in part on experiences his friends, Jean and Richard Hughes, had had in providing a home for unwed teenage mothers, in a little more than four months. In spite of all he had heard about the difficulty of finding someone to publish one's first novel, Peck neatly piled his manuscript of *Don't Look and It Won't Hurt* into a small box and hand delivered it to George Nicholson, then editor in chief of juvenile books at Holt, Rinehart and Winston. On the following day, Peck's phone rang, and George Nicholson said: "You can start your second novel." That first novel sold more than a half million copies during its first ten years in print.[63]

To further support himself during 1972 and 1973, he wrote occasional pieces on travel, local history, and the architecture of historical neighborhoods for the *New York Times* and published articles in *Saturday Review*, *House Beautiful*, and *American Libraries*, along with a poem in the *Chicago Tribune*. A book begun earlier with Mortimer Smith and George

Weber at the Council for Basic Education—*A Consumer's Guide to Educational Innovations*—was also released in 1972.

But writing novels for young adults was Peck's main interest. In quick succession, he wrote *Dreamland Lake* and *Through a Brief Darkness*, both published in 1973. To date, Richard Peck has produced at least one young adult novel almost every year of his writing career. In a year when a young adult novel was not published, more often than not Peck produced a novel for adults, a collection of poems, or a nonfiction text for teachers instead.

Although the writings resulting from Peck's last twenty years as an author have focused more exclusively on young adult novels, he has also found time to educate teachers with his memoir/social commentary/writing manual *Love and Death at the Mall: Teaching and Writing for the Literate Young* (1994), a well-regarded text revised and reissued under the title *Invitations to the World: Teaching and Writing for the Young* (2002).

What Peck does best, however, is write for young people. Since 1995, he has published eleven new titles for young adult readers, ranging in scope from the political (*The Last Safe Place on Earth*, 1995) and social (*Strays like Us*, 1998) to the technological (*Lost in Cyberspace*, 1995 and *The Great Interactive Dream Machine*, 1996) and historical, currently Peck's favorite form of writing. Despite his prolific career, Peck remains ever humble, asserting, "I've just kept going, hoping to have the next book accepted before the last book can be reviewed."[64]

NOTES

1. "Best of the Best Books 1970–1982," *Booklist*, 15 October 1983, 351–54.

2. *Nothin' but the Best: Best of the Best Books for Young Adults 1966–1986* (Chicago: American Library Association, 1988). See also *Booklist*, 15 October 1988, 403.

3. Betty Carter, "Best of the Best: Twenty-Five Years of Best Books for Young Adults," *ALAN Review* (Fall 1994): 67–69.

4. Donald R. Gallo, "Who Are the Most Important YA Authors?" *ALAN Review* (Spring 1989): 18–20.

5. Richard Peck, in Viking Press publicity brochure, n.d.

6. Richard Peck, Speech presented at the Children's Book Council/American Booksellers Association meeting, New Orleans, 24 May 1986. Also printed as "Young Adult Books" in *Horn Book* (September–October 1986): 619.

7. Richard Peck, Speech presented at the Children's Literature Festival, University of Southern Mississippi, Hattiesburg, 19 March 1981.

8. Lou Willett Stanek, "Just Listening: Interviews with Six Adolescent Novelists: Patricia McKillip, Robert Cormier, Norma Klein, Richard Peck, S. E. Hinton, Judy Blume," *Arizona English Bulletin* (April 1976): 32.

9. Peck, Children's Literature Festival, University of Southern Mississippi.

10. Peck, Children's Literature Festival, University of Southern Mississippi.

11. All quotations of Richard Peck's statements throughout this book that are not attributed to a specific published source come from Don Gallo's personal interviews with him that took place in his New York City apartment in early June and late December 1987 and over the telephone on 19 January 1993 or from our more recent letters and e-mail correspondence with him.

12. "Richard Peck," *Fifth Book of Junior Authors* (New York: H.W. Wilson, 1983). See also "EPA's Top 100 Authors," Educational Paperback Association, www.edu paperback.org.

13. Marilou Sorenson, *Deseret News*, 29 January 1984.

14. *Kirkus*, 1 May 1987, 724.

15. Cynthia K Leibold, *School Library Journal* (April 1985): 9.

16. Evie Wilson, *Voice of Youth Advocates* (June 1987): 82.

17. Hazel Rochman, *Booklist*, 1 September 1998, 113.

18. Connie Tyrrell Burns, *School Library Journal*, 1 April 2006, 146.

19. Richard Peck, "A Writer from Illinois," *Illinois Libraries* (June 1986): 392.

20. Richard Peck, "Love Is Not Enough," *School Library Journal* (September 1990): 153.

21. Peck, "A Writer from Illinois," 393.

22. Richard Peck, in *Something about the Author Autobiography Series*, vol. 2, ed. Adele Sarkissian (Detroit: Gale Research, 1985), 178.

23. Peck, *Something about the Author Autobiography Series*, vol. 2:177.

24. Peck, *Something about the Author Autobiography Series*, vol. 2:178.

25. Peck, "A Writer from Illinois," 393.

26. Richard Peck, "The Invention of Adolescence and Other Thoughts on Youth," *Top of the News* (Winter 1983): 182.

27. Peck, "A Writer from Illinois," 393.

28. Nancy Gilson, "Seeding the Suburban Desert: Author's Books Tug at the Blinders Worn by American Teen-Agers," *Columbus Dispatch*, 20 September 2001, 08G.

29. Peck, *Something about the Author Autobiography Series*, vol. 2:178.

30. Roger Sutton, "A Conversation with Richard Peck," *School Library Journal* (June 1990): 38.

31. Peck, "The Invention of Adolescence," 183.

32. Peck, "The Invention of Adolescence," 183.

33. Richard Peck, *Anonymously Yours* (New York: Julian Messner, 1991), 7.

34. Richard Peck in *Speaking for Ourselves*, ed. Donald R. Gallo (Urbana, IL: National Council of Teachers of English, 1990), 165.

35. Peck, "A Writer from Illinois," 394.

36. Peck, "A Writer from Illinois," 394.

37. Peck, *Something about the Author Autobiography Series*, vol. 2:180.

38. Peck, *Something about the Author Autobiography Series*, vol. 2:181.

39. Peck, *Something about the Author Autobiography Series*, vol. 2:181.

40. Peck, *Anonymously Yours*, 2.

41. Peck, *Something about the Author Autobiography Series*, vol. 2:181.

42. Peck, *Something about the Author Autobiography Series*, vol. 2:182.

43. Jennifer M. Brown, "A Long Way from Decatur," *Publishers Weekly*, July 21, 2003, 170.

44. Peck, *Anonymously Yours*, 79.

45. Peck, Viking Press publicity brochure.

46. Peck, *Something about the Author Autobiography Series*, vol. 2:183.

47. Peck, Viking Press publicity brochure.

48. Richard Peck, "Coming Full Circle: From Lesson Plans to Young Adult Novels," *Horn Book* (April 1985): 209.

49. Peck, *Something about the Author Autobiography Series*, vol. 2:183.

50. Peck, "Coming Full Circle," 210.

51. Peck, "Coming Full Circle," 211.

52. Nancy Gallt, telephone interview, 22 July 1988.

53. Peck, "Coming Full Circle," 212.

54. Peck, "Coming Full Circle," 213.

55. Richard Peck, quoted in *Contemporary Authors*, 85–88, ed. Frances Carol Locher (Detroit: Gale Research, 1980), 459.

56. Mona Kerby, "Richard Peck," *The Author Corner*, www.carr.org/mae/peck.

57. Peck, Viking Press publicity brochure.

58. Peck, Viking Press publicity brochure.

59. Curt Schleler, "Peck Is Author Whose Dreams Came True," *Grand Rapids Press*, 25 July 1982.

60. Peck, *Anonymously Yours*, 95.

61. "A Conversation with Richard Peck," Dell Publishing publicity brochure, n.d.

62. "Richard Peck's Scholastic Interview Transcript," *Scholastic*, www.books.scholastic.com/teacher/authorsandbooks/authorstudies.

63. Schleler, "Peck Is Author Whose Dreams Came True."

64. Richard Peck, "Newbery Medal Acceptance," *Horn Book* (July 2001): 397.

· 2 ·

The Writer

*R*ichard Peck begins his day this way:

> I get up in the morning; I get dressed; I go out and drink coffee in public,
> walk around the block, and come back and pretend that I have arrived at
> my office. One of the great advantages of writing for yourself is that you
> don't have to commute. But once you're a writer, you go out and pre-
> tend to be a commuter.

His "office" is one room of a modest and very neat New York City
apartment on 72nd Street, attractively furnished with antiques from the
early 1900s and accentuated by the vibrant red of several small Oriental
carpets. A large window with a southern exposure in his workroom provides a ninth-floor view of neighborhood roofs and mostly nondescript
buildings—nothing inspiring or distracting. In contrast to the antique
furniture, Peck's desk consists of what he describes as "a slab of unhistoric
Formica held up at both ends by filing cabinets." On a metal stand beside
his desk sits an IBM Wheelwright electric typewriter. Although he has a
laptop computer for e-mail correspondence, he prefers the typewriter for
composing. He says, "I still need the typewriter sound and the turning
pages in the three-ring notebook as the novel thickens." As with almost
everything else, Richard Peck prefers the comfort and reliability of older
things.

Peck is almost always working, whether at home in his office or
elsewhere. He argues, "I'm reading or writing all my conscious hours."
He explains, "I never go out for a cup of coffee without taking a book
with me. When I pack to travel, I pack the book and notebook before

the clothes."[1] When he is at the typewriter, he seems to accomplish more later in the day. "I'm not a morning person," he asserts. "That's the time I answer my mail." He is most productive between 4:30 and 6:30 p.m. when no one else is. "I think that comes from teaching. My idea of night is to go back in there and get ready for tomorrow—which is pretty much what schoolteachers do."

While most writers purport to prefer isolation, without phone calls, without interruptions of any kind, Peck welcomes them as a respite from the solitude of writing. In the beginning of his literary career, the isolation proved particularly difficult. Peck asserts, "I was used to being surrounded by students and other teachers from dawn on. Life had been divided into segments by ringing bells and interrupted by fire drills. I was used to being besieged by voices, activity." "The idea that a novel is written one word at a time hit me like falling masonry,"[2] he admits. Now, he jokes straight-faced, "I pay people to call me up."

Richard Peck starts slowly on a new novel, but he works longer the further he gets into it. "I *gather* enthusiasm as I write." Then he doesn't want the phone to ring. At that point, he says, "my own life has no meaning; I'm in the world of my book. I just wish I could move that up to the beginning of the novel."

Peck, however, is unable to write while on the road. "I'd be terribly distracted if I tried to write when I'm outside New York." Ironically, Peck finds no distractions living in one of the busiest cities in the world. "I've lived in New York long enough not to have anyplace to go," he explains. Nevertheless, Peck credits the loneliness of living in New York City with making him the kind of writer he is. "Living in New York—which has no sense of community—makes me want to create one on the page. . . . If I were writing in a tight, involved, involving, sociable community somewhere else, I might be a little too busy to get my work done."[3]

GENERATING THEMES

There is a pattern to the way Peck goes about starting, developing, and revising a novel. He begins with theme. "Again, that's the schoolteacher's view: what is the story trying to divulge? . . . Not what's the story about, but why was it written?" Many of Peck's themes, especially those

explored in his earlier novels, come from teenagers themselves. His satire
Secrets of the Shopping Mall resulted from comments young people made
in their letters to him about how much time they spend in shopping cen-
ters after school, or instead of going to school. He wrote *Remembering the
Good Times* because he heard about a seventh-grade boy who told twelve
of his classmates he was going to kill himself; they did nothing about it,
but the boy did what he promised. And it was junior high readers who
kept asking Peck when he was going to write a story about the supernatural. "They wanted WEIRD while I was trying to be understanding of
their problems." Spurred by their interest, he wrote *The Ghost Belonged
to Me*, featuring the ghost of a dead girl who haunts the loft of a barn. "I
would never have thought of a ghost story," Peck admits. "And I never
had more fun in my life."[4]

"I try to write what young people ask for," he says, "but I don't
give them *everything* they want. I don't want to tell them that marrying
means living happily ever after. I don't want to tell them that there is
justice in the world and all you have to do is be nice. It's a compromise
. . . between what I want and am able to say and what they are willing
to read."[5]

Peck understands, too, that "at your typewriter you're aging every
minute while, mysteriously, your readers remain the same age. Worse
yet, they change their protective coloring, their fads in clothes and
speech and music, every semester."[6] What, Peck asked himself, is the best
way to find out about those elements of real-life teenagers?

"You really have to go to the kids themselves."[7]

So, early in his writing career, Richard Peck started a habit of travel-
ing across the country, speaking in up to sixty schools and libraries a year.
He has talked with young people in wealthy Connecticut suburban
junior high schools and in poor inner-city high schools in Cleveland; he
has discussed his books with rural students in a sheep station high in the
Colorado Rockies and on a raft in a logging community in Ketchikan,
Alaska. He benefits by going directly to the source. In writing *Princess
Ashley*, for example, he went to Courtney Hughes, then attending New
Trier High School in Winnetka, Illinois.

> Being a senior, she really knew her way around that school. Also, she was
> on her way out—she would graduate before the book came out. When
> I needed something, I could call her up and say, "What do you call

this? . . . What happens in the school if this situation comes up?" She's very verbal and she told me about high school life. And she did something else that helped more than anything else: every time the high school newspaper came out, she sent me a copy. So I knew what was really important to those students at that time.[8]

In creating this setting, Peck insisted upon authenticity, arguing, "I wanted nothing in the novel that wasn't directly based on what was in fact happening among the students in that school, their patterns and parties, their home lives and school lives, the vast open stretches of their free time."[9] He adds, "I kept digging until I had a brief, euphoric, eerie moment of being on the other side and thought I really did know what it's like to be there, in young shoes."[10]

His concerns about kids and their academic and social development have served as inspiration for Peck's more recently written titles. His worries over inadequate education and the pervasive influence of video games and other technologies are both heartfelt and disheartening. Peck has little hope that, in the face of these obstacles, kids will develop and maintain a passion for reading. In typical Peck fashion, however, he channels this frustration into his work as a writer. Compelled to help young people find themselves in history, he aspires to use literature to instill in readers a rich sense of time and place they lack as a result of living in a fast-paced, unstable world. Ever the teacher, he wants readers to come away from his novels as more knowledgeable human beings: "I hope my novels can spark some interest in history and geography. After all, I fell in love with the Civil War by way of Scarlett O'Hara."[11]

"My favorite kind of story is now set in the past, a novel, perhaps, that bootlegs a little history for a readership who won't be learning history in school, or college to come."[12]

CREATING CHARACTERS

With a new novel's theme in mind, Peck searches for an effective spokesperson for the book. "I go shopping for a theme and then start auditioning the characters. I can't tell these stories myself."[13] Although he looks for real-life situations—present or past—Richard Peck does not look for real-life models for his characters. "Real people are never enough, and real people never do what you want them to do in the novel."[14]

In selecting the appropriate voice for his story, Peck says, "I know it has to be young." In his first novel, *Don't Look and It Won't Hurt*, he tried out three different voices before finding the right one. "I thought the unwed mother had a right to tell her own story; she couldn't—she was too self-delusive. Then I thought her younger brother would be the right distance; he wasn't—he was a boy who couldn't handle his emotions. Then I came up with a younger sister who hadn't gotten herself into trouble and therefore looked at her older sister with a critical eye, and that gave the cutting edge to the novel."

In *Are You in the House Alone?* Peck felt that only the victim could tell the story, and she did. But when he began *Remembering the Good Times* in the voice of the eventual suicide victim, it didn't work. If Travis had been able to express himself and explain what was happening to him, he probably wouldn't have had to kill himself. The story was better told, Peck discovered, by a friend—a boy friend rather than a girl friend.

Even so, the task of capturing the ever-changing voices of young readers proves daunting. Peck is "unnerved by how quickly language alters, how suddenly a phrase passes its sell-by date, and how easily adult authors reveal their years and show their hands when they fail to capture the changing rhythms of young speech."[15] His solution is to become a word sleuth, to keep abreast of new terms as they enter the vernacular of his young readers. When Peck listened and learned, for example, that he could not understand a word of "a linguistically barbaric new pseudo-language called 'computer talk,'" he acquired a copy of *Webster's New World Dictionary of Computer Terms* and began reading *Byte* magazine to allow himself to speak to adolescents who had already become experts in this language.[16] Although contemporary language has not been necessary in any of Peck's recent historical novels, he nevertheless strives for accuracy, utilizing phrases and expressions of times past in the re-creation of each story's setting.

Whether he is writing about the past or the present, dialogue is Peck's favorite part of constructing a novel. He attributes that to his interest in listening to people, going back to his Illinois childhood where he eavesdropped on the conversations of relatives. But he doesn't feel comfortable creating the dialogue out of his own imagination. "I can't speak in my own voice. I have the wrong vocabulary, the wrong memories, and the viewpoint of somebody's father or of the old schoolteacher I still am in my heart."[17] And so, he says, "I carry a notepad. I sit behind people in buses and listen in shopping areas and take dialogue down. I can't think up a lot of that dialogue: I've got to use the language I hear."[18] Writing, he says, "depends upon snooping, though we call it 'research.'"[19]

ESTABLISHING SETTING

From theme and characterization, Peck moves to setting next, in the same way an English teacher might lead students through a novel. He asks: "What does this novel tell about the life of its time? Very few people ask that question about a novel, but teachers *do*."

In his early novels, Peck's settings are most often somewhere in suburbia, because, he says, "that's where my readers live." Nostalgia toward his Midwest upbringing has led Peck to look closer to home in his more recently published novels; he chooses to set these stories in rural communities inhabited by people similar to the relatives and neighbors of his youth. In writing *A Long Way from Chicago*, for example, Peck went directly to his sources, traveling home to Decatur for Thanksgiving, rounding up "extended family, country cousins, those living on their ancestral acres, people younger than I," and asking them to share their memories:

> It was not long before their stories flowed. Someone said, "Oh, I had a great aunt who was so prissy she carried a rose to the privy to cut the smell." And then my cousin's son's girlfriend said, "My granddad is really impatient. He can never wait for the pecans to fall." When I asked what he does, she rewarded me with, "He puts a rubber tire on the front of his tractor and runs into the tree!" That's when I saw Grandma, but it wouldn't be her tree, and it wouldn't be her tractor. I could actually see the moonlight on her hair so I said to these relatives, "Tell me another one."[20]

Peck's memories of visiting his grandparents' farm, his father's memories of childhood, the stories shared around the holiday table, and his desire to encourage young readers to immerse themselves in the creation of meaningful memories shape the tales he writes now. Thoughts of these times are "fueling the end of my career,"[21] he says.

RESEARCHING THE DETAILS

One of the most pleasurable activities for Richard Peck is the research. In addition to serving as a primer for his pump, as he has put it,[22] it's a process with which he has felt comfortable since his university days. "Nobody ever taught me how to write a novel," he declares, "but I was trained by graduate school professors to do research; to take notes and to be able to read them later; to draw upon the world." Then he adds, with a smile in his voice: "I even know how to use the library."[23] Adamant in his belief that writing is a means to communication rather than self-expression, he argues for the necessity of writers to possess strong observation and investigative skills, claiming, "Our characters regularly find themselves in situations we writers have never experienced and had to go to the library to research."[24]

This penchant for research combined with a curiosity about all things old aligns nicely with the requisite work of writing historical fiction. "If I'm writing a novel about 1937," Peck says, "I spend all day in the library, because that's where 1937 is hiding."[25] In the six months prior to writing *A Year Down Yonder*, Peck read every issue of *Time* magazine published that year. "I needed to know the world my readers would be living in," he argues and adds, "That summer aviator Amelia Earhart vanished without a trace. I had to mention that in the book—because that is what people were talking about"[26]

"Then I went through all the catalogues, the Lane Bryant catalogue of course, and what we used to call the Monkey Ward catalogue. These were very helpful because they tell you what things cost."[27] It wasn't until he compiled five hundred pages of notes that he was ready to begin the drafting process.

Similarly, Peck dedicated two years to researching the stories of the mixed-race women who fled their homes in the early years of the Civil War before he sat down to write his own interpretation in *The River between Us*. Peck wondered about the fate of the women who traveled north and, with their light skin, managed to blend in. "I hugged myself with glee, thinking of all those northern families who said, 'My grandmother came from New Orleans' without knowing why."[28]

Gathering information about the 1893 World's Columbian Exhibition that ultimately made its way into *Fair Weather* allowed Peck to visit the Chicago Historical Society Museum, read newspapers and magazines from 1893, and delve into his own collection of world's fair books. On the wall of his apartment, he hung a map of the 600-acre fairgrounds and, for the year it took to craft the story, imagined the landscape come to life.[29]

DEVISING PLOT

As his writing process progresses, Peck turns (reluctantly) to plot:

> The day comes when you have to call a halt to your research and go home to sit before a mute typewriter until you begin to hear voices in the room. Voices that never were. Young voices, but a little wiser, a little less self-delusive than the young.
>
> When those voices become coherent and then insistent, you begin to type.[30]

But plot intimidates him, he admits. "I don't like plot. I don't read for plot. And I think a novel that is overplotted is weak." His approach is to start somewhere and see where it goes:

> There are some elements of the plot that I just can't foresee; I couldn't outline the book. I try sometimes but I don't get very far. And I realize now that I *don't* want to do that: it would put [the characters] in a straightjacket; it would also make them marionettes, dancing to my tune. A lot happens in a novel that I didn't perceive. . . . It's the unexpected event that has to be woven in seamlessly as if you saw it coming the day you started writing the novel.

In developing his stories, Richard Peck never rushes through an entire first draft just to get the basic story down before he goes back to rework it. He starts with the opening scene and develops the novel scene by consecutive scene. Once the drafting process is under way, Peck engages in a recursive process of creating and revising, writing (and retyping) each page six times. When Peck feels satisfied with the result, he then removes an additional twenty words.[31]

In the completion of the final piece, then, he writes an average of seven drafts, although the earlier chapters in the developing novel are rewritten far more times, the first chapter as many as twenty-five times,

Peck estimates. He wonders sometimes if his decision to rewrite the beginning so many times is wise. "I should just *leave* the first chapter after six or seven tries, go on, and then come back at the end. But, oh no, if I don't go back over every word of the first chapter I can't figure out how the rest goes."

Yet, despite his commitment to creating a foundational first chapter upon which the rest of the novel will stand, Peck makes a habit out of scrapping this very chapter upon the completion of the finished piece. When the novel is seemingly done, he says, "I'll take this first chapter, and without rereading it, I'll throw it away and write the chapter that goes at the beginning. Because the first chapter is the last chapter in disguise."[32]

ENDING (AND BEGINNING ANEW)

Unlike some writers who share their works in progress with a close friend, trusted colleague, or sympathetic editor, no one sees Richard Peck's latest novel until he is satisfied. The only exception is when he occasionally reads a specific scene to students and asks them what they think will happen next.

Although Peck delivers his completed manuscript to his editor with the false assumption that it is ready for printing, he is always grateful for the editor's viewpoint, especially when that editor finds something the writer has missed. "You think you've got that scene there and you go back and look at it and you say, 'Oh, that scene: I wrote it in my head, I didn't write it on the paper.' And that's useful." But he does not want to share the creative process of developing the novel with an editor. "I want to give the editor as finished a product as possible so we can get down to smaller fine points and not big concepts. . . . I want to do all the editing within a month and get on to production."

While the selection of a novel's final title might seem to be one of these smaller fine points, the resulting decision carries great weight with Peck. He frets, for example, over the title of his Newbery-winning tale, arguing that the use of the term "yonder" was a terrible mistake given the unfamiliarity of the word to his intended readers. He says, "Titles are a tyranny. They are the advertisement for the book because our readers don't read reviews."[33] How does Peck select the ideal title, then? "I make long lists," he says. "I once submitted 24 titles before they accepted one."

Following a book's release come the reviews—an uneasy period for Peck. "That's one more group of adults you have to work through," he says with a little pique in his voice. Though most reviews of his novels have been positive, he exhibits that insecure feeling most writers—and probably all creative artists—seem to have when their latest creation is unveiled. He explains, "I don't want a good review to please me because I wasn't writing for the reviewer—he didn't pay for the book, and he's the wrong age, and he's reading too many books. And I don't want a bad review to make me mad."

Peck's most important responses come from young readers. Although he keeps no record of the number of letters he gets in a typical week, he does notice patterns during the year. The best letters, he says, come in the summer, "because they're self-solicited." It's easy to notice when teachers have assigned students to write a letter to an author. "Most teachers are so glad to see students write anything that they will not only grade their rough drafts, they'll mail them! In fact, I will get letters that are marked by the teacher." He answers all of the letters that he can decipher, he says, giving more thoughtful responses to those he receives in the summer "because they're not coming in droves."

Whichever way and at whatever time they come, those letters complete the process of creation that Peck began as much as two or more years earlier. And the responses and ideas they contain help regenerate the process as Peck searches for new ideas for the theme of his next book and listens for clues to the language and interests of today's young readers.

NOTES

1. "Richard Peck's Scholastic Interview Transcript," *Scholastic*, www.books.scholastic.com/teacher/authorsandbooks/authorstudies.

2. Richard Peck, "In the Beginning Was The . . . ," *ALAN Review* (Spring 1997): 2–4.

3. Roger Sutton, "A Conversation with Richard Peck," *School Library Journal* (June 1990): 38.

4. Richard Peck, Speech presented at the Children's Literature Festival, University of Southern Mississippi, Hattiesburg, 19 March 1981.

5. Richard Peck, Interview at Montclair, New Jersey, Public Library, 9 December 1987.

6. Richard Peck, *Something about the Author Autobiography Series*, vol. 2, ed. Adele Sarkissian (Detroit: Gale Research, 1985), 184.

7. Jean W. Ross, *Contemporary Authors*, New Revision Series, vol. 19, ed. Linda Metzger (Detroit: Gale Research, 1987): 367.

8. Peck, Interview, Montclair Public Library.

9. Richard Peck, "Huck Finns of Both Sexes: Protagonists and Peer Leaders in Young Adult Books," *Horn Book* (September/October 1993): 554–58.

10. Peck, "Huck Finns of Both Sexes," 554–58.

11. "Richard Peck's Scholastic Interview Transcript."

12. Richard Peck, Speech presented at the Florida Association for Media in Education Conference, Orlando, 20 October 2005. Also printed in *Florida Media Quarterly* (Winter 2005), www.floridamedia.org/FMQWinter2005RichardPeckat2005 Conference.htm.

13. Deborah Kovacs, *Meet the Authors* (New York: Scholastic, 1995), 78.

14. Peck, Interview, Montclair Public Library.

15. Peck, "In the Beginning," 2–4.

16. Peck, "In the Beginning," 2–4.

17. Richard Peck, *Anonymously Yours* (New York: Julian Messner, 1991): ix.

18. Ross, *Contemporary Authors*, vol. 19:370.

19. Peck, *Anonymously Yours*, ix.

20. Nancy J. Johnson and Cyndi Giorgis, "2001 Newbery Medal Winner: A Conversation with Richard Peck," *Reading Teacher* (December 2001/January 2002): 392–97.

21. Linda Castellitto, "Lessons Learned," *First Person Book Page*, www.bookpage.com/0310bp/richard_peck.html.

22. Richard Peck, "The Invention of Adolescence and Other Thoughts on Youth," *Top of the News* (Winter 1983): 186.

23. Peck, "The Invention of Adolescence," 186.

24. Richard Peck, "Nobody but a Reader Ever Became a Writer," in *Authors' Insights: Turning Teenagers into Readers and Writers*, ed. Donald R. Gallo (Portsmouth, NH: Boynton/Cook-Heinemann, 1992), 80.

25. Catherine Gourley, "Richard Peck: Researching Fiction," *Writing!* (November/December 2001): 26.

26. Gourley, "Richard Peck: Researching Fiction," 26.

27. Johnson and Giorgis, "A Conversation with Richard Peck," 392–97.

28. Castellitto, "Lessons Learned."

29. Judy Green, "Richard Peck Looks Back in a Changing World," *Sacramento Bee*, 13 January 2002, E1.

30. Peck, "The Invention of Adolescence," 187.

31. Jennifer M. Brown, "A Long Way from Decatur," *Publishers Weekly*, 21 July 2003, 169.

32. Brown, "A Long Way from Decatur," 169.

33. Johnson and Giorgis, "A Conversation with Richard Peck," 392–97.

· 3 ·

The Teacher

$\mathcal{A}$lthough Richard Peck left the education profession in 1971, his appetite for teaching has never left him. "I am an old schoolteacher," he admits, "and I do want to give lessons."[1] The teacher in him can't quite be squelched: "Teaching is a job you never quit. You just go on and on trying to turn a life into lesson plans. Every word I read and every word I write causes me to ask: How would I present that in class? Would they accept this? How would they see this?"[2] Peck's "mythical students," as he calls them, as well as those that live and breathe, are ever present—and come in all ages. In addition to visiting his youngest readers in schools across the country, Peck teaches university courses in young adult literature in the Louisiana State University's School of Graduate Librarianship. He has also been a lecturer and teacher of creative writing on cruise ships to Europe, the Far East, and South America.

Speaking about his cruise experiences, Peck identifies readily the parallels between his eldest and youngest students. "A ship full of passengers is like a school full of students," Peck remarks with a grin in his voice; "everybody [is] dressed alike and waiting for lunch."[3] These mostly retired people "act exactly like children: they wait to be told everything." And "you have to tell them everything three times, and then they swear they never heard it (though in their case it's often true)."[4] While on board, Peck taught daily writing classes and lectured on such topics as "Your Day in Colombo, Sri Lanka" or "Madagascar, the Mystery Island" or "Blood-Soaked Panama, from Balboa to Noriega," all designed to impart essential destination information to passengers prior to the ship's approach to each port of call.

Regardless of the age of the participants, watching him speak to a group gives observers the impression that teaching comes naturally to Peck. In any presentation he makes, he is well prepared with specific ideas and helpful advice, but he is also fast and sharp with responses to questions. His statements are pointed if not barbed. He tells listeners:

- As are the end of education. Nobody learns from an A.
- Watching television is what you do with your life when you don't want to live it.
- Writing is not self-expression; writing is communication. Nobody wants to read your diary except your mother.
- Puberty is deciding at the age of twelve or so to divorce your own parents, charging irreconcilable differences.
- Never write what you know. Write what you can find out.[5]

A newspaper reporter in Alaska wrote, "Richard Peck rattles off streaks of wisdom like a barrage of Northern Lights."[6] A writer in Indiana observed that, when talking with students, Peck "strangles their ideals with a satin sash. A gentle charm helps soften his attacks on the extended adolescent, the unimaginative or just plain uninteresting kid."[7] If the audience is slow to respond, Peck uses some old and effective teaching methods for involving the group: posing questions, calling on individuals for their opinions, asking for a raise of hands.

No matter what his approach, Richard Peck enjoys performing before a group. In fact, he would rather speak than write. "I feel more myself in giving a speech," he acknowledges. "Making a speech is the only place in my life I've found where I didn't know about the past and the future—it's just now. . . . You get immediate response. The deadline is already there . . . oh, yes. Speaking is the reward for having written."

LESSONS FOR STUDENTS
(AND THEIR PARENTS)

At a gathering of about three dozen students and a few adults—teachers and librarians, and a parent or two—in an overheated room in the Montclair, New Jersey, Public Library in December 1987, Richard Peck talks about himself, since that is part of what he was invited there to do. But he wants students to participate, and so, from time to time, he asks them open-ended, fill-in-the-blank questions:

> The most important thing you can give your friend is . . .
> Every poet needs to be . . .

Or he presents a situation that occurs at the start of one of his novels and asks members of the audience what they think will happen next. There is a "right" answer, of course, because the inquirer is leading into an issue he has already addressed in one of his novels, but Peck doesn't let off-target answers escape him. The students' responses reveal what's important to them, and Peck is likely to store those in his mind (or later in his notes) for future reference. He also never tells a student that his or her answer is wrong. He may give the respondent a quizzical look or a crooked smile, but like any good teacher, he doesn't want to inhibit additional responses.

A second purpose today is to respond to students in the audience who, through their teachers, sent him poems and stories they had written weeks before. He diligently wrote comments on every one, copied some of the best verses and descriptive paragraphs onto a sheet of paper, had that duplicated, and distributed copies to everyone in attendance. Throughout the afternoon session, he continually refers to those examples, while also noting elements of his own writing, teaching the audience what good writing is and suggesting ways to help the students develop their own ideas. Praise is foremost in his comments about the students' work. But he does not allow students to settle for today's accomplishments. "You are all good writers," he says, "and you can all be better."

As he moves through his presentation, he continues to give advice to young writers: "The one voice your story never needs is yours," he says. "If you want to be a writer, you need to read three books a week. You need to see how other people do it. You need to see what the publishers are accepting."[8]

In other speeches, as well as in articles he has written, Peck recommends that students study Latin and also learn five new words every day.[9] In "Nobody but a Reader Ever Became a Writer," Peck states forcefully: "The young in the nineties . . . are verbally anorexic and getting away with it." Therefore, "No student should be admitted to class without a dictionary under one arm and a thesaurus under the other."[10]

In another place at another time, he has advice for parents about motivating their children to read:

> Never imply by word or attitude that reading and writing are "woman's work.". . .
>
> Never worry about a book corrupting a child. And never blame a book for having given sex education you haven't gotten around to. Worry if your children are not getting ideas from books. . . .
>
> Let kids observe adults who read books, magazines and newspapers that reflect various tastes and interests. Independent reading is the badge of adulthood, and the young are hungry for the advantages of maturity.[11]

LESSONS FOR TEACHERS

To English teachers, he explains what he tries to do in his novels:

> Today I'm still trying to hold the attention of the young, to deal with a diminished attention span, to explore subject matter of immediate and manifest relevance, to vie with the distractions of television and peer-group pressure and the disarray of permissive home lives. I don't suggest that my novels are didactic—or dare to be. We live in an age and country in which we approach our young by indirection.[12]

In his recent speeches to teachers, he recommends books for them to teach, maintaining that these are books he would use if he were teaching today. His suggestions vary as new novels come to his attention, but first on his list is always Robert Cormier's *The Chocolate War.* "I wouldn't let anyone get through high school without reading that book because it's on one of the most important issues today—that is, what happens when power shifts to the young, away from adults."[13] His next recommendation is M. E. Kerr's *Night Kites*, "because of its structure," not just because it deals with the timely topic of AIDS. Third is Chris Crutcher's *Running Loose*, "because it's one book on the subject of what are we going to do about a school that is run by the coach, not the principal."

Peck also has provided English and reading teachers with "Ten Questions to Ask about a Novel." They include:

What would this story be like if the main character were of the
opposite sex?
Why is this story set where it is (not what is the setting)?
Reread the first paragraph of Chapter 1. What's in it that makes you
read on?[14]

And he has suggested specific pedagogical methods for teaching these
books, asking these questions, and more, encouraging teachers to prominently display a Word for the Day; send word lists from assigned reading
home to be reviewed and learned by parents and students; read more
poetry; require more memorization; and devote more time to reading
and writing and less to class discussion ("now that we've learned class
discussion doesn't cure the young of 'like' and 'you know,' you
know?").[15]

According to Peck, we must teach kids to read and write well, or
we wrong them. Students deserve to know that "without literacy, you
will fail at whatever you want to do. . . . If you can't use language, it *will*
be used against you."[16]

LESSONS FOR LIBRARIANS (AND THE AUTHORS THEY PROMOTE)

Peck feels his greatest affinity with young adult librarians, because, as he
tells a convention gathering of them, "in the 1980s we writers and librarians have come into our own. We are the people left willing to know
the young. Everyone else in their lives has recoiled from them and is still
looking for ways to abdicate authority." Since then and with increasing
regularity, Peck has articulated his frustration with the current schooling
system and the role students play in their learning—or lack thereof. He
describes schools as failing institutions inhabited by administrators and
teachers who cater to parents and students who cater to themselves: "The
power the young have had over their choices in education, over what
they choose to learn and what they choose not to learn, has diminished
their education entirely."[17]

He worries that, in an ever-changing world, schools are not keeping
pace. In reference to the events of September 11, 2001, in particular, he
says, "Every time I go to the airport now, I know that something hap-

pened and changed everything. But [in the schools] nothing has happened. Nothing. No sudden, 'Okay, that didn't work. Now we've got to have foreign languages and geography and history.'"[18] He worries, too, about the disconnect between students and their communities and the world at large, as evidenced by this excerpt from his Newbery Acceptance Speech:

> Powerful forces divorce the young from their roots and traditions: the relentlessness of the video game that is the pornography of the prepubescent, a violent virtual reality that eliminates the parent who paid for it. And the peer group that rushes in to fill the vacuum of the teacher's vanished authority and an awesome parental power failure.[19]

Peck defines adolescence as "the gnawing need to lose your innocence while retaining your illusions" and would love to tell teens a few key truths: "all mass movements . . . are designed to keep you down"; "love may be eternal, but romance has a time limit"; "you will be held responsible for the consequences of your actions."[20]

To meet the needs of adolescents and reveal these truths in a way that avoids didacticism and keeps teens listening, Peck believes that librarians and the books they know and recommend to kids are crucial. Writers and librarians must "spot for survivors"[21] in this lost generation. But to succeed with teenagers, writers and librarians must be crafty. "Our job seems to be," he says, "to plant a challenge in a novel that looks reassuring; put a new book behind cover art that looks comfortably clichéd, and bootleg inspiration in a format of escape."[22]

Peck argues that, together, writers and librarians can reach some young people through compromise. He advocates for the power of fiction as a means to educate the young and reintroduce them to their historical and cultural traditions. As an author, Peck assumes this role of teacher through the stories he creates. Taking readers back in time through his historical fiction, for example, provides them a window into a world unlike their own, one that might shake them up or help them see that how it is now is not how it's always been—or needs to be. Fiction expands one's perspective, enlarging one's sense of self, time, and place and allowing for alternate explanations and understandings of the world. Peck says, "Kids today are controlling their own screen time and are going to live in the smallest world possible; whereas, I'm always going to write a novel about a young person who suddenly walks through a door, and there's the world."[23] For Peck, stories offer hope and a revision of an otherwise dreary vision of the future:

> Story will survive even these dark times and our schools where literacy has become an elective, when academic standards have been replaced by "self-esteem," schools full of students who believe they are gifted because their parents paid so much for the house.[24]

PECK'S PRAYERS FOR A MORE HOPEFUL FUTURE

One day early in 1986, Richard Peck was searching for an ending to a speech that would be both instructive and entertaining. In desperation, he claims that he thought, "Help me, God." Inspiration came to him in an instant: a prayer! So he wrote "A Teenager's Prayer" to end that speech. It later appeared in print in *Horn Book*.[25] In its eleven lines, the prayer asks, among other things, for "freedom from television because I'm beginning to suspect its happy endings," "the knowledge that conformity is the enemy of friendship," and "the understanding that nobody ever grows up in a group." Since then, Peck says, "I think that 'Teenager's Prayer' has probably been read by far more people than ever read a novel of mine!"

He later followed that prayer with "The Fervent Prayer of a Teenager's Parent," with such lines as "Embolden my heart as I unplug the telephone from my child's room so that the peer group that rules the school all day will not rule our nights as well" and "Stay my hand when I am tempted to buy my children's love with credit cards in their names, or mine." Later came "A Teacher's Prayer" that asks God to "Send me a couple of administrators who care more about standards than they do about their jobs" and "I want to make bricks. Could you send me some straw?"

NOTES

1. Richard Peck, Interview at Montclair, New Jersey, Public Library, 9 December 1987.

2. Nancy J. Johnson and Cyndi Giorgis, "2001 Newbery Medal Winner: A Conversation with Richard Peck," *Reading Teacher* (December 2001/January 2002): 392–97.

3. Richard Peck, *Anonymously Yours* (New York: Julian Messner, 1991): 115.

4. Richard Peck, "Love Is Not Enough," *School Library Journal* (September 1990): 153.

5. Richard Peck, "Nobody but a Reader Ever Became a Writer," in *Authors' Insights: Turning Teenagers into Readers and Writers*, ed. Donald R. Gallo (Portsmouth, N.H.: Boynton/Cook-Heinemann, 1992), 88.

6. Randi Sulkin, "Richard Peck: Writing Is Communication," *Ketchikan Daily News*, 3–9 March 1984, 2.

7. Patrice Smith, "Author Aims at Teen-Age Ideals," *Evansville Courier*, n.d.

8. Richard Peck, Workshop at Montclair, New Jersey, Public Library, 9 December 1987.

9. See, for example, Richard Peck in *Speaking for Ourselves*, ed. Donald R. Gallo (Urbana, Ill.: National Council of Teachers of English, 1990), 166.

10. Peck, "Nobody but a Reader Ever Became a Writer," 82.

11. "Tips That Get Kids Reading," *Ketchikan Daily News*, 3–9 March 1984, 3.

12. Richard Peck, "Some Thoughts on Adolescent Lit," *News from ALAN* (September–October 1975): 4.

13. Peck, Interview, Montclair Public Library.

14. Richard Peck, "'Ten Questions to Ask about a Novel," *ALAN Newsletter* (Spring 1978): 1.

15. Richard Peck, "In the Beginning Was The . . . ," *ALAN Review* (Spring 1997): 2–4.

16. Peck, "In the Beginning," 2–4.

17. Matt Berman, "Peck's Peak," *Times-Picayune*, 7 April 2002, Living 1.

18. Jennifer M. Brown, "A Long Way from Decatur," *Publishers Weekly*, July 21, 2003, 170.

19. Richard Peck, "Newbery Medal Acceptance," *Horn Book* (July 2001): 397.

20. Richard Peck, "The Invention of Adolescence and Other Thoughts on Youth," *Top of the News* (Winter 1983): 188.

21. Peck, "Newbery Medal Acceptance," 397.

22. Peck, "The Invention of Adolescence," 189.

23. Dean Schneider, "Richard Peck: 'The Past Is My Favorite Place,'" *Book Links* (September 2006): 56.

24. Richard Peck, Speech presented at the Florida Association for Media in Education Conference, Orlando, 20 October 2005. Also printed in *Florida Media Quarterly* (Winter 2005), www.floridamedia.org/FMQWinter2005RichardPeckat2005 Conference.htm.

25. Richard Peck, "A Teenager's Prayer," in "Young Adult Books," *Horn Book* (September–October 1968): 621.

· *4* ·

Early Novels

When Richard Peck faced the mute green keys of his Royal typewriter at the start of the summer of 1971, he had only a vague idea of his direction. He was determined to write a novel. He wanted to write for teenagers because that was the audience he knew from his teaching. He had things he wanted to say to kids, though he knew he could not preach to them. And he did not want to write a story about his own personal experiences. Moreover, "I knew I couldn't tell it about the kids that I had just come from in teaching," he says. "I was overheated on that subject. I was not only burned out but I was also a bit angry. I was too close to it."

DON'T LOOK AND IT WON'T HURT

Looking for a story that met these criteria, Peck thought about the young pregnant girls he had met at the home of friends in Evanston, Illinois. There, a doctor and his wife, Richard and Jean Hughes, housed girls from a local residence for unmarried mothers-to-be. Asking his friends if they observed anything the girls had in common, he learned there was a clear profile: The girls all say they will keep the baby, marry the father, and never return home. In the end, they do just the opposite. With that information, Peck was ready to write. Although *Don't Look and It Won't Hurt* began as a story about an unmarried pregnant teenager, Peck developed it into something more. It's a novel about responsibility, the disintegration of a rural, small-town family, and human relationships.

Carol Patterson, almost sixteen, is the middle sister in a poor family.

Her father is a ne'er-do-well who left the family years before. Her mother works the evening shift at a restaurant on the edge of their Illinois town. Overwhelmed by her own struggles, she relinquishes responsibility, leaving Carol feeling responsible for her nine-year-old sister, Liz. Carol watches, too, as her irresponsible seventeen-year-old sister, Ellen, falls for a twenty-year-old who says he's helping draft evaders escape to Canada during the Vietnam War when, in fact, he's a drug dealer who is soon arrested and sent to prison for ten years. Ellen leaves for Chicago to have the baby, communicating only with Carol, and that rarely. Fearing that Ellen won't ever come back home and feeling responsible for keeping the family together, Carol takes the overnight bus to find her sister and convince her to return.

This is a dark novel for a writer known for humor. It's not about suburban youngsters, there are no ghosts or shopping malls, and no one rescues the girls and makes their lives better. In fact, there are no clear resolutions in the novel, a fact that disappointed the reviewer for *Library Journal*.[1] It isn't certain that Ellen will return home after the baby is born, that Carol will pursue the contact she made with her father, or that the injured leg of the stray cat Liz brought home will heal. And Carol is still the sister in the middle feeling responsible. This sensitive novel does show, however, that Carol has come to understand herself and others better. That is, after all, a realistic and satisfying outcome. As in real life, there are raw edges in this novel.

Twenty years after this book was published, it inspired a highly praised feature film written and directed by Allison Anders called *Gas Food Lodging*, though anyone familiar with Peck's novel will hardly recognize it in this contemporary production. (See appendix B for additional commentary on the film.)

Although the *Kirkus* review of *Don't Look and It Won't Hurt* wasn't very complimentary,[2] *Publishers Weekly* proclaimed this "an extraordinarily good" first novel,[3] and most other reviewers agreed. A surprising negative response came several years later in a book about teaching young adult literature. Educator Sheila Schwartz, herself a writer for teenagers and adults, proclaimed Peck's first novel "poor adolescent literature" because it "contains no concepts of value for the teenager today."[4] Believing the novel's key message tells readers to close their eyes to painful things, Schwartz concludes that Peck gives young people "a potentially harmful philosophical perception."[5] No other reviewers interpreted the title that way, nor do readers in their letters sent to Richard Peck. In contrast to the book's title, the text's commitment to the theme of individual responsibility is unmistakably evident.

DREAMLAND LAKE

That same theme of individual responsibility lies beneath the mysterious elements of Richard Peck's second novel, *Dreamland Lake*, which won the Edgar Allan Poe Mystery Award in 1973. Although the novel opens with two boys discovering a decomposed body at the edge of a lake where an amusement park had once been, and mysterious events related to a classmate's behavior are found throughout the novel, Peck maintains that he did not intend the story to be a mystery. In fact, the narrator says on page two: "If some of [the story] sounds like a murder mystery or something, remember, it isn't." Rather than quibble, it's wiser to adopt the approach of the *School Library Journal* reviewer who wrote that readers will be "captivated first by the mystery, and then by its deeper levels of meaning."[6]

It does not matter how the old man died, only that his remains are discovered by two seventh graders, Brian and Flip (Philip), and that their discovery of the body is observed by a friendless classmate, Elvan Helligrew, who, like "a damn big dog that hangs around waiting for you to kick it," goes to unusual lengths to get attention. Beginning with the corpse, the story recounts Brian's loss of innocence as it progresses through other deaths, ultimately ending with the horrifying death of Elvan. Brian, recounting the story two years later and acknowledging his guilt, blames Flip for what happened but blames himself for being a follower. The death of Elvan marks the end of the friendship between Brian and Flip; in fact, Brian says that he hasn't had a close friend since.

In spite of its grim ending and somber theme, there is humor sprinkled throughout the novel, with lively glimpses of the boys' paper-route escapades and a description of their English class. The adventures come in rapid succession, with enough foreshadowing to keep normally reluctant readers moving through the story.

Reviewers praised the "finely tuned"[7] novel's "emotional depth"[8] and "superior . . . characterizations."[9] In addition, the relationship between the boys, with its "ambiguous mixture of nostalgia and guilt," reminded reviewers for *Kirkus*[10] and *Booklist*[11] of the bond between boys in John Knowles's *A Separate Peace*. Letters Peck received in response to the novel consistently reflect the interest and engagement of readers, most of them boys. Because of those letters, Peck believes that *Dreamland Lake* is one of his best books, in spite of—or perhaps because of—the fact that many of the letter writers resist the message of the book. Peck explains, "They say, 'I don't understand the book,' but you can tell from the letters that they do. They don't *accept* the message."

THROUGH A BRIEF DARKNESS

Thinking independently is not a major theme in *Through a Brief Darkness*, Peck's third novel for young adults, but it is a significant element. Sixteen-year-old Karen Beatty, motherless daughter of a big-time New York mobster, has always done what her father or his secretary told her to do. Forced to attend boarding schools, she remains blind to her father's shady activities. Her complaisance allows her to be easily kidnapped and flown to London, supposedly to stay with cousins whom she has never met. Karen is unaware that her father has been attacked by rival mobsters who set him afire; he remains in a coma in the hospital. Learning that her "cousins" are agents of her father's enemies, she vows to solve the mystery, as "there'd already been too many times in her life when she'd been expected to follow blindly." With help from a childhood friend studying at Eton and a fortuitously appearing old woman, she makes her escape and joins her father. Ultimately, though, Karen must act independently to survive.

Peck establishes the suspense early in this novel and maintains it effectively to the end, thus keeping the novel moving rapidly. A hint of romance adds to the adventure. And glimpses of London and the British countryside, as well as a description of a rough crossing of the English Channel, provide a depth to the setting that few other young adult novels of the time offer. However, as one reviewer noted, the extensive description of Jay's life at Eton seems out of place and unnecessary.[12]

The plotting in this novel is more contrived than that in any of Peck's other books, except perhaps for *Amanda/Miranda*. But Peck intended both novels to be Gothic adventure-romances, which traditionally employ melodrama and rely on stereotyped characters and

chance encounters. In *Through a Brief Darkness*, Jay happens to be studying at Eton and to be in London at the right time; his parents happen to
visit at that moment; and when Jay and Karen need help, they happen
upon Jay's grandmother, who, in spite of having had no previous contact
with these American teenagers, calmly and completely takes over the
management of Karen's escape from her captors. A critical reader has the
choice of faulting Peck for his contrived plotting and stereotyped characters, as the *School Library Journal* reviewer did,[13] or praising him for writing "a tightly drawn romantic melodrama" that "wisely relinquishes any
pretense to relevance or depth," as the *Kirkus* reviewer did.[14]

Peck himself says that, after writing two serious novels, he wanted
to write something light. "I believe in books for increasing the pleasure
of reading books," he says. Young readers had a deeper reaction to the
novel than Peck expected. The letter writers, Peck says, "are very caught
up in the relationship . . . between the girl and her father. . . . I thought
that the fact that the father and the daughter could not communicate in
here simply set up the plot. . . . But they don't see it that way." "That
taught me something," Peck admits, "that my opinion doesn't really
count here. And that's okay."

REPRESENTING SUPER DOLL

Although there is adventure in *Representing Super Doll*, the action is not
life threatening. This novel explores the topic of female beauty—
contrasting one sixteen-year-old who has it with another who does not.
Reviewers praised the "natural, often snappy dialogue and convincing
characterizations"[15] of this "swift, funny, and touching story."[16] Zena
Sutherland emphasized the book's "deeper treatment of a theme than
most beauty-contest books achieve."[17] But Jean Alexander in the *Washington Post*, believing that the beautiful Darlene and not the "smug"
Verna is the heroine of the novel, states that Peck "fails to make his
point."[18]

Peck acknowledges the novel is about Darlene Hoffmeister, "the
dumbest, most beautiful girl that anyone ever heard of," but it's narrated
by Verna Henderson, a level-headed, intelligent "country mouse." But
it's fruitless to argue about who the main character is because both girls
are needed to explore the theme of this novel: "the terrible tyranny of

glamour."[19] Peck says about Verna: "She didn't *mean* to be having an adventure of her own; she meant to tell you about this girl she went to school with . . . but of course she has to get involved; otherwise she's too much the author standing in the wings."

After winning the titles of Miss Hybrid Seed Corn and Central United States Teen Super Doll, Darlene, with Verna as a traveling companion, embarks on a three-day public relations trip to New York. As part of the tour, Darlene appears on the television panel show *Spot the Frauds* (patterned after the real *To Tell the Truth*, on which Richard Peck used to appear as an impostor). Verna, at the last minute, must substitute for a missing Teen Super Doll impostor. She is viewed, as one panelist says, as "the kind of girl who would be chosen to represent young people" and fools everyone, while Darlene appears to have nothing but good looks. Verna realizes her intelligence is worth more than Darlene's beauty and that, with a new hairdo and the right clothes, she is more attractive than she ever imagined. While visiting New York City, Verna sees a world that is much wider than her small Midwest community, and she is anxious to explore it in the future. In the end, Darlene possesses enough sense to realize that she has been unhappily doing what her pushy mother wants, and she refuses to enter any further beauty contests.

This is a lighter book with more humorous scenes than Peck produced in any of his first three novels. Particularly funny are the scenes when Verna's town friends visit her farm home and when Verna and Darlene arrive in New York City and have to deal with taxis, subways, bag ladies, nasty waitresses, restaurants that "don't do malteds," and television news programs that specialize in violent crimes (that prompt Verna to say, "I just sat there feeling privileged to be left alive").

Richard Peck's next novel was to be even lighter and more humorous, its success leading to a string of novels about the now infamous Blossom Culp and introducing the element of the supernatural into his writing repertoire.

NOTES

1. Peggy Sullivan, *Library Journal*, 15 December 1972, 4080.
2. *Kirkus Reviews*, 15 August 1972, 949.
3. *Publishers Weekly*, 25 September 1972, 60.

4. Sheila Schwartz, *Teaching Adolescent Literature: A Humanistic Approach* (Rochelle Park, N.J.: Hayden, 1979), 201–2.

5. Schwartz, *Teaching Adolescent Literature*, 202.

6. Alice H. Yucht, *School Library Journal*, 15 November 1973, 53.

7. *Kirkus Reviews*, 15 June 1973, 648.

8. *New York Times Book Review*, 13 January 1974, 10.

9. *Publishers Weekly*, 6 August 1973, 65.

10. *Kirkus Reviews*, 15 June 1973, 648.

11. *Booklist*, 15 November 1973, 342.

12. Margery Fisher, "Fashion in Adventure," *Growing Point* (April 1976): 2844–48, in *Contemporary Literary Criticism*, vol. 21, ed. Sharon R. Gunton (Detroit: Gale Research, 1982), 298.

13. Peggy Sullivan, *School Library Journal* (February 1974): 72.

14. *Kirkus Reviews*, 1 December 1973, 1314.

15. *Booklist*, 1 October 1974, 159.

16. *Publishers Weekly*, 9 September 1974, 68.

17. Zena Sutherland, *Bulletin of the Center for Children's Books* (November 1974): 51.

18. Jean Alexander, *Washington Post Book World*, 10 November 1974, 8.

19. Paul Janeczko, *From Writers to Students: The Pleasures and Pains of Writing*, ed. M. Jerry Weiss (Newark, Del.: International Reading Association, 1979), 80.

· 5 ·

Fantasy and the Supernatural

THE GHOST BELONGED TO ME

$\mathscr{T}$here was nothing supernatural about how Richard Peck came to write *The Ghost Belonged to Me*, but the evolution of the novel and what followed it involve the intersection of several forces.

After completing his fourth book for young adults, Peck was eager to write about something different. By that time, he had also received a letter from a boy asking why Peck had never written a ghost story. And in talking with junior high school students, Peck found out that lots of boys were fascinated by the *Titanic*. "It was their favorite disaster."[1] In addition, he thought his next novel might explore the relationship between "a young boy just entering life and an old man he admires who is just leaving life."[2]

As he considers writing a new novel, Peck says he reviews the characteristics of his previous novels and lists ways in which he wants the new novel to be different. His list at this point included a ghost, the *Titanic*, an old man and a young boy, and the past versus the present. Peck says: "Originally the novel was to be a love story between a contemporary New York baseball-playing boy and the ghost of a girl who was killed on the *Titanic*. When they finally confronted each other, the story fell apart."[3]

Saving the *Titanic* incident for another time, Peck dropped the love story, retained the old-man–young-boy relationship, and set the new novel entirely in the early 1900s in Bluff City, Peck's re-creation of his hometown of Decatur, Illinois, at the turn of the century. He also made it a comedy. Somewhere during the development of his story about Alexander Armsworth and his great-uncle Miles, Peck realized something more was needed. So, he says, "I took the character of Huckleberry Finn and gave him a sex change."[4] When Peck looked up from his typewriter, "there in the door stood Blossom Culp."[5] Later, Blossom remarks that because "a boy gets into more scrapes than he can get out of," Alexander "just naturally needs me to steer him right."[6]

After *The Ghost Belonged to Me* was published in 1975, Peck was surprised to receive more letters about Blossom than about Alexander. In the next novel, published two years later, Blossom became the primary protagonist, Alexander became a sidekick, the sinking of the *Titanic* resurfaced as a key incident—and *Ghosts I Have Been* outsold its predecessor. Two other Blossom Culp novels followed during the next seven years, interspersed between Peck's more serious contemporary novels. For Peck, the Blossom Culp novels provided a needed "flight from the young adult novel as a contemporary problem novel." Peck recalls, "I was afraid I was going to burn out on writing on the same terms that I had burned out on teaching—going from problem to problem trying to put out fires."[7] For Peck, Blossom provided distance and perspective.

Blossom is "the poorest, plainest, most bedraggled girl" in Bluff City.[8] She's also the ugliest. She has big, nearly black, round eyes, dark kinky hair, and legs so skinny that Alexander says she has "a spidery look." Blossom and her toothless, fortune-telling mother live alone in a decrepit two-room row house on the other side of the tracks. Above all, Blossom ranks among the spunkiest characters in contemporary literature for young people. "She's unattractive, she has a poor mother, no father, nothing, except wonderful spunk."[9] She says, "I've always lived by my wits."

In spite of having illiterate parents, Blossom is, as she puts it, "a quick study." While her grammar isn't perfect and clichés abound in her tales, she's an excellent speller, even though she spends as little time in school as possible. Her language is colorful and clever, her voice a combination of the countrified female voices Richard Peck heard from his relatives in Illinois.[10] Most important, she has not only inherited her mother's clairvoyant ability, but Blossom's talents are even greater—for, in the four novels in which she appears, she travels both backward and forward in time.

Focusing on the comedy in the supernatural, Peck attains, as Kip and Christen Hartvigsen note, "just the right mix of chills and chuckles."[11] And, as Alleen Nilsen and Kenneth Donelson point out, "it is a relief to occasionally turn to" Peck's Blossom Culp novels because of their comic elements.[12] Moreover, they recognize that Blossom uses her supernatural talents not to hurt others (well, maybe Letty Shambaugh a little) but "to become more and more compassionate."[13] Blossom's purpose in traveling through time is always to help or comfort someone in distress.

Barbara Elleman in 1985 proclaimed *The Ghost Belonged to Me* one of the "50 Books Too Good to Be Missed" from the previous twenty years.[14] *School Library Journal* declared it "a light romp with engaging characters, plenty of laughs, and enough shivery moments to qualify as a mystery too."[15] *The Junior Bookshelf* called Blossom "a splendid creation."[16] Most importantly, this was one of the novels that the American Library Association cited for presenting Richard Peck with the Margaret A. Edwards Award in 1990.

Granted, none of the parents in any of the Blossom Culp novels provides a positive model, but Blossom herself is "a strong and resourceful heroine,"[17] one that offers an alternative to females steeped in the limited vision of girlhood advocated by popular culture. She refuses to develop "into a slim femme fatale, but, instead, learns more about who she is through her adventures."[18] Despite the challenges she faces, whether socioeconomic, familial, or otherwise, "she got on by her smarts" and by her sense of humor, debunking "the sexist trope still floating around, the one about women not being funny."[19]

Although the most interesting adults in Richard Peck's novels are often old women, the most interesting adult in *The Ghost Belonged to Me* is an old man, Alexander's great-uncle. Uncle Miles, patterned closely after Peck's real great-uncle by the same name, is a free-spirited, eighty-five-year-old carpenter "who's lived just the way he's wanted to" and knows everything about everybody else's business. It is Uncle Miles's story about Captain Thibodaux that explains the ghosts of young Inez Dumaine and her damp dog that haunt the brick barn. And it is Uncle Miles who accompanies Alexander to New Orleans (with Blossom tagging along) in order to give Inez a proper burial. In the process, the ghost of Inez informs Alexander about a tragedy about to happen with a train and a bridge and a man with one hand, saving lives and making Alexander famous as a result.

GHOSTS I HAVE BEEN

Having discovered Blossom's popularity, Peck wisely wrote *Ghosts I Have Been* in Blossom's voice. Later, Blossom remarks that although he had made "a grave error by letting Alexander tell the [first] story, . . . Mr. Peck had the sense to step aside and let me tell this story . . . in my own way."[20] This is also where the *Titanic* came in.

In the fictional fall of 1913, a few months after the ending of *The Ghost Belonged to Me*, Blossom Culp describes herself as having "the talent for involving myself in other people's business." She gets involved in plenty. First she scares Alexander and his mischievous buddies on Halloween night as they attempt to overturn Old Man Leverette's outhouse. Then she is invited to an after-school meeting of the Sunny Thoughts and Busy Fingers Sisterhood led by Letty Shambaugh, where she first fakes a "Second Sight" incident and then really does have a vision of a boy being run over by an automobile. She quickly has other visions of both past and future events, most of which she can't comprehend. One of them is a vision of World War I; in another, she sees men walking on the moon. Blossom, "always an astute observer and critic of hidden motivations and guarded sentiments," writes Tony Manna, uses these experiences to moralize about society—"each of her visions an increasingly intense indictment of a society gone and about to go haywire."[21]

Invited to tea by the eccentric Miss Dabney, Blossom and Alexander encounter the ghost of a serving girl who had hanged herself in the kitchen years earlier. Later, forced by her school principal, Miss Spaulding, to prove her ability to "see the Unseen," Blossom passes back nearly two years in time to find herself aboard the sinking *Titanic*, where she comforts a young boy who is about to slip beneath the icy waters. She returns to reality with a wet blanket on which is woven the word "Titanic." Both Blossom and the town become famous. Blossom's mother's "business" flourishes, and Blossom receives a commendation from the Queen of England and an invitation to visit.

Everyone loved this novel; it earned best-book-of-the-year honors from the ALA, *School Library Journal*, and *New York Times*; it later was named one of the ALA's Best of the Best 1970–1982 and went on to appear on ALA's Best of the Best Books for Young Adults 1966–1986 list. Walt Disney Productions also made a television movie out of it, *Child of Glass* (see appendix B). *School Library Journal* praised the "hilarious" first-person narration and its combination of "humor, occult adventure, and a thoroughly engaging heroine."[22] *Horn Book* singled out the "unmistakable American accent" of this "effervescent comedy."[23] And more than one reviewer likened Peck's style to that of Mark Twain, although the *KLIATT* reviewer opined that "the wit and insight of the narrator will be missed by most of the audience the book is intended for."[24] Maybe so—but that also suggests that adult readers might find this book as entertaining as young adults do. Most importantly, this was another of Peck's novels that the ALA cited for presenting him with the Margaret A. Edwards Award in 1990.

THE DREADFUL FUTURE
OF BLOSSOM CULP

Compared to its predecessors, *The Dreadful Future of Blossom Culp* was a letdown to some reviewers, mainly because its commentary on contemporary society is so negative. Nevertheless, Kip and Christen Hartvigsen rate this book the best in the series because of its exploration of "the theme of peer conflict and rejection."[25]

In this novel, Blossom is zapped through a time warp from 1914 to 1984 to discover that Bluff City has changed significantly. With the exception of Jeremy, with whom she shares a mutual attraction, the world of the 1980s is "a real interesting place to visit, but I wouldn't want to live there."[26] Jeremy, a solitary teenager from a broken home, spends most of his time playing computer games. His father lives in a singles condo complex; his mother is so busy with her own life that she doesn't even notice Blossom's presence. His sister, Tiffany, dresses punk, spends most of her life at the mall, and speaks Valley Girl argot, "like totally." Blossom finds her fascinating: "I never heard tell of a girl named for a lamp before," she says, "though this one was none too bright."

School in the 1980s is a sham. The middle school building is architecturally sterile. Attendance is optional. Kids who are reading "at or near grade level" are termed "Gifted," and everyone is "heavy into computer math." The classes are totally out of control because it's Halloween, and everyone is in costume (which allows Blossom to attend in her own clothes)—though Blossom says, "I doubt things were much better on a regular day." Blossom wisely wants to return to 1914.

That kind of caustic commentary by Peck led Patricia Lee Gauch, herself a young adult novelist, to conclude her review in the *New York Times Book Review* with "Blossom is too good a character to end up chiefly a vehicle for social commentary on the sterility and loneliness of our contemporary adolescent world."[27] In all fairness to Peck, though, there's much to smile at in those scenes where Blossom tries to comprehend the meaning of Cuisinart and microwave, along with television, in general, and Pac Man and Atari 2600 VCS, in particular. Jeremy, in fact, is so immersed in video games that when Blossom first appears, he asks her: "What *game* are you from?"

Fortunately the 1980s take up only about one-fourth of the book, with the rest being about Blossom and Alexander's other exploits in 1914 Bluff City. In the beginning of the novel, for example, Blossom once again foils the plans of Alexander and his cohorts, Bub and Champ, to victimize Old Man Leverette. In the end, while telling fortunes in the old haunted Leverette farmhouse, Blossom uses her talents to expose the duplicity of her history teacher, Mr. Ambrose Lacy.

Even though this book does not live up to the standards set by *Ghosts I Have Been*, it is still a fun read, providing "tons of gentle laughter that will charm even a punk rocker," said a reviewer in the *Ocala Star Banner*.[28] And the *Parents' Choice* reviewer, delighted with the novel's "three belly laughs and two second-thoughts per chapter," proclaimed it "one of the best teenage novels of the year."[29]

BLOSSOM CULP AND THE SLEEP OF DEATH

"After an uncomfortable brush with technology in *The Dreadful Future of Blossom Culp*, it is good to see our doughty heroine back where she belongs, in 1914,"[30] wrote Patty Campbell on the publication of Peck's fourth Blossom Culp book in 1986. The ALA liked *Blossom Culp and the Sleep of Death* better than the previous series title, too, naming it a Notable Book for Children. Other reviewers agreed. Michael Cart called it "an entertaining and generally well-crafted diversion with moments of inspired humor . . . and abundant examples of Peck's gift for turning the humorous phrase,"[31] and *Publishers Weekly* called it a "fast, feverish, funny, altogether satisfying escapade."[32]

Blossom tells readers: "Though the past and future are often open books to me, I have more trouble than most getting through the present." But, in this novel, she deals adroitly with problems of both the present and the past. In the present, her rival, Letty Shambaugh, and her mother attempt to discredit the new ninth-grade history teacher, Miss Fairweather, because she was a suffragette and therefore "a dangerous agitator." From the past appears the shade of Sat-Hathor, the daughter of the Egyptian goddess of love, who has been dead for nearly 4,000 years and whose tomb has been desecrated.

It just so happens that the ninth-grade history class is studying ancient Egypt. And although Blossom has recently accidentally burned down Old Man Leverette's privy with Alexander trapped, for a time, inside it, she convinces Alexander to work with her on a class project. Fighting all the way, Alexander tries to deny his talent of Second Sight, but soon, along with Blossom, he gets involved with the *ka*, or spirit, of Sat-Hathor.

After locating the princess's mummy and other possessions and using them for their project, Blossom and Alexander travel back in time to return them to Sat-Hathor's tomb, scaring away grave robbers in the process. Along the way, Blossom prevents Alexander from foolishly giving his fraternity pin to Letty Shambaugh, both Letty and her mother receive a surprising comeuppance that ties in perfectly with the rest of the story, Miss Fairweather attracts a male admirer, Blossom discovers that her talents for "seeing the Unseen" are greater than those of her disagreeable Mamma, and readers learn much about mummification and the desecration of Egyptian tombs. As Blossom might say, "The story's as busy as a swarm of flies on spilt chicken fat."

VOICES AFTER MIDNIGHT

Leaving Blossom Culp behind, Richard Peck continued to craft novels about the supernatural, with *Voices after Midnight* marking another important step in the development of his writing. In *Voices*, he draws on the supernatural, as he did in the four Blossom Culp novels, but presents it in a serious manner. The Blossom Culp novels were intended to be funny and essentially frivolous; *Voices* contains the same kind of cleverness, along with a pile of Peck's usual humorous incidents and aphorisms, but it's not at all frivolous. Like the Blossom stories, however, *Voices* employs the main characters as rescuers of characters from the past. In this case, the characters from the past turn out to be ancestors of the present-day characters.

From California, sixteen-year-old Chad (the narrator), along with his eight-year-old brother, Luke, his sixteen-year-old sister, Heidi, and Luke's dog, Al, move to New York City with their parents for two weeks during the summer while their father is temporarily employed there. They soon discover that the multistoried brownstone house they rent on East 73rd Street near Central Park has an unusual history, and all three of the kids find themselves able to slip from the present to the past and back again, usually just by opening the right doors in the house. The ever-insightful Luke remarks after their first forays into the past—1928, 1776, 1849—"everything that ever happened is still going on, inside us."

For most of the novel, only Chad and Luke travel through time. When they ultimately focus on the period to which they seem drawn— the winter of 1887–1888—they are surprised to discover their sister at a New Year's Eve ball, dancing with the much-talked-about Tyler Dunlap. Until this incident, the boys have been only observers of the past; now all three kids are participants in the action. They discover they must rescue Tyler and his sister, Emily, who have been trapped in a birdcage-like elevator due to a loss of electricity during the Great Blizzard of 1888.

This exciting novel is filled with surprising twists and unexpected revelations about the family histories, as well as several interesting notes about New York City landmarks and historical events. Along the way, the usual Peck trademarks are evident: witty observations about people; humorous comments about the vagaries of teenage life; the power of peer pressure; references to literature and popular culture; the support of an elderly character; and the use of specific names to identify clothing labels (Banana Republic pants), objects (Acura Integra car), television shows (*The Wonder Years*), and celebrities (Tom Cruise). In addition, Peck pays homage to Dame Barbara Cartland for the romantic elements in this novel and to various characters—real and fictional—associated with contemporary horror and supernatural movies, such as Stephen King and Freddy Krueger.

Most significantly, this is the first novel Richard Peck wrote with a New York City setting, and it isn't coincidental that the action takes place just a few blocks from Peck's own apartment building. Following through on his intent to take young people on a journey to self-discovery, Peck sends his characters on a visit into Manhattan's past. Along the way, his young characters discover lessons about themselves "that would remain forever unlearned back in their twentieth century and in a subdivision no older than they are."[33]

The quality of Peck's time-travel fantasy was uniformly praised by reviewers, especially for the "device of having time manipulate the characters (rather than the traditional reverse situation),"[34] though several reviewers (notably Betsy Hearne[35] and *Publishers Weekly*[36]) were disturbed by the manipulation of logic that enables the two characters rescued from death in 1888 to be the rescuers' great-great-grandfather and his sister, thus ensuring the existence of Chad, Luke, and Heidi. If, however, the present is tied to the past, why not tie the past to the present, as Peck has done so cleverly?

LOST IN CYBERSPACE

Peck explores further his interest in both the supernatural and New York City in *Lost in Cyberspace* (1995) and its sequel, *The Great Interactive Dream Machine* (1996). He describes these titles as "innocent little satire[s]" that play with "the *lingua franca* of a new generation more computer-literate than literate." In the creation of Josh, his narrator, Peck claims he "tried to imagine Bill Gates at puberty, which wasn't, somehow, so difficult."[37]

In the first of the two titles, we meet Josh Lewis and Aaron Zimmer, sixth-graders at the elite Huckley School for Boys. Josh lives with his newly career-oriented mother and high-maintenance twelve-year-old sister, Heather. Due to his parents' recent separation, his father has taken up residence in Chicago and interacts with Josh through phone conversations on Sunday nights. To provide the necessary care for her children, given her increasing absence from home, Josh's mother contracts with a London-based au pair agency, which results in a series of disastrous helpers who are quickly dismissed from the position. Josh's best friend, Aaron, lives in the penthouse of the same apartment building but spends most of his in- and out-of-school time in the Huckley computer lab. When Aaron's penchant and passion for computing uncover the key to time travel, the boys find themselves in the living room of a house built in 1921 and owned by the monied Osgood Vanderwhitney family, the house that years later becomes their school.

Josh and Aaron learn unwittingly that the time-travel process works in reverse when they transport Phoebe, a servant from the historic home, into their modern-day school. Unable to determine how to send her back, the boys decide that Phoebe must assume the au pair role at the Lewis household until matters are sorted out. Unlike her predecessors, Phoebe excels in her work and plays an integral role in keeping this distanced family together. In the end, Josh and Aaron discover a link through time, not one that results from their tinkering on the computer, but one that exists through the living generations of people who inhabit their community.

Lost in Cyberspace was generally well received by reviewers, who praised, per usual, Peck's ability to craft believable characters. Bruce C. Appleby encapsulated these accolades when he said that the tales are "peopled with interesting characters" and stated, "Peck has created young characters who are real and whose very flaws make them more interesting."[38] Appleby admired, too, Peck's use of Internet jargon, arguing that this provides "insights into how young adults understand cyberspace more realistically than do adults."[39] Another reviewer, however, worried that, while "the title will immediately appeal to cyber-freaks, students who are not highly computer literate may be turned off."[40] That is not a likely comment a reviewer would make today, however, given the high rate of computer literacy among young readers.

There was also some dissension among reviewers regarding the effectiveness of the time-travel element as a literary device in the novel. One *Publishers Weekly* reviewer argued that Peck's "mechanisms seem almost plausible; even better, they don't overpower the story."[41] But a *VOYA* reviewer argued that the novel represents "science fiction fluff from a well-established author" that "devotes little space to the actual time spent in either the past or the future."[42] Some, like Carolyn Phelan, found value in the text beyond the device, noting, "Elements of the plot may intrigue those who wonder about the nature of time, but most readers will be happy reading this witty, fast-paced novel just to see what happens next."[43]

THE GREAT INTERACTIVE
DREAM MACHINE

In *The Great Interactive Dream Machine*, Aaron and Josh's cyber adventures continue. Only this time, Aaron's computer savvy and Josh's accidental meddling result in the creation of a dream-granting machine—with one catch: nobody knows whose wish will come true or when. As a result, the boys find themselves at the whim of others' fantasies: Heather wants to scout out boys in the Hamptons; the spinster downstairs wants to go back in time to be with her lover; Aaron's poodle just wants to go outside. Josh and Aaron are simply along for the ride. They do occasionally enjoy a dream-come-true of their own making, most humorously when they both imagine themselves bigger and older than the class bullies. The resulting vision of the boys as senior students equipped with razor stubble, sausagelike fingers, and underwear that feels more snug than usual is wryly portrayed with wit and sensitivity.

These wish-fulfillment activities keep Josh and Aaron from completing their summer school project on World War II. All hope is not lost, however, as the boys, again, learn the power of history, not through technology, but in the form of a living person, the spinster downstairs. Lonely Miss Mather, who has forged a relationship with the boys, teasing them with cookies and stories of her work in the Women's Voluntary Services during World War II, visits their classroom when oral report day arrives and shares her story with their classmates.

Reviewer response to *The Great Interactive Dream Machine* was generally positive, despite a few intimations that the book lacks depth and complexity. Reviewers across the board complimented Peck on the story's pace and style, citing the effectiveness of the novel's "clever one-liners,"[44] "biting prose,"[45] and "fast-paced action and witty conversations."[46] Others argued, however, that the novel is hindered by the technologically inspired organizing device; a *Booklist* reviewer noted, "The day-to-day talk of private school bullies and family troubles is more involving than the many techno-speak and culture-of-the-nineties references."[47]

As with *Lost in Cyberspace*, Peck's use of computer language affected reviewers in diverse ways. According to a *Publishers Weekly* reviewer, "Aaron's technical jargon sheds no light on the logic of the 'dream machine' and his lengthy discourses may bore some readers."[48] Instead, Joyce A. Litton identified this as a selling point, claiming, "One need not understand computers to like this book, although technical language provides added pleasure for the would-be hacker."[49] Interestingly enough, at the time of this novel's publication, Richard Peck owned no computer and was not what anyone would call "computer literate."

NOTES

1. Richard Peck, Workshop at Montclair, New Jersey, Public Library, 9 December 1987.

2. Richard Peck, Speech presented at the Children's Literature Festival, University of Southern Mississippi, Hattiesburg, 19 March 1981.

3. Paul Janeczko, "An Interview with Richard Peck," *English Journal* (February 1976): 97.

4. Richard Peck, *Anonymously Yours* (New York: Julian Messner, 1991), 23.

5. Richard Peck, "An Exclusive Interview with Blossom Culp," Dell publicity brochure, 1987.

6. Peck, "An Exclusive Interview with Blossom Culp."

7. Jennifer M. Brown, "A Long Way from Decatur," *Publishers Weekly*, 21 July 2003, 170.

8. Peck, "An Exclusive Interview with Blossom Culp."

9. Deborah Kovacs, *Meet the Authors* (New York: Scholastic, 1995), 76.

10. Richard Peck, in *Something about the Author Autobiography Series*, vol. 2, ed. Adele Sarkissian (Detroit: Gale Research, 1985), 178.

11. M. Kip Hartvigsen and Christen Brog Hartvigsen, "The Divine Miss Blossom Culp," *ALAN Review* (Winter 1989): 33.

12. Alleen Pace Nilsen and Kenneth L. Donelson, *Literature for Today's Young Adults*, 2nd ed. (Glenview, Ill.: Scott, Foresman, 1985), 153.

13. Nilsen and Donelson, *Literature for Today's Young Adults*, 153–54.

14. Barbara Elleman, "50 Books Too Good to Be Missed," *Learning* (April–May 1985): 28.

15. Judith Atwater, *School Library Journal* (September 1975): 109.

16. *The Junior Bookshelf* (June 1977): 183.

17. Richard Peck, in *Contemporary Authors Online* (Detroit: Thomson Gale, 2006), http://galenet.galegroup.com.

18. Arthea J. S. Reed, *Reaching Adolescents: The Young Adult Book and the School* (New York: Merrill, 1994), 50.

19. Reyhan Harmanci, "Blossom Culp Never Loses Her Spirit, Appeal," *San Francisco Chronicle*, 28 August 2005, C6.

20. Richard Peck, "A Personal Letter from: Blossom Culp to: Whom It May Concern," Dell publicity brochure, n.d.

21. Tony Manna, *ALAN Review* (Fall 1979).

22. Linda Silver, *School Library Journal* (November 1977): 61.

23. Ethel L. Heins, *Horn Book* (February 1978): 56.

24. Jane B. Jackson, *KLIATT Young Adult Paperback Book Guide* (Fall 1979), 12.

25. Hartvigsen and Hartvigsen, "The Divine Miss Blossom Culp," 35.

26. Peck, "A Personal Letter from Blossom Culp."

27. Patricia Lee Gauch, *New York Times Book Review*, 18 December 1983, 21.

28. *Ocala Star Banner*, 25 December 1984.

29. Anne Eliot Crompton, *Parents' Choice* (Spring–Summer 1984): 5.

30. Patty Campbell, *Wilson Library Bulletin* (March 1986): 51.

31. Michael Carl, *School Library Journal* (May 1986): 108.

32. *Publishers Weekly*, 21 March 1986.

33. Richard Peck, "Traveling in Time," *ALAN Review* (Winter 1990): 2.

34. Barbara Elleman, *Booklist*, 1 October 1989, 353.

35. Betsy Hearne, *Bulletin of the Center for Children's Books* (October 1989): 41.

36. *Publishers Weekly*, 29 September 1989, 69.

37. Richard Peck, "In the Beginning Was The . . . ," *ALAN Review* (Spring 1997): 2–4.

38. Bruce C. Appleby, *ALAN Review* (Spring 1996), 29.

39. Appleby, *ALAN Review*, 29.

40. Terri Evans, *VOYA* (April 1996): 43.

41. *Publishers Weekly*, 2 September 1996, 131.

42. Evans, *VOYA*, 43.

43. Carolyn Phelan, *Booklist*, 15 October 1995, 402.

44. *Publishers Weekly*, 2 September 1996, 131.

45. *Kirkus Reviews*, 1996, http://clcd.odyssi.com.

46. Carolyn Phelan, *Booklist*, 1 September 1996, 131.

47. Phelan, *Booklist*, 131.

48. *Publishers Weekly*, 2 September 1996, 131.

49. Joyce A. Litton, *ALAN Review* (Spring 1997), 34.

·6·

Problem Novels

For most of the 1970s and early 1980s, the field of books for adolescents was dominated by "problem novels"—novels that explored contemporary topics easily categorized in bibliographies—drugs, divorce, physical handicaps, abortion, and death. The worst of those novels deal with a single topic in a manipulative or didactic manner, using shallow characters and arriving at an unrealistic solution. The best of them engage readers in a realistic, multidimensional story, with well-developed characters whose major problem is not necessarily resolved completely by the end of the story. In the decade between the mid-1970s and mid-1980s, Richard Peck published four problem novels that are among the best of that type.

ARE YOU IN THE HOUSE ALONE?

Teenage rape is the focal problem in *Are You in the House Alone?* though the book is also about friendships and communication; relationships between teens, parents and children, and students and teachers; and social class differences in a "snug, smug" Connecticut town. Gail, the sixteen-year-old victim and narrator, does not live in a vacuum, and the aftermath of her attack reveals the true colors of various members of her community. The chief of police refuses to prosecute the attacker, Phil Lawyer, because he is the son of the town's most prominent family. Gail's best friend, Alison, denies her own boyfriend's guilt. Gail's middle-class mother wants to put the incident behind her as quickly as possible, and her father, recently laid off from his job, feels powerless in his inability to protect his daughter or to bring the criminal to justice. The school guidance counselor is incapable of dealing with the problem or Gail's feelings about it because she's trained to deal only with test results. The mother for whom Gail babysits wants no more contact with Gail because she doesn't want to be reminded of what happened in her house. The lawyer is willing to take the case to court but knows only too well that Gail is likely to be victimized again because she and her boyfriend have had a sexual relationship, there were no witnesses to the rape, and the accused rapist can plea-bargain to a lesser charge. Given these circumstances, the reader feels increasingly frustrated along with Gail, who, Peck is certain to point out, did nothing to encourage the attack. It's not a pretty portrait, but it is truthful.

Peck avoids didacticism and creates a story that moves along inexorably: each disturbing phone call, each disgusting note left in Gail's locker takes the reader along with Gail toward the inevitable attack by a psychotic acquaintance. The story contains some bright spots, too. Gail's family is drawn closer together as a result of the rape. Madame Malevich, Gail's colorful drama teacher, is as helpful as a teacher can be. And Gail survives the experience with insightful determination not to be handicapped by the resulting pain.

Peck was inspired to write the novel after receiving review copies of several nonfiction books about rape, all of which identified a teenage girl as the most likely victim. But then, Peck says, "each book dropped her like a stone and went on to discuss the victim as a figure in the adult world."[1] And so Peck set out to set the record straight. As he explains: "I had to do a lot of research and interview a lot of people and go to a lot of places. I had to talk to doctors and lawyers and police personnel and victims. I had to deal only in the truth. I couldn't put a happy ending on this story because we don't have any happy endings to this problem in our society."[2]

There were other things that Richard Peck wanted readers to know, he says. He wanted to include a rape crisis center but decided against it because he feared that many readers might not have access to such places. (Remember, this was 1976.) He also wanted to include a courtroom scene but did not write one because, he says, "The typical case is never reported, much less brought to trial."[3] The novel does not describe the forced intercourse (Gail is knocked unconscious), but it does graphically describe the pelvic examination that follows when Gail is brought to the hospital. "Research indicated that the typical rape victim never goes for medical treatment and attention. I wanted my readers to know what this treatment is and why it's vital."[4]

Although determined to publish the novel, Peck worried that it would ruin his career. However, with the exception of *Kirkus*, reviewers praised it highly, calling it "sensitive, tasteful,"[5] "honest and perceptive,"[6] and "neither sensational nor pornographic."[7] J. W. Levy, writing in the *Journal of Reading*, went so far as to recommend that the novel "be required reading for all teenagers."[8] The American Library Association named this one of the Best of the Best Books 1970–1982 and later honored it as a Best of the Best Books for Young Adults 1966–1986. It also received the Edgar Allan Poe Mystery Award in 1977. Most important, this was one of the novels that the ALA cited for presenting Richard Peck with the Margaret A. Edwards Award in 1990. Peck reported that the combined support of students, teachers, and librarians made this his best-selling novel until his award-winning *A Long Way from Chicago* and *A Year Down Yonder*.

FATHER FIGURE

Although *Father Figure* has not sold as well as most of Peck's other novels for young adults, it contains some of his best writing. Peck views it as one of his best books, and *Publishers Weekly* in 1978 said it was "assuredly one of the best for all ages in many a moon."[9] Surprisingly, it did not make as many best-books lists as some of Peck's other novels, although *Booklist* and *School Library Journal* each gave it a starred review and the ALA named it a Best Book for Young Adults in 1978. Years later, however, the ALA Young Adult Services Division named it one of the Best of the Best 1970–1982. Ultimately *Father Figure* was another one of the novels cited by the ALA for Peck's Margaret A. Edwards Award.

This is a quiet, intense book for the most part, though it's not somber, even if it is about how an insecure teenager deals with the death of a parent. Nothing exciting happens, and Jim Atwater, the seventeen-year-old cynical and reflective main character and narrator, typically maintains a cool exterior, even at his mother's funeral.

Coming to terms with his mother's death is only one of Jim's problems. Jim and his eight-year-old brother, Byron, have been living with their uncommunicative, cool maternal grandmother in Brooklyn Heights since their father abandoned them eight years earlier. From the time when their mother became incapacitated with her illness, Jim has assumed responsibility for Byron. Now, suddenly, the two boys are being sent to Florida to live with their father, a man they know nothing about. Throughout the summer, Jim punishes his father for past transgressions while preventing him from becoming the central parental figure in Byron's life. The conflict provides an unusual twist in the archetypal coming-of-age plot: in order to grow up, Jim has to relinquish his parental role. Once he does that, he can finish his senior year in high school and make plans for college and life as an adult. In the process, Jim comes to terms with his father as well, providing an emotional, upbeat finale to the novel.

The novel's effective examination of the father-son relationship is a rarity in books for young adults. Peck had a strong desire to explore the topic of male emotions in this novel, a topic he later examined further in *Close Enough to Touch* and *Remembering the Good Times*. In fact, in *Contemporary Authors*, Peck stated his intent to "do a body of work" exploring the feelings of boys and men that will enable them to show their more sensitive side and to communicate with others more effectively.[10]

CLOSE ENOUGH TO TOUCH

Close Enough to Touch was inspired by a seventh-grade boy in a Toronto library who asked, "Say, listen, have you written anything on dating?"[11]

"They want love stories? All right, I'll try one, but I won't play their game," Peck decided.[12]

First, he wrote this teenage love story about a boy, and it remains to this day one of the few told from a male's point of view. Second, the story is not about finding the right girl but about, as Peck puts it, "that long dry spell between girls."[13] And it's not just about losing a girlfriend; this one left without warning, dying from an aneurysm. Moreover, it's about male emotions, specifically grief, self-pity, loneliness, and the inability to communicate those feelings.

As in *Father Figure*, the father-son relationship is an important part of *Close Enough to Touch*, even though the novel's main concern is how a teenager copes with the sudden death of his girlfriend. Matt Moran, a high school junior, narrating his own story in the present tense, is a more relaxed, less cynical version of Jim Atwater. Matt's father, a former military man, is sensitive and understanding. After Matt gets drunk and cries for the first time, for example, he and his father have an important talk. Matt tells the reader: "Dad always thinks what he has to offer isn't good enough. It's good enough for me." By explaining to his father how much he loved Dory, that they had such great plans for the future, and that, now, there is nothing, Matt feels relieved. His father's significant, albeit clichéd, exit line is "A boy needs his dad." And, of course, Matt does.

Supported in his grief by his father, his equally sensitive stepmother, Beth, and his energetic grandmother, Matt continues to deal with his self-pity. Intending to spend the rest of the school semester at his family's lakeside cottage, Matt meets Margaret Chasen—a cocky, candid, nonconformist high school senior—who has been thrown from her horse. In the process of helping the injured Margaret, he realizes he is attracted to her. Returning to school, he begins a lengthy process of pursuing her and leaving dead Dory behind. Symbolically, this turning point occurs on Easter weekend, a time of rebirth. It's not an easy process, to be sure, especially because Matt and Margaret do a lot of verbal sparring. But some of the book's most humorous lines occur during this part of the novel, and the book ends with a quirky, joyful scene.

Unlike *Father Figure*, this novel received a varied response from critics. No one was cool toward it, however. On the enthusiastic side were the *New York Times Book Review, Publishers Weekly*, and the *Bulletin of the Center for Children's Books*. The latter called the novel "compelling and bittersweet."[14] Norma Bagnall, in the *ALAN Review*, wrote that the story "could have leaned towards the maudlin except for Peck's superb infusion of humor and his emphatic, yet unsentimental, tone."[15] But a *School Library Journal* reviewer found the narrator's worldly wisdom inconsistent with his immature actions and labeled the book "predictable."[16] The most cutting attack came from a *Bestsellers* reviewer who called the story "trivial" as well as "shallow and tedious," recommending it only for "light casual reading for some callow freshmen."[17] The ALA obviously did not share that opinion, because they listed *Close Enough to Touch* as one of 1981's Best Books for Young Adults. It remains one of the best of the very few books available on the subject of male emotions.

REMEMBERING THE GOOD TIMES

While both *Father Figure* and *Close Enough to Touch* begin with a death and end with the rebirth of the main character, *Remembering the Good Times* does the opposite: it begins with the birth of a foal (in a barn that is later bulldozed out of existence) and ends with the suicide of one of the book's three main characters. The novel filled a serious void in the bibliographies of problem books by examining the symptoms of teenage suicide, and in the process, it received more reviews than any other book Peck had written up to that time.

There was little disagreement among critics about *Remembering the Good Times*. Except for one who foolishly faulted Peck for not providing the answer to why teenagers commit suicide[18] and another who took issue with the way school is portrayed,[19] everyone else praised this novel highly, valuing it for its depth of character development, "finely honed style,"[20] "quiet intensity,"[21] and unsentimental examination of suicide. *Publishers Weekly* boxed off its review for emphasis and called the novel Peck's "best book so far."[22] Although one reviewer predicted that teenagers will neither identify with the characters in this novel nor "stick with this book,"[23] high school students participating in the Iowa Young Adult Book Poll selected *Remembering the Good Times* as one of the best books they had read in 1986.[24] And, in a survey administered in 1992 by Ted Hipple—with eighty-seven teachers, college professors, and publishers active in the Assembly on Literature for Adolescents of the NCTE (ALAN) responding—*Remembering the Good Times* was ranked among the top ten best young adult novels published in the 1980s. *Remembering the Good Times* was also another of Peck's novels that was cited in naming him the recipient of the 1990 Margaret A. Edwards Award.

Peck wrote the book in response to student reaction to *Close Enough to Touch*. When he asked teenagers what a boy might do in responding to the kind of loss Matt experiences when his girlfriend dies, Peck was shocked when they answered, "Kill himself."[25] Hearing the identical response wherever he talked with students across the country, Richard Peck immediately began to research the causes and signs of teenage suicide as the basis for his next novel.

Instead of writing a book that focuses on the suicide itself and how it affects those left behind—as Fran Arrick's *Tunnel Vision* and Susan Beth Pfeffer's *About David* had already done effectively—Peck focused instead on the friendship that develops among three young teenagers during a period of nearly four years (more time than young adult novels usually cover), thus allowing readers not only to become involved with the characters but also to observe the subtle clues that portend one troubled boy's fatal act. In addition, this book is also about several topics that Peck deals with in his other novels: class differences, conformity, the inadequacies of school programs and their administrators, the importance of caring adults in teenagers' lives, and, with noted effect, the suburbanization of rural areas. Peck enriches the story of these three young people by "dramatically introducing interrelated themes of change and violence and show[ing] how these phenomena flourish in the suburban community where the friends live—an impersonal town so new that its developers are still carving it out of a pastoral landscape and uprooting the past in the process."[26] As the community becomes more impersonal, violence becomes more regular, with Tray's culminating act providing the link between the two.

As in *Father Figure* and *Close Enough to Touch*, the relationship between fathers and sons and the need for boys to express feelings are key to the novel. While the bright, self-driven Tray Kirby refuses to communicate with his affluent parents, the less intellectual Buck Mendenhall, who lives with his hardworking father in a trailer at the edge of town, learns to express his emotions. Buck's father, in fact, revealing his own sensitivity, tells Buck how he feels about him and later encourages Buck to let out his emotional pain so that, at the end of the book, everyone—including a sensitive reader—has a purifying cry.

Buck, who tells this story in retrospect, is an unusual—and refreshing—teenage narrator. He's an excellent observer, but it takes him a while to understand what he sees. According to one reviewer, "His insights never match his observations, . . . and he's neither as clever and charismatic as Kate nor as bright and driven as Tray."[27] Three other characters enlarge this novel, making it more entertaining and insightful. One is Skeeter Calhoon, the psychopathic bully who harasses not only Buck but also a first-year English teacher. Sherrie Slater, the new English teacher, is hopelessly unprepared to deal with junior high kids, especially without a supportive school administration. And Polly Prior, Kate's great-grandmother—a balding, cranky, wheelchair-bound old lady who cheats at cards—provides snatches of wisdom as well as a significant link to the past that helps make this novel so vibrant. Peck envisioned her as

"Blossom Culp, grown old, but still herself."[28] Polly's pear orchard also provides a symbolic link to a past that is being wiped out by spreading subdivisions and shopping malls. The inevitability of this incursion helps to drive Tray to hang himself from a branch of one of those pear trees. Memorable characters all. "In fact," a *Los Angeles Times* reviewer wrote, "all the characters shimmer."[29]

Richard Peck still views *Remembering the Good Times* as his best novel—and the most difficult to write, not only as an author engaging in a craft but as a person feeling very real emotions. When speaking of the novel, he says, "I wrote it in grief. Every time I created something more about the character, I knew I was creating a human sacrifice."[30] In his 1991 autobiography, *Anonymously Yours*, he states that the novel "is the young adult book of my own that means the most to me."[31] But he never explained why. When pressed for an explanation during a telephone interview in early 1993, Peck offered this self-analysis:

> I must say I can account for not any of the time that I spent writing that book. I felt as if I had walked into it and was living it. . . . Those characters also meant more to me than other characters have meant. . . . I just somehow reached down more for that one in ways I didn't realize. I think the father of Buck in this story is drawn more from my own father than I had ever meant to use. It just meant so much to me. . . . It was a very emotional experience for me, in ways I'm not sure I understand.

NOTES

1. Richard Peck, "Richard Peck Discusses Adolescent Rape," Dell publicity release, n.d.

2. Richard Peck, Interview by Paul Janeczko, "An Interview with Richard Peck," in *From Writers to Students: The Pleasures and Pains of Writing*, ed. M. Jerry Weiss (Newark, Del.: International Reading Association, 1979), 81.

3. Richard Peck, "Rape and the Teenage Victim," *Top of the News* (Winter 1978): 175–76.

4. Peck, "Rape and the Teenage Victim," 175.

5. Janet Leonberger, *Young Adult Cooperative Book Review Group of Massachusetts* (February 1977): 89.

6. Zena Sutherland, *Bulletin of the Center for Children's Books* (March 1977): 112.

7. Paul Heins, *Horn Book* (February 1977): 60.

8. J. W. Levy, *Journal of Reading* (April 1978): 655.

9. *Publishers Weekly*, 17 July 1978, 168.

10. Richard Peck, quoted by Jean W. Ross in *Contemporary Authors*, New Revision Series, vol. 19, ed. Linda Metzger (Detroit: Gale Research, 1987), 369.

11. Richard Peck, "People of the Word: A Look at Today's Young Adults and Their Needs," *School Library Media Quarterly* (Fall 1981): 20.

12. Richard Peck, "The Invention of Adolescence and Other Thoughts on Youth," *Top of the News* (Winter 1983): 186.

13. Peck, "The Invention of Adolescence," 186.

14. *Bulletin of the Center for Children's Books* (November 1981): 53.

15. Norma Bagnall, *ALAN Review* (Winter 1982): 21.

16. Kay Webb O'Connel, *School Library Journal* (September 1981): 140.

17. *Bestsellers* (January 1982): 403.

18. Ann A. Flowers, *Horn Book* (July–August 1985): 457.

19. Mary R. Oran, *Book Report* (September–October 1985).

20. Cynthia K. Leibold, *School Library Journal* (April 1985): 99.

21. Hazel Rochman, *Booklist*, 1 March 1985, 945.

22. *Publishers Weekly*, 17 May 1985, 118.

23. Oran, *Book Report*.

24. John W. Conner and Kathleen N. Tessmer, "1986 Books for Young Adults Poll," *English Journal* (December 1986): 60.

25. Richard Peck, "Suicide as a Solution?" Dell publicity brochure, n.d.

26. Michael Cart, *From Romance to Realism: 50 Years of Growth and Change in Young Adult Literature* (New York: HarperCollins, 1996), 173.

27. Lenore Skenazy, *Advertising Age*, 18 April 1985, 13.

28. Richard Peck, *Anonymously Yours* (New York: Julian Messner, 1991), 113.

29. Kristiana Gregory, *Los Angeles Times Book Review*, 10 August 1986.

30. Deborah Kovacs, *Meet the Authors* (New York: Scholastic, 1995), 77.

31. Peck, *Anonymously Yours*, 90.

· 7 ·

Departures from the Usual

$\mathcal{O}$ne of the qualities that makes Richard Peck so important as a writer is that he isn't satisfied to churn out only one kind of book. Each of the novels examined in this chapter represents a significant departure from his other novels.

SECRETS OF THE SHOPPING MALL

Published exactly midway between his four problem novels, *Secrets of the Shopping Mall* (1979) was unlike any of Richard Peck's other works until *Bel-Air Bambi and the Mall Rats* was published in 1993. It won no prizes and made no one's best-books list. Yet it engendered more reviews than all but one of his previous novels, and almost all of the reviewers made negative remarks. It is also his least well-crafted novel. But it resulted in more letters to the author than any of his earlier novels and outsold most of his previous novels that did make best-books lists. *Secrets of the Shopping Mall* is not an impressive literary work, but younger teenagers seem to love it, though not for the reasons that Peck wrote it. But in 1990, this was one of the six novels cited as integral to Peck's receiving the Margaret A. Edwards Award in recognition of his contributions to young adult literature.

What makes this novel unusual are its setting and its concept, which are almost the same. The concept is a brilliant one, the reasoning behind it perfectly logical: today's climate-controlled shopping malls contain everything to sustain life. Many contemporary teenagers use their local mall as their chief gathering place, going there after school or, as Peck says, often instead of school. If not ordered to leave at closing time, a person could live inside a mall indefinitely—if he or she hid somewhere until the security guards left. That's exactly what Peck's characters do. A "nutty premise" Patty Campbell called it, but an "especially delicious" one.[1]

Escaping from the vicious King Kobra gang at their chaotic, graffiti-covered, inner-city junior high school, loners Teresa and Barnie spend their last two dollars on bus fare to Paradise Park, New Jersey, where they hide out in a large department store. Sleeping beneath the beds in the Beds and Bedding department by day and roaming the darkened store by night, they feed themselves from the refrigerated deli unit in the Gourmet department and "borrow" clothing from whatever department suits their fancy. Their families won't miss them because thirteen-year-old Teresa lives with an aunt who doesn't care, and Barnie—"too smart for the seventh grade and too short for the eighth"—lives in a foster home that probably won't even report him missing. In the mall, they at last feel safe. Besides, there is no school to attend, no adults to set limits for them—no one to tell them what to do.

They find out otherwise. The store houses other runaway teenagers, though from permissive, affluent, suburban homes. Like Teresa and Barnie, they roam the store by night, wearing the latest name-brand fashions, and they hide by day, often "freezing" like store mannequins. Their names identify the departments over which they watch: Swank from Cuff Links, Crystal from Stemware, and so on. They are ruled by the beautiful blond Barbie and the immaculately dressed preppie Ken, who look "like an advertisement for a modeling school." They all go along with the dictatorial Barbie because it's easier than thinking for themselves. In essence, they exchange one gang at school for a different one at the mall, one authority figure for another, which proves to be even worse than the one they initially fled.

Being independent thinkers, Teresa and Barnie wrangle themselves legitimate jobs in the department store, then rally some members of the group to rebel against Barbie's dictatorial decisions, after which all the kids decide to go back home while Teresa and Barnie stay on to enjoy their new, productive lives.

"A bizarre farce," one reviewer called it.[2] An "offbeat comedy/mystery/fantasy . . . too frantic, and occasionally confusing," another one wrote.[3] *Kirkus* labeled it a "ham-handed satire."[4] *English Journal* reviewers wrote: "What Peck was probably aiming for was the ultimate satire on suburbia, but unfortunately where he landed is somewhere beyond realism but short of fantasy."[5]

Whatever its label, Peck says he intended the story as "a commentary on being young in the 1980s, an age in which the young no longer go from home to school, but go from the TV set to the shopping mall."[6] And, he states, "I wrote it as a satire, with these kids as pioneers on the last American frontier."[7] *Time* magazine called it "Lord & Taylor of the Flies."[8] Peck, hoping to expose—or at least poke some fun at—the teenage penchant for conspicuous consumption, says, "I don't think it did any good but I decided it would be good to be on record. Nobody has ever challenged kids' crassness, and asked them what they're really trying to buy."[9]

But young readers don't necessarily read the book the way Peck intended. A number of readers—adults as well as teenagers—misinterpret part of the action. Because Teresa and Barnie at first think the mannequins have come alive, some readers read the story as science fiction. In addition, many young readers don't see the point that "it can still be a gang even if they're well-dressed and the girls are picture-perfect models. They don't get that; they don't want to," Peck declares.

Nevertheless, some of Peck's usual themes are sure to come through to some readers: the need to act independently and not blindly follow the leader of a group; the importance of genuine friendship; being an outsider; the inability of educators to educate kids; the overemphasis on designer labels in our society. And even if readers don't "get it," they can have fun fantasizing a life in their own mall.

BEL-AIR BAMBI AND THE MALL RATS

Some readers liked *Secrets of the Shopping Mall* so much that their letters urged Richard Peck to write a sequel. In an age of series books in 1987, Peck said: "There ought to be a series called Mall Rats. I'm not happy with that setting, but . . ." Four years later, he was hard at work on a story that he entitled *Bel-Air Bambi and the Mall Rats*, published in the fall of 1993, his seventeenth novel for young people.

One need not read very far into *Bel-Air Bambi* to see that it is clearly a satire, with exaggerated characterizations and loads of Peck's usual humor, much of it bitingly sharp. But instead of focusing on a gang hiding out at the mall, Peck extended the situation and created a small, rural, middle-American community in which a group of high schoolers take over not only the mall but also their own homes, their school, and the entire town.

The supreme irony in this clever novel is that, in an age in which middle-American "family values" and morals have received so much attention, the town of Hickory Fork provides the opposite. "The only whole, functioning, cohesive family in the story is a group of rich Hollywood people from Bel-Air," Peck says, for "in this wholesome middle-American small town, there is nothing left—the family structure, the school, the community have all collapsed!"

That Hollywood family—the Babcocks—consists of an eleven-year-old narrator, Buffie, six-year-old Brick, thirteen-year-old Bambi, and their parents, Beth and Bill. And if all those B's don't give you a clue to the lengths that Peck has gone to be funny in this novel, consider these other characters: the football star, Jess Neverwood; the helpful good guy, Justin Thyme; the school principal, "Stretch" Wire and his oversized son, Bob Wire; Coach "Bear" Bottoms; the female leader of the Mall Rats, Tanya Hyde; and a ditsy, incompetent sixth-grade teacher, Miss Jean Poole—who is heard to say, "Me and the principal generally have lunch in his office."

Ever the teacher himself, Richard Peck pokes not-so-subtle barbs into a number of his favorite shibboleths of teenage as well as adult society. For example, when the family moves to Hickory Fork, Bambi refuses to set foot in the new school before she knows what the proper dress is. Peck writes that Bambi "hadn't shopped in two days and was developing a twitch." In school, when Big Tanya learns that Bambi and Buffie are from L.A., she asks them to reveal their signs and colors, thinking they must be in a gang like the Bloods or the Crips. Bambi naively replies, "Sagittarius" to the first question and "I'm best in beige" to the second. Realizing her mistake, she explains, "Oh, for Pete's sake, we're from *Bel Air*. We don't have gangs. We have fund-raisers." And to that surprising news, Tanya inquires, "Then if there's no gang, who runs the school?"

There's no doubt who runs the school in Hickory Fork. And the Babcocks, with some assistance, set out to correct the situation by using their natural talents for acting and making horror films. In the end, the world is set right once again by the Hollywood crowd, and everyone (well, *almost* everyone) lives happily ever after.

Middle school readers find much to enjoy in this novel, even if they don't fully understand or appreciate the satire. The satirical elements even posed problems for one adult reviewer who found the story in need of "a little less satire and a little more heart," arguing that "what starts as an extravagant tale goes over the top very quickly. Even outrageous humor needs a story to cling to, but overthrowing the mall rats is not enough story to support the frenzied goings-on."[10] Other reviewers praised the satire, calling the novel "a honey of a funny ride through small-town America gone horribly awry,"[11] and "a clever, intelligently written, and very funny spoof."[12] No matter the response, for Peck, the novel was a kick to write, providing a perfect venue for him to take his characteristic jabs at society.

PRINCESS ASHLEY

Two of Richard Peck's novels are not easily categorized. *Princess Ashley* is part problem novel, part romance. It's about peer pressure and conformity; parent-child relationships and lack of adult control; and school, friendship, alcoholism, and self-concept. *Those Summer Girls I Never Met* addresses the relationships between brothers and sisters, children and parents, and young people and old people, while it examines nostalgic elements from the past. It also addresses death and male emotions. On top of it all, it's overflowing with Peck's usual humor.

The themes in *Princess Ashley*—conformity and parent-child relationships—are vintage Peck. But they are not just part of the story as they are in his previous novels; here they *are* the story. Peck is his most direct in this novel; no teenage reader can possibly miss the point that it's unwise to follow a self-appointed leader blindly; no adult reader can possibly miss the point that it's unwise for parents to pamper their children and give up control with the hope that kids will do the right thing on their own. Adults play a large role in this novel, especially the narrator's mother, who becomes the spokesperson for much of Peck's philosophy. At the end of the novel, Mrs. Olinger—ironically, a school guidance counselor—says to her daughter: "I've been too much like any other parent, and you've been too much like any other child. We give you all this space and time, and you do nothing with it but damage."

The danger in this approach, of course, is that the novel becomes didactic. Peck can be a little heavy handed. Note, for example, when his sixteen-year-old narrator says, "At fourteen you can believe anything you want," and "in tenth grade you like rumors better than the truth anyway." But for the most part, the action illustrates clearly enough that the teenagers are out of control. They reach a crisis point in the middle of the novel when Gloria, the school's most volatile female student, smashes Mrs. Olinger in the face with a metal wastebasket, and again at the climax of the novel when Craig, the school's most out-of-control male student, crashes his sports car after drinking irresponsibly. It's easy to accept the adults' advice to their children because the book's previous events enable the reader to see how right the adults are—even if readers wouldn't follow the advice. When Craig's father says, "When we couldn't control him, we just hoped for the best," readers see the parents' regret because, by then, Craig is lying brain damaged and paralyzed in the hospital.

Peck's choice of narrator works well here, too. Rather than serving as a perceptive interpreter of life, as many narrators of young adult novels are, Chelsea has a serious blind spot: she's an insecure teenager who wants to belong in her new school, and so she doesn't comprehend what she's doing or why. A typical teenager, she also wants no contact with her parents. Once school starts, Chelsea blindly follows the manipulative Ashley Packard, who has "been in charge from the first day she set foot in the sandbox." Chelsea doesn't see her misjudgments until two hundred pages, two years, and two tragedies later. It's an effective technique, masterfully executed.

Letters to Peck from teenage readers, however, seem to indicate that many of them "prefer the manipulative and possibly psychotic Ashley" to the more sensible and finally independent Chelsea.[13] The first letter Richard Peck ever received about *Princess Ashley* was from a young girl who said, "I just read *Princess Ashley* and I loved it. This is just like me and my best friend." And in response to a teacher's assignment to write about a character in one of Richard Peck's books with whom they identified, an eighth-grade girl wrote, "Oh, I'm definitely Ashley. I'm a full-time manipulator." Responses like these sadden the author, who says, "They just don't get it. I write one thing and they see another."

This novel's harsh look at teenage life reflects Peck at his angriest. "It's my toughest novel," Peck admits.[14] He has said, "I think the real fuel for all writing is anger." When asked if he feels angrier now than when he first started writing, Peck's unhesitating reply is, "Oh, infinitely." Janice K. Tovey, writing about *Princess Ashley* in her master's thesis on Richard Peck, concludes: "After numerous novels in which he asked questions of [readers], he seems to want to shock them into questioning their own values and attitudes. He seems less tolerant of their attention to their peers and angry that they relinquish their own identity."[15]

This novel, however, is not all serious, for Peck knows very well that teenagers want to be entertained when they read. There is considerable humor in this novel, and the most reliable source of it resides in the character of Pod Johnson, an insightful, oddball student who, though bright and rich, projects the image of a bumpkin. His efforts at writing poetry in English class alone are enough to make him memorable. Pod, the *Los Angeles Times* wrote, is "one of the most winning characters in young adult fiction."[16]

In addition to high praise from various reviewers, such as *Kirkus*, which singled out Peck's "unusual wisdom and empathy for the teen condition,"[17] *Princess Ashley* received *VOYA*'s highest possible rating for quality and popularity[18] and was named one of 1987's Best Books for Young Adults by the ALA as well as *School Library Journal*.

THOSE SUMMER GIRLS I NEVER MET

Humor dominates *Those Summer Girls I Never Met*, though sorrowful situations lurk behind the exterior adventures of two teenagers. Drew (for Andrew) Wingate, just weeks away from being sixteen years old and expecting to have the summer of his life as soon as he gets his driver's license, has a colorful view of the world and a talent for portraying it with exceptional wit. He describes his fourteen-year-old sister, Stephanie: "Steph's the all-suburban champion door banger for her weight and class. She practices." She also spends a lot of time in her room, "with her Walkman in one ear and her Trimline in the other and a VCR running." Like a typical teenager, she tries to avoid adults. "Eating with her nearest relatives kills her appetite." She, of course, finds Drew as obnoxious as he finds her, and that makes their mother's announcement even more horrifying: instead of enjoying the summer of their dreams, they will be spending two weeks on a cruise ship leaving from England with their sixty-four-year-old grandmother, whom they haven't seen in ten years.

Their grandmother turns out to be Connie Carlson, a vivacious jazz singer from the 1940s—"the Madonna of her particular generation"—who entertains the mainly elderly passengers in the ship's nightclub. She wishes to be reacquainted with her two grandchildren before it's too late, for she has a grim secret that the kids discover as they visit Copenhagen, Leningrad, Helsinki, Stockholm, and Oslo. One of Drew's greatest adventures during the trip is meeting Holly, the ship's dance instructor. She's a gorgeous twenty-two, and trying his best to look as old as possible, he pursues her lustfully, with amusing results.

Over the course of the journey, both Drew and his sister mature, come to love their bizarre grandmother, find out something about their previously unaccounted-for grandfather, learn to understand their mother a little better, see a bit of Europe, and tune in to music from an age they once thought was prehistoric. Peck skillfully interweaves a serious story with a humorous one, with humor being much more dominant than in any of his other serious novels.

Though almost all reviewers praised this novel for its balance between the silly and the somber, they were not uniform in their assessment of its other aspects. One critic identified a lack of depth in characterization, noting especially the "exaggerated qualities" of the females.[19] Another was displeased with the depiction of the cruise ship setting and the cities visited along the way, declaring them no better than "painted backdrops."[20] While detailed descriptions of Copenhagen and the other Baltic ports might be attractive to adult readers, Peck knows enough about his young readers to limit such particulars. Because most teenage readers are interested in a story, "the novel can't evolve into a lesson plan on Scandinavian ports of call and the political history of Leningrad," Peck notes. "Novels are about change and the people capable of it."[21] And both Drew and his sister undergo significant changes in their views of people and themselves on their sea journey.

Drew's insights, however, do seem a bit too sophisticated for a sixteen-year-old boy, as Hazel Rochman noted in *Booklist*.[22] Roger Sutton concurred, asserting that Peck's own strong voice "overwhelms his narrator, who has too much adult perspective on himself and the world."[23] Both of those reviewers nevertheless praised Peck's portrait of Stephanie's rebellious behaviors, with Sutton proclaiming hers "a perfect portrait."[24]

Peck has blended his experiences working on a cruise ship, knowledge of foreign cities, and nostalgic feelings for the past with some of his most common young adult themes—relationships between young and old, taking independent action, and viewing the world from a wider perspective—to produce a novel that is both funny and sad, instructive without being didactic, and, above all, uplifting.

UNFINISHED PORTRAIT OF JESSICA

Never one to play it safe in his writing, Richard Peck used *Unfinished Portrait of Jessica* to delve into a topic that no other young adult book writer had yet explored in depth: a young girl's anger at her mother when her father leaves. Peck says, "This business of anger against the mother from the daughter has been a silent neurosis." But an essay written by a girl whose paper "burned with anger and self-pity" about her mother's inability to hold on to her father and her father's remarriage[25] served as a catalyst for Peck to bring the issue forth.

During her parents' marriage, Jessica's father, a "brilliant photographer," was regularly absent from their home on Lake Shore Drive in Chicago. She remembers that, wherever he went, "there were ladies waiting to draw him even farther away." Jessica, nearly fourteen years old, retreats into a world of romance novels and a romanticized view of her father, using the walls and door of her room as barriers to keep her mother at bay—until her mother suggests that Jessica spend Christmas vacation with her father, who is living in Acapulco with Lucius Pine, Jessica's great-uncle and a famous painter.

With its lush flowers and warm sea breezes, the exotic Acapulco setting provides another romantic vision for Jessica. But it is here that Jessica's illusions are shattered. Her father fails to meet her at the airport when she arrives (he's out fishing). He doesn't comfort her when she gets ill and even forgets her fourteenth birthday. And he tries to seduce a young woman who has befriended her. Wiser, Jessica returns early to Chicago and slowly learns to appreciate the mother she had unfairly shunned, ultimately learning that her mom is the author of the romance novel she's been so fond of.

Peck has thoughtfully selected an older, more experienced Jessica as the novel's narrator, capturing her voice a few years after the Mexico trip when she is able to look back with more understanding of herself and her parents, a point apparently missed by one reviewer. Hazel Rochman found the last section of this novel "disappointing," "almost an addendum," and "an ending as facile as the miniseries Peck's been undercutting all along."[26] To which the author replies: "If I hadn't carried it on beyond that first Mexico scene, the implication there would have been that learning to do without your father and learning not to blame your mother is the work of a moment. You can do that over the holidays."

Peck explains further that Jessica has to be ready years later when her father comes back—which of course he would, because he's the kind of person who can never find what he is searching for. And when he comes back, the daughter has to have matured by then in order to deal with him.

Rochman, however, did praise "the compassion, the dreaming, and the humor" of Peck's novel and singled out "the perfectly tuned voice" of Jessica.[27] Peck reports that acerbic critic Roger Sutton echoed these sentiments regarding Jessica, telling the author, "At least you got the voice right."

Although this novel elucidates one of Richard Peck's several ongoing themes—you need to stop shifting blame—it differs from most of his other novels in several respects. First, the story is not set in the typical suburbs of most of Peck's previous novels. Like *Those Summer Girls I Never Met*, most of this novel doesn't even take place in the United States. Peck says he chose the Mexico setting for its lushness and excitement, and because he had been in Acapulco four times on a cruise ship during the winter of 1989–1990 and "the place really got to me."

> I was so appalled by the town—and that terrible contrast between poverty and luxury—that it worked nicely to represent the world to which Jessica's father would retreat. Besides, I saw the house in the story from a sailboat in Acapulco Bay, and even then I knew I had to have it, one way or another.

Second, the main character has no peers in the story. Even more than in *Father Figure*, peer-group interaction, perhaps Peck's most common subject, is nonexistent. Third, adults and adult problems are the focus of much of the novel, though we see those problems through Jessica's eyes. In fact, Richard Peck reports that *Unfinished Portrait of Jessica,* among his first eighteen novels for young people, was the book that received "the most immediate response from adults."

> The people who came to me first said, "I am that mother," because a lot of librarians and teachers have been in that circumstance—and some of them were in tears. Over and over again . . . somebody says, "That was my daughter."

With such a strong personal response from adults, one might expect this novel to have won several commendations from English teachers and librarians. But it didn't even appear on the 1991 Best Books for Young Adults list from the ALA, an appalling omission. Published reviews, however, were full of high praise for the "depth and nuance"[28] of this "richly textured" novel[29] and its "exposure into the worlds of art, artists, and Mexican culture."[30] Virginia Monseau says that "Peck uses his pen as a paintbrush, deftly splashing his canvas with vivid depictions of the Mexican landscape, using it as a backdrop for Jessica's journey toward self-realization."[31]

Some of those passages are artistically beautiful. Early in the novel, describing the painting called *Unfinished Portrait of Jessica,* Peck writes: "Her hair was brush strokes of silver-blond and her dress a cool pillar of ice-blue." And later, describing dinner, Peck writes: "Candles burned in big glass chimneys the same color as the sea. We sat in the pools of this underwater light, and the conversation came and went in waves."

Most importantly, this is a contemporary story that, as Peck says, "begins in anger and ends in hope, and it is called *Unfinished Portrait* because all our novels are unfinished portraits."[32] And, like all of Peck's novels, this one ends "at a new beginning after one necessary step forward."[33]

THE LAST SAFE PLACE ON EARTH

Like the other novels described in this chapter, *The Last Safe Place on Earth* (1995) tells a contemporary story; unlike these other titles, it is intentionally political, a critique at its core. Peck weaves into the narrative a deadly car crash involving teen drivers, an alcoholic parent, a delinquent and abusive child, the death of two parents, reference to AIDS, and threats on free speech through several acts of overt and covert censorship. Despite the compelling and weighty issues he raises, however, Peck allows readers to come to the surface and escape, at least temporarily, the hazards of living in a seemingly perfect community through the character he creates in Todd Tobin, "a first-person narrator with immense appeal and a fine sense of humor."[34]

A high school sophomore counting the days until he is old enough to attain his driver's license and enjoy the freedom he assumes will accompany it, Todd is believably rendered. He is fascinated and frustrated by girls and his inability to get one for himself. Objects of his affection are everywhere, however, inhabiting his town and his thoughts at almost every moment: "I see girls in the shapes the tree trunks make and in the formations of the clouds. I see a lot of girls this fall. I'm not obsessed. I'm in tenth grade." This characteristic play on language provides several opportunities for Peck to infuse his wit throughout the story, often at the expense of readers he understands—and wants to pay attention.

Peck's biting commentary on the community in which Todd and his family live runs throughout the text. The Tobin family has settled into a Christmas-card home on Tranquility Lane in Walden Woods, a picture-perfect place where, according to Peck, families have gone "not to face up to life's problems, but to avoid them."[35] The Tobins discover that their seemingly idyllic locale cannot protect them from forces potentially more destructive than those they attempted to escape. Todd's younger sister, Marnie, finds herself under the spell of her religious fundamentalist babysitter, Laurel, a quiet and demure girl who hides behind her fanatical faith to conceal the truth about her dysfunctional family. Selecting a teenage "enemy of freedom" was important for Peck, who argues, "Teenagers are too likely to shift all blame onto adults"[36] and thus not pay attention when grown-ups are the perpetrators. Terrified that her family members will go to hell for not being true believers, Marnie is plagued with nightmares and daytime fears. Laurel's mother extends the influence of the church into the school when she and her fellow prayer-group members attempt to remove *The Diary of Anne Frank* and Robert Cormier's *The Chocolate War* from the library.

The fraying edges of this community are further ripped apart when a drunken joyride results in the death of a high school student, several cars are stolen and crashed throughout town, and drug deals going down in the local park keep passersby at a safe distance. Peck, pulling no punches, hits his teenage audience hard in the way he describes their response to these events. When students learn that the teen who perished in the accident is to be buried on a Saturday, they are disappointed; "they'd wanted a half day off from school for her funeral." A week later, a junior student arrives at school wearing in a grotesque, blood-riddled Halloween costume; rumor has it, he has come dressed as this same victim of the crash.

For some, Peck's warnings to teens are sometimes too transparent. As Hazel Rochman says, "the didacticism is loud and clear, and the foreshadowing is heavy."[37] Nevertheless, the novel demonstrates the need for teens to realize that there is no safe place, passivity is never harmless, and others will not change their views simply because we want them to. The novel's chilling ending reinforces this well. Despite all the damage Laurel has done to the Tobin family (and herself) in her willing acceptance of her mother's beliefs, she holds true to what she thinks is right and good and true.

Adult readers found much in the story to like, as evidenced by ALA Best Book and Quick Pick recognitions. Reviewers called the novel a "perceptive, chilling look at censorship and religious fanaticism,"[38] "a taut, suspenseful,"[39] and "truly terrifying novel."[40] Reviewers were consistent in their praise of Peck's depiction of the religious right, congratulating him on creating fundamentalist characters that defy oversimplified categorization; they are not pure evil, though they are "both frightened and frightening."[41] And Donna Pool Miller of *Book Report* credits Peck for exploring "the nature of fear and how it can drive people to hide behind religion rather than take responsibility for their lives."[42]

STRAYS LIKE US

Strays like Us, an ALA Best Book for Young Adults, marks the start of a key transition in Peck's body of writing—a shift from contemporary to historical fiction. While *Strays like Us* remains set in modern times, the setting shifts from suburbia to small-town Missouri in one of those places where, Peck says, "Old people never left and everybody knows everybody.''[43] Twelve-year-old Molly Moberly lives here with her great-aunt Fay, a home-visiting nurse. Molly waits patiently for her drug-addicted mother to return and reclaim her as soon as her mother recovers and is released from a hospital elsewhere. Molly is befriended by another seeming stray, a peer named Will, who lives next door with his grandparents. His father, Molly is told, is in jail. The two form a loose friendship, in part out of survival and the need to have at least one companion on the walk to school and in the cafeteria during lunch.

Molly prefers to remain on the fringe, hiding quietly in the sea of classmates, hoping her teachers will never learn her name, and not allowing anyone to get too close, knowing she'll be leaving soon. This outsider status affords Molly the opportunity to keenly observe those around her. She notices her first-year English teacher's sad eyes behind her animated smile, the once-youthful beauty masked by the thick makeup of old Mrs. Vorhees (a patient of great-aunt Fay's), and the loneliness felt by Tracy Pringle (a home-schooled girl Molly meets in the public library) despite her cute clothes and seemingly devoted mother. This small community, Molly learns, holds more than its share of secrets, some necessary, others complicated, and still others devastatingly destructive. Members of this town, however, share a history, a kinship (by blood or otherwise) that allows them a sense of connection and subsequent security as these secrets are revealed. When Molly learns the truth about Mrs. Vorhees's identity, Will's father's illness, and Tracy Pringle's dangerous yearning for companionship, one might expect her to come unraveled at the seams. It's too much to handle. In this setting, however, the rich relationships built by previous generations provide a safety net. As a *VOYA* reviewer notes, Molly is able "to re-evaluate her detached existence and reach out to those around her."[44]

As he does in his later historical fiction, Peck draws here on the elderly in the community, the wise ones who support the children in a way their parents are unable or unwilling to do. The young people in the story who have the support of an elderly member of the community manage to make it. Molly learns to appreciate the patience and diligence of her great-aunt, even going so far as to emulate her dialect and phrasing. Will is provided a place to live, and Rocky Roberts, while a delinquent and rabble-rouser, still has someone pick him up from school when he gets into trouble. It is Tracy Pringle who offers a sad alternative. She attempts to burn down the school building in a desperate cry for the attention her mother, the only significant adult in her life, fails to provide in their sterile, sheltered world.

Peck wrote this novel from firsthand observation of kids lacking community, conceiving *Strays like Us* during a visit to a consolidated country school. From the window of the library on the morning of his presentation, he watched as students exited the bus: 70 percent of this school's population were among the "millions of kids searching for homes because they are the children of an aimless and failed genera- tion."[45] Discarded by their mothers and fathers, they were sent to live with members of their extended family, mostly grandparents. Here, he garnered his "first glimpse of a vast, nomadic young population, adrift in search of home and family," and wondered if he could "write a story that might give them some identity, and dignity."[46] And so he did.

Given Peck's emotional response to these children, it's no surprise that reviewers called *Strays like Us* "tender"[47] and "heartwarming,"[48] a "wry, unsentimental story of three generations in small-town Missouri: their roots, their failures, their loving kindness."[49] Several attributed the effectiveness of the novel to its plain-talking narrator, a *Publishers Weekly* reviewer noting that Peck "paints a richly detailed portrait of Molly. He draws indications of her assimilation with subtlety and exquisite pac- ing."[50] But a few reviewers found the novel too preachy and criticized Peck's overemphasis on parental incompetence. A *Kirkus* reviewer asserted: "The novel becomes something of a treatise about a generation of children who have been cast aside by their parents."[51] Although Ste- phen Davenport claimed the novel "reads like an afterschool TV spe- cial," he went on to praise Peck's creation of a complex, intriguing character in the form of great-aunt Fay, whom he described as "a healer and a midwife. What she heals are bodies and spirits; what she delivers are the stories, the secrets she gets people to tell."[52]

In multiple forms, all suited to their function, Peck composes tales wherein characters tell their stories, their secrets, in a way that makes us want to lean over and listen in.

NOTES

1. Patty Campbell, *Wilson Library Bulletin* (October 1979): 122.
2. Joan Foster, *Danbury News-Times*, 3 February 1980.

3. Marilyn Kay, *School Library Journal* (November 1979): 92.

4. *Kirkus Reviews*, 15 October 1979, 1213.

5. Dave Davidson et al., *English Journal* (May 1980): 95.

6. Richard Peck, Speech presented at the Children's Literature Festival, University of Southern Mississippi, Hattiesburg, 19 March 1981.

7. Jean W. Ross in *Contemporary Authors*, New Revision Series, vol. 19, ed. Linda Metzger (Detroit: Gale Research, 1987), 368.

8. J. D. Reed, "Packaging the Facts of Life," *Time*, 23 August 1982, 6.

9. Deborah Kovacs, *Meet the Authors* (New York: Scholastic, 1995), 78.

10. Ilene Cooper, *Booklist*, 1 September 1993, 62.

11. *Kirkus Reviews*, 1993, http://clcd.odyssi.com.

12. Lucinda Snyder Whitehurst, *School Library Journal* (September 1993): 234.

13. Richard Peck, *Anonymously Yours* (New York: Julian Messner, 1991), 103.

14. Richard Peck, Workshop at Montclair, New Jersey, Public Library, 9 December 1987.

15. Janice K. Tovey, *Writing for the Young Adult Reader: An Analysis of Audience in the Novels of Richard Peck*, master's thesis, Illinois State University, 1988, 82.

16. Carolyn Meyer, *Los Angeles Times*, 11 June 1987.

17. *Kirkus Reviews*, 1 May 1987, 724.

18. Evie Wilson, *Voice of Youth Advocates* (June 1987): 82.

19. Margaret A. Bush, *Horn Book* (January/February 1989): 79.

20. *Kirkus Reviews*, 15 August 1988, 1246.

21. Richard Peck, "Traveling in Time," *ALAN Review* (Winter 1990): 2.

22. Hazel Rochman, *Booklist*, 1 October 1988, 259.

23. Roger Sutton, *Bulletin of the Center for Children's Books* (September 1988): 17.

24. Sutton, *Bulletin of the Center for Children's Books*, 17.

25. Peck, *Anonymously Yours*, 107.

26. Hazel Rochman, *Booklist*, 15 September 1991, 137.

27. Rochman, *Booklist*, 137.

28. Zena Sutherland, *Bulletin of the Center for Children's Books* (September 1991): 18.

29. Lucinda Snyder Whitehurst, *School Library Journal* (August 1991): 195.

30. John H. Bushman and Kay Parks Bushman, *English Journal* (April 1992): 84.

31. Virginia Monseau, *ALAN Review* (Spring 1992): 27.

32. Peck, *Anonymously Yours*, 50.

33. Peck, *Anonymously Yours*, 108.

34. Carol A. Edwards, *School Library Journal* (April 1995): 154.

35. Richard Peck, *Invitations to the World: Teaching and Writing for the Young* (New York: Dial, 2002), 156.

36. Richard Peck, "The Last Safe Place on Earth," *Book Links* (September 1995): 25–26.

37. Hazel Rochman, *Booklist*, 15 January 1995, 913.

38. Reviewer on Amazon.com.

39. *Publisher's Weekly*, 19 December 1994, 55.

40. Edwards, *School Library Journal*, 154.

41. Edwards, *School Library Journal*, 154.

42. Donna Pool Miller, *Book Report* (March/April 1995): 39.

43. Nancy J. Johnson and Cyndi Giorgis, "2001 Newbery Medal Winner: A Conversation with Richard Peck," *Reading Teacher* (December 2001/January 2002): 392–97.

44. *VOYA* (June 1998): 124.

45. Johnson and Giorgis, "A Conversation with Richard Peck," 392–97.

46. Peck, *Invitations*, 182.

47. *Publishers Weekly*, 13 April 1998, 76.

48. *VOYA*, 124.

49. Hazel Rochman, *Booklist*, 1 April 1998, 1325.

50. *Publishers Weekly*, 13 April 1998, 76.

51. *Kirkus Reviews*, 1998, http://clcd.odyssi.com.

52. Stephen Davenport, *Journal of Adolescent and Adult Literacy* (December 1999/January 2000): 387.

· 8 ·

Historical Fiction

$\mathcal{L}$ong before receiving his Newbery and Margaret A. Edwards Awards, Richard Peck was a well-respected author for teens. In his seven most recent historical novels, however, he has come home, finding new subject matter and renewed purpose. Peck clearly feels comfortable in the past: "I'm reaching the age of nostalgia now when my beginnings are more vivid to me than all the years between."[1] His commitment to the past fuels his most recent works and, he promises, those to come: "I have made a commitment that the rest of my career will be in historic fiction because of 9/11."[2]

Disappointed that visits to schools revealed no discernible curricular change as he hoped to see following such pivotal events, Peck aims to provide the missing teaching through his writing. "Stories set in historical periods have a special job for this generation of young people who really don't know history,"[3] he says. Peck claims that, while he "can't rectify" the state of education, he can "write a story with a historic setting"[4] and perhaps teach readers something about the line that runs between the then and the now.

A LONG WAY FROM CHICAGO

Set in rural Illinois during the Great Depression, Peck's first historical novel for young readers features two Chicago kids, Joey and Mary Alice, who every year for seven summers spend a week in the country visiting their grandmother. What began as a short story, "Shotgun Cheatham's

Last Night above Ground," grew into a collection of stories surrounding these visits—all told from Joey's changing perspective over time. In each visit, Peck says, the kids "see a different woman in their grandmother, though she never changes. . . . It takes Joe more than a few summers to begin to see that Grandma Dowdel's moral code transcends mere laws, and the men who enforce them. It takes him longer than that to learn that she's capable of anything, even irony. He's almost a man before he sees how much she loves him."[5]

Joey watches Grandma foil the plots of those nasty Cowgill boys, feed hungry drifters the fish she catches illegally in waters owned by the self-righteous members of the Rod and Gun Club, rig a contest to wheedle her way into the seat of a biplane, aid and abet an eloping couple despite parental disapproval, save the house of a poor neighbor, and undermine the banker's wife while providing due credit to an elderly codger others have written off. Joey watches—and learns the value of eccentricity, the satisfaction of social justice, and the power of love.

Grandma Dowdel is one of the most memorable characters—elderly or otherwise—in literature. Peck says, "She is the American tall tale in a Lane Bryant dress. There's more than a bit of Paul Bunyan about her, and a touch of the Native American trickster tradition: she may just be Kokopelli without the flute."[6] Peck calls this feisty and independent woman his "retort to all those cloying little old ladies nodding by the fire in traditional children's picture books."[7] Her spunk is perfectly appropriate, given her origins and childhood. Peck lets us in on a little secret: "Grandma Dowdel's first name is Blossom."[8] Like the Widow Douglas and Aunt Polly before her, Grandma Dowdel lives beyond the page. As one *Kirkus* reviewer puts it, "Grandma Dowdel, with her gruff persona and pragmatic outlook on life, embodies not only the heart of a small town but the spirit of an era gone by."[9]

Grandma Dowdel speaks in a composite of voices Peck heard while hanging out on the porch and around the stove as a child. Peck says, she "speaks in the voices of all my great aunts, farm women born in the 1860s and 70s who ruled the world from their kitchens, spoke in her cadences, and wore her aprons."[10] A few details of the novel, however, are grounded directly in his grandmother's history. Peck explains:

> I took [Grandma Dowdel's] circumstances, but not her personality, from
> my grandmother. My grandmother was the sole survivor of a smallpox

epidemic. As an infant she was found alive in a house with two dead parents and a dead twin sister beside her in the crib. She lived to be 93. That's really why Grandma Dowdel had to live with Aunt Puss, but I don't give out that story because it's too serious for the book.[11]

Critical response to *A Long Way from Chicago* was overwhelmingly positive. Reviewers called the novel "warmly nostalgic, beautifully written, humorous, and full of thought-provoking interpersonal relationships."[12] A *Kirkus* reviewer describes the work as "remarkable and fine," noting, in particular, the way in which Peck "skillfully captures the nuances of small-town life" and "weaves a wry tale that ranges from humorous to poignant."[13] Critics loved not only the story but also the storyteller's craft. Peck's characters are described as "larger-than-life funny,"[14] his conversational style filled with "wit, humor, and rhythm,"[15] his selection of details perfect in "subtly evoking the era."[16] Reviewers were also quick to praise Peck's ability to avoid sentimentality. He is "neither condescending nor picturesque. With the tall talk, irony, insult, and vulgarity, there's also a heartfelt sense of the Depression's time and place."[17] "Although firmly rooted in the past, there's no nostalgia here: issues such as bank foreclosures, Prohibition, and hungry drifters play a large part in Grandma's schemes."[18] Peck succeeds in telling a good tale grounded in good history.

These accolades help to explain why the title was selected as both a Newbery Honor Book and a National Book Award finalist.

A YEAR DOWN YONDER

This sequel to *A Long Way from Chicago* shifts from Joey's voice to Mary Alice's. The recession of 1937 hits, her brother heads west to join the Civilian Conservation Corps, her father loses his job, her parents move into a place big enough for two, and she heads back to Grandma's—this time for an entire school year. Disappointed at the thought of leaving her family, friends, and modern conveniences behind, Mary Alice assumes the worst as she imagines herself, "a city girl," enrolling "in the hicktown school" and living in a place "that didn't even have a picture show."

Frustration turns to admiration then to emulation, however, as

Mary Alice learns to respect, and assume, the ways of her caregiver. As did Joey in the first novel, Mary Alice watches. She watches Grandma punish the Halloween pranksters, steal nuts and fruits only to give them back in the form of baked goods, scare up donations to support a poor neighbor and her invalid son, alter the luncheon guest list typically limited to those with cash and clout, and play matchmaker to an unlikely couple. But Mary Alice does more than watch; she takes action, too, writing social commentary as the author of "Newsy Notes from Our Communities" in the *Piatt County Call*, forging Valentine cards to exact revenge on the class snob, and garnering personal attention from cute Royce McNabb by asking him to be her math tutor.

A Year Down Yonder is more than a second title in a series. Yes, it takes place after *A Long Way from Chicago*. Yes, it is set in the same small town. And yes, it features some of the same characters. "But, emotionally," as writer Marc Talbert says, "it is a prequel, giving us, through Mary Alice, a window into the kind of girl Grandma Dowdel must have been so many years before, shaped differently by different times and places but emotionally parallel to this budding young woman from Chicago."[19]

Most critics praised Peck for that "same combination of wit, gentleness, and outrageous farce"[20] achieved in *A Long Way from Chicago*. Many attributed the power of the novel to Grandma Dowdel once again, describing her as "just as feisty and terrifying and goodhearted and every bit as funny,"[21] "her usual crusty, hell-raising self,"[22] a "Depression-era Robin Hood,"[23] and "the heart of the book."[24] Kitty Flynn stands alone in her less complimentary commentary, claiming that "Grandma, who was an indefatigable source of surprise and bewilderment to her grandchildren in the first book, doesn't come across as such a mythic figure this time around, perhaps because some of her shock value has worn off."[25]

Other reviewers recognized and praised Peck's use of Grandma as the impetus for Mary Alice's development. Deirdre Baker of the *Toronto Star* notes that Peck gives us "a glimpse of Mary Alice trying out her Grandma's methods for herself, growing from a homesick girl into a force to be reckoned with, a woman like Grandma."[26]

A few critics were less enamored with the final chapter of the novel, titled "Ever After," in which Mary Alice returns to Grandma's house for her wedding to Royce McNabb, claiming it "odd"[27] and "sentimental."[28] Members of the Newbery Medal selection panel, however, were quite content with the novel's beginning, middle, and end, awarding *A Year Down Yonder* the 2001 Newbery Medal, reaffirming Peck's commitment to reaching present-day readers by writing about the past.

Given his success with these novels—and the character of Grandma Dowdel, in particular—readers regularly query Peck as to whether Grandma will make a return in any future works. Peck answers, "I guess not. She has been so good to me that I don't want to beat her to death." But young readers continue to push for her revival, recommending that Peck send Joey or Mary Alice's kids back to Grandma's house for a week during the summer. Peck, having learned to listen to the advice of his young readers, reconsiders his initial refusal, saying, "I don't know whether we could have Grandma taking on the McCarthy hearings with a TV in her house. I can't quite picture it. Although the more I think about it, the better I like the thought of it."[29]

FAIR WEATHER

Peck's next two novels required that he delve not only into his family history but the library stacks as well. *Fair Weather* (2001), set in 1893, takes readers to two geographic locations: rural Illinois and Chicago. It traces the literal and metaphoric journey of Rosie Beckett, a thirteen-year-old farm girl, who, with her younger brother, older sister, and spirited Granddad Fuller, travels to the World's Columbian Exposition. Rosie has never ventured beyond the immediate vicinity of her community. She is elated and afraid when her wealthy Aunt Euterpe extends an invitation to visit her in Chicago and attend the grandest event of the century. Rosie ventures out into the wider world and returns forever changed.

In his conception of the novel, Peck rethought the narrative premise employed in his two previously published novels: "I intentionally turned *A Year Down Yonder* and *A Long Way from Chicago* inside out to create *Fair Weather*. . . . Since Grandma Dowdel's grandkids come from Chicago, I decided to send rural grandkids to Chicago, and the great event of all times would have been that fair, and so the setting of the story was going to be 1893."[30]

His decision also hinged on his interest in the fair itself. "I went for the fair," he says, "because I wish I'd gone to it."[31] Peck's mother, pregnant with him, attended the next World's Fair in 1933, also held in Chicago. Peck likes to say he was technically present, especially in the way he played a role in his mother's experience there: "My mother says I went to the fair and that prevented her from going on the sky ride, but I was prenatal and can't be held responsible. Still, it must have left its mark."[32]

The fair leaves its mark on Rosie, too. Peck's selection of Rosie as the narrator suits his thematic goals for the novel. The narrator was female, he says, because "there was the Women's Pavilion at the fair, and it was one of the first great statements of American women."[33] The fair offers alternative perspectives, shaping those who allow themselves to experience it fully. As Peck tells it, "Rosie finds her future in the Women's Building at the fair. The murals on its walls are by Mary Cassatt. The speaker of the day is Susan B. Anthony. It's where Rosie learns that women can paint pictures and make speeches and take stands."[34]

Another character of note in the novel is Rosie's grandfather, Granddad Fuller. Loud, adventurous, eccentric, Granddad Fuller hitches a ride on the train to the fair to avoid being left out of the fun. Donning a "once-cream-colored suit, badly creased, and a curly-brimmed Panama hat, a high celluloid collar, and a silk cravat," he encourages the kids to make the most of every minute, even if it means seeing the scantily clad dancer Little Egypt, listening to the singing of Lillian Turner, a "fallen woman" married three times, or visiting the Midway, den of immorality.

Granddad's character was created in response to the critical acclaim garnered by Grandma Dowdel, Peck says. "Grandma Dowdel became such a towering figure that I thought she would overwhelm any other grandmother I'd create, so I came up with Granddad Fuller."[35] While most reviewers found much to enjoy in Granddad, claiming his "antics steal the show"[36] and noting his ability to "hold his own"[37] against Grandma Dowdel, Nancy Gilson of the *Columbus Dispatch* was less complimentary: "Granddad simply isn't as outrageous or as memorable as Grandma Dowdel. Granddad is all bluster, while Grandma Dowdel spoke softly and carried out imaginative pranks."[38] Nevertheless, Granddad Fuller joins the distinguished assemblage of fascinating older people in Peck's novels for young people. Besides, Peck notes that Granddad Fuller is his "most nearly autobiographical character,"[39] both of them wishing they were Mark Twain.

To re-create the setting for these characters, Peck immersed himself in books, magazine articles, and newspapers of the time to learn all he could about the World's Fair. Given his unwillingness to believe that technology can replace old-fashioned research, he refused to garner information from online sources. He did, however, conduct a little experiment: "I asked a computer literate person what he could find in the Net about the World's Fair, and it was 104 pages, but it was the same material in all these different sources, and very superficial—you couldn't have gotten a haiku out of it, let alone a novel."[40]

So Peck went right to the source: "I went through all the official records of the World's Fair, all written down with much civic pride."[41] Here he discovered Mrs. Potter Palmer, wife to the owner of the famous Palmer House Hotel and town celebrity, and the popularity of Buffalo Bill's Wild West Show held on the fringes of the fairgrounds. At the Chicago Historical Society, he discovered, too, a rich visual history of the fair documented through photographs taken at the time. Thus, as Rosie writes postcards to her parents, readers view not only the notes she crafts but the pictures on the flip side—photographs of the Midway, Women's Building, and Lillian Turner.

In addition to weaving rich historical details into the narrative, Peck further educates readers through a final chapter, "After the Fair: A Note from the Author." Here he discusses how the World's Columbian Exposition "altered the future and changed the face of the nation in large ways and small"—from the inspiration it provided architect Frank Lloyd Wright and *Wizard of Oz* author Frank Baum to the lasting presence of hamburgers, Cream of Wheat, and Juicy Fruit gum, all introduced in the pavilions and along the Midway. Peck wants readers to be duly impressed despite their jaded twenty-first-century sensibilities. He declares, "There is nothing that the young could see today that would be that impressive. I took people to the fair who had never seen a lightbulb, and yet they saw 600 acres blazing in the midnight brighter than noon. There is no place we can go today and be that awed. Disneyland doesn't cut it."[42]

Reviewers hailed *Fair Weather* as a "marvelously funny . . . human-interest story"[43] that "paints a charming portrait"[44] as a result of Peck's "no-nonsense Midwestern narrative voice and his humorous touch."[45] What particularly impressed reviewers, however, was the scope of the research Peck conducted in the crafting of the tale. Elizabeth Change of the *Washington Post* wrote: "1893 Chicago comes alive in a way that you almost feel as though you were at the fair, soaking in the marvels of a new age."[46] In her *New York Times* review, Ilene Cooper praises Peck for his ability to help readers envision the fair but remembers, too, his ability to give his characters roots: "Yet as dazzling as the city and its Columbian Exposition are, Peck balances all that newfangled excitement with the familiar domesticity—and bone-wearying work—of home. . . . The matter-of-fact description of farm life, peppered by Rosie's droll voice, makes it clear that eking out a living in rural 19th-century Illinois was hard and unending."[47]

THE RIVER BETWEEN US

In his fourth historical novel, a book that Peck views as one of his best, he demonstrates again his ability to make the factual fantastic in his re-creation of history. *The River between Us* (2003) is written as a framed story. The opening and closing chapters are set during the summer of 1916, when young Howard Leland Hutchings, his father, and two brothers travel to the home of Dad's Aunt Delphine to pay their respects before she passes away. The trip offers the opportunity to listen to the voices of those who came before, to get "caught in the grip" of a place, to feel "the weight of its history, and mystery." Upon seeing his elderly relatives, Howard finds himself wondering what these folks were like when they were young and just "how quiet you'd have to be to hear the voices of those times."

Readers are offered a vision of those times in the middle chapters of the novel, set during the early years of the Civil War, when members of the Pruitt family, living in the small town of Grand Tower, Illinois, welcome into their home two mysterious young women fleeing New Orleans. Tilly, the thoughtful and perceptive narrator, paints the picture of the newcomers: Delphine, outspoken, gorgeous, and sophisticated in her splendor, represents a way of life both foreign and fascinating; Calinda, her darker-skinned companion, is guarded and serious, protective of a truth she and Delphine wish to conceal. While Tilly observes Delphine and Calinda, caught up in their glittering ways, she also observes her older brother, Noah, caught up in the war. Soon after Noah leaves to fight, word of the deplorable living conditions faced by soldiers in his regiment arrives. Unable to bear the thought of losing her son (having already lost her restless husband), Tilly's mother demands that Tilly find

Noah and bring him home. Out of love for Noah, Delphine accompanies Tilly to the military station at Cairo, Illinois. Here, the filth, decay,
disease, and hopelessness of war become reality.

The River between Us is a war story, but it is one that examines the
cost of life on the front and off. Peck gives readers a clear understanding
of the social implications for those who never take up arms, in this case
Delphine and Calinda. As the novel progresses, the secret these two
women harbor is ultimately revealed: the girls, sisters, are freewomen of
color, members of what Peck describes as a New Orleans "community
that gathered economic clout and considerable—though precarious—
prominence,"[48] most typically by becoming mistresses to white men and
bearing mixed-race children. Ironically, a Northern victory would mean
loss of status for these women. The escape from New Orleans saves their
lives but, ultimately, requires that they live lives of lies. Calinda, passing
as Spanish, travels to California and is never heard from again. Delphine,
fearing those in town might learn her identity, refuses to call her son her
own out of a belief that "it could have closed too many doors" for him.
In the end, as a result of his willingness to listen, Howard is ready to
understand and accept the truth: Delphine's son is his father.

To weave together these multiple stories, Peck conducted two years
of research. When the time came to write, he was reluctant. He says, "I
could have spent the rest of my life researching that time. People do. But
I had to carve out a place for my young characters to stand."[49] They
stood on the banks of the Mississippi River for both practical and personal reasons. The mysterious young women have come north from
New Orleans and need a northern destination; the familiar hometown of
Peck's friend, Richard Hughes, provided the perfect locale.[50]

These choices were validated by reviewers who admired Peck's
employment of a framing device as a means to bridge time and place.
"Not only is [the novel] a gripping yarn—but it is nearly as intricately
structured as *Wuthering Heights*, with multiple narrators and tales-within-
tales enhancing both the mystery and the wistfulness of long-ago
events,"[51] says Elizabeth Ward of the *Washington Post*. Peter Sieruta of
Horn Book adds: "When Tilly's reminiscence is complete and grandson
Howard takes over the narrative for one final chapter, many readers will
question whether this framing device was necessary. But there is one
more twist to the tale—a revelation that both affirms the past and deter-

mines the present—bringing this powerful novel to a stunning conclusion."[52]

Reviewers also found Peck's writing poignant and well suited to the novel's setting. Hazel Rochman of *Booklist* argues, "Peck's spare writing has never been more eloquent."[53] Lynne Perri of *USA Today* reiterates these claims, writing, "Few modern writers for adults or children wield a pen with the surgical precision Peck brings to every sentence. Each paragraph has a cadence that speaks of long experience and attention to detail, and that carries his passions in succinct, poignant rhythms."[54] And Matt Berman of the *Times-Picayune* likens Peck to a master: "He writes life-changing scenes reminiscent of the Atlanta pilgrimage that Scarlett O'Hara makes in *Gone with the Wind*."[55] Given this praise, it comes as no surprise that *The River between Us* was selected as a National Book Award finalist and winner of the Scott O'Dell Award for Historical Fiction.

THE TEACHER'S FUNERAL: A COMEDY IN THREE PARTS

Peck's fifth historical novel echoes *A Long Way from Chicago* and *A Year Down Yonder* in its rendering of the daily realities of small-town life. Living in rural Indiana in 1904, fifteen-year-old Russell dreams of lighting out to the Dakotas, joining a wheat-threshing crew, and escaping school. When old Myrt Arbuckle "hauls off and dies" just before she is expected to start up another year as teacher in the one-room schoolhouse, Russell is hopeful that his dream might become a reality even sooner. He fears his worst nightmare has come true, however, when he learns that his older sister, Tansy, will assume control of the classroom. But Tansy foils his plot by proving to be a truly effective teacher. Patient, creative, humble, and downright smart, she guides her motley crew of students through their reading, writing, and arithmetic, fostering an appreciation for schooling, even in her little brother. By the end of the school year, Russell and his classmates have found they know "way more than we wanted to." Says a reviewer from the *Washington Post*, "School has rarely been paid a more backhanded, or more effective, tribute."[56]

The Teacher's Funeral reveals Peck at his comedic best. Particularly effective is Russell's deadpan narration. He is droll and unknowingly wise in his description of his community. Explaining why Miss

Arbuckle's death is for the best, Russell notes that she was hard of hearing in one ear and had arthritis in her elbow. "When you get right down to it," he says, "if you can't hear and you can't whup, you're better off dead than teaching." Later, when the very large Aunt Fanny Hamline falls in a ditch outside the school and needs pulling out, Russell chronicles the complicated process and concludes, "Getting Aunt Fanny Hamline out of the ditch became one of Tansy's most famous days of teaching. It was a lesson in engineering too. It should have been studied at Purdue University." As one *Publishers Weekly* reviewer noted, "Events on their own are enough to keep readers in stitches, but Russell's pithy descriptions of characters add another dimension of humor. Following the tradition of Mark Twain, Peck gently pokes fun at social manners and captures local color while providing first-rate entertainment."[57]

For all its humor, the novel is emotionally touching. In one scene, Russell's father, savvy to his son's intention to sneak out and catch a train to the Dakotas, drives him to the tracks. When Russell sees a drunk tramp, "weaving in half circles, swinging a bottle," and other drifters, "rough customers, crouched in the boxcar doors, smoking," he realizes, "It wasn't like I'd pictured it, nor anywhere I wanted to be." However, still unwilling to let go of the dream he's held so long, he assures his dad that he would have sent home some of his earnings. His dad responds, "I'd sooner have you home."

Reviewers describe *The Teacher's Funeral* as "full of life"[58] and "rich with colorful characters, Midwest dialect and poignant plot twists; a rollicking glimpse of adolescent pranks and dreams in a simpler time."[59] In this "masterfully crafted ode to a strong teacher and a bygone era,"[60] Peck "lovingly details a vanished way of life in twentieth-century rural America"[61] and "evokes the smells and sights and practices of period farming as if he'd been there himself."[62]

Although Patrick Jones, writing in *VOYA*, admired the novel's depiction of time and place, he questioned its appeal to adolescent readers, claiming, "It is hard to imagine any teen reading this book unless already a fan of Peck's writing . . . because of Peck's attraction with historical re-creation, not fast action or funny dialogue."[63] A reviewer for the *Washington Post* disagreed, drawing a connection between kids then and now: "The novel may be rooted in the remote and ancient world that is 1904 rural Indiana, but the kids—especially 15-year-old Russell

Culver, who narrates—are as alert as any modern suburban teenager would be to the bright side of Miss Myrt Arbuckle's sudden demise."[64]

HERE LIES THE LIBRARIAN

Peck picks up the pace in his sixth historical novel, beginning the narrative with dead bodies thrown from their coffins in a tornado and ending with a nail-biting road race on a dusty track. Peck guides readers from start to finish by telling the story through Peewee, a fourteen-year-old tomboy (whose given name is Eleanor) living with her big brother, Jake, in a small Indiana town in 1914. Peewee's mother died in childbirth, and her father, unable to bear the grief, fled years ago. When she's not in school, Peewee helps Jake run a mechanic shop out of an old livery stable owned by their Civil War veteran neighbor, Colonel Hazelrigg. Their quiet life is disrupted by the arrival of Irene Ridpath, a wealthy Indianapolis girl and librarian-in-training who, along with her three best girlfriends, wheedles her way into running the run-down town library.

With Irene and her friends come cars, nice cars—the Peerless, the Packard, the Pierce-Arrow, the Stutz, and the Stoddard-Dayton—all purchased by the girls' well-to-do fathers. These cars play a key role in Peewee's development; ultimately, it is behind the wheel of one of them that Peewee proves herself to her brother and herself.

As Peewee witnesses the charm, grace, and power the young librarians wield as they revitalize the library, win the hearts of the men, and dash around in their best attire, part of her feels compelled to emulate Irene and come out from under the car, wipe off the grease, and become a civilized young girl. She is secretly excited to don the beautiful frock Irene buys for her, and she enjoys her role as hostess during the library tea. Although Peewee fears having to forsake that part of herself that has made her who she is, Irene helps her understand that she need not feel obligated to choose either tomboy or lady in determining the girl she will ultimately be.

Peck was intentional in his use of Irene as a guide for Peewee. He says: "This is a novel, of course, about empowerment; it's not about dying librarians at all. . . . It's a story about a girl who worships her brother, so much so that she'd like to be him. But, as it turns out, she is empowered by a new generation of young women who have found freedom through education and the automobile."[65]

Reviewers were mostly positive toward the novel, likening it to Peck's other successful titles in its "signature combination of quirky characters, poignancy, and outrageous farce"[66] and Peck's characteristically effective use of "one-liners, colorful physical comedy, and country dialect."[67] A *Publishers Weekly* reviewer praised the unique elements of the novel: "Offering plenty of action and a cast of larger-than-life characters, the book pays tribute to the social and industrial revolution, which awakens a sleepy town and marks the coming-of-age of an unforgettable heroine."[68]

Other critics, while complimentary, critiqued Peck's creation of character, citing the people who inhabit these pages as "wonderfully quirky" but "not fully developed,"[69] or noting that they are "often silly but ultimately relatable."[70] Stephanie Zvirin found the novel lacking in coherence: "Even with some exciting scenes of old-time dirt-track racing, the pace lags, and the story is choppy." She also thought it was unlikely to interest teen readers: "Young fans of Danica Patrick, today's *Queen of the Road*, may want to read this, but it will probably be librarians who'll have the most fun."[71] Given the book's dedication to "living librarians everywhere," perhaps that's a most suitable accolade.

ON THE WINGS OF HEROES

Written as a tribute to his father, a World War I veteran, Peck's thirtieth novel for young adults is his most nostalgic. "My dad was there for me every moment of my growing up," says Peck, "and so he's with me still, and something of him shared in these pages."[72] Set in small-town Illinois at the start of World War II, this tender story is related through the eyes of Davy, a boy now grown and reflecting on his childhood. He remembers warm summer evenings playing hide and seek, the branchy box elder tree in front of the Hisers' house as home base, his father joining the fun, dashing from his hiding spot, carrying the littlest participants to safety. He remembers, too, Halloween nights thwarting tricks attempted by neighborhood rabble-rousers, watching them slip, slide, and tumble on ball bearings placed surreptitiously on the sidewalk between them and the pumpkin on the porch. And he remembers moments when he feels like he can hear his dad thinking and worrying about Bill, Davy's older brother away in St. Louis taking the Civil Aviation Administration course.

When World War II begins and Bill enlists as a pilot, some of Davy's innocence fades away, but all is not lost. Although Davy describes the resulting pull on his emotions—pride in and fear for his brother—he finds small joys despite big changes in his life. He and his best friend, Scooter, find an old jalopy in a falling-down barn and meet its owner, Miss Titus, a gun-toting, "dried-up woman with a face like a walnut," who later turns out to be their teacher—the best they've ever had. He relishes the story of how Miss Titus uses a well-placed rattrap to spoil an attempt at thievery in the classroom, putting the culprits (and classroom bullies) in their place. And he recalls the arrival of his distant grandparents at the family home; they've come to serve as a distraction, to keep thoughts from straying to Bill, who has gone missing in action. This is neither a simple war story nor a family tale; Peck has created a novel in which these elements are so tightly intertwined, one could not exist without the other.

Peck is at his best in his ability to weave period details into the narrative. He educates readers as to air-raid drills conducted in classrooms; the increasing number of "eight to five orphans," kids who move to town and bring their lunch to school, unable to travel home because their mothers are working in new war plants; the value of a dime used toward the purchase of War Savings Stamps; the push to collect and donate rationed items for the war effort; the propaganda used to recruit and maintain morale; and telegrams that brought word of a soldier's death or survival.

Reviewers rewarded Peck for his commitment to rekindling the past through his fiction. A *Kirkus* reviewer called the novel "an ode to a father, a big brother and an era captured by a writer at his peak."[73] Sheldon Fogelman of *Publishers Weekly* added, "Peck concocts another delicious mixture of humor, warmth and local color in this period piece."[74]

Even those reviewers who offered criticism of the novel couched their comments in respect for Peck's writing; he has earned their admiration. Geri DiOrio of *VOYA*, for example, noted, "The story is so slow and safe and contains so many contextual references to the 1940s that one might wonder who the audience really is." Yet she also offered this praise: "Peck is a master. His language is lovely, his story has great depth, and his humor is always apparent, even in a wartime novel. This book made this reviewer laugh out loud and get misty-eyed all in one sitting."[75] Similarly, Michael Cart of *Booklist* offered an honest assessment demonstrating the name Peck has made for himself in the field: "No one does nostalgia better than Peck, and this episodic story of a boy's life on the home front just before and during World War II is a charmer. . . . Yes, some scenes seem a bit sketchier than usual, and some jokes a bit wheezy, but the pages are still filled with gentle humor and wonderful turns of phrase. All in all, there remains no more genial guide for a trip down memory lane than the redoubtable Peck."[76]

WHAT MATTERS MOST

When Peck, a resident of New York City, witnessed the events of September 11, 2001, he refused to shake them off and resolved instead to shake readers up. Peck allows this date to serve as a persistent reminder of why history matters, of why telling stories of the past is an essential act in the shaping of a future. Language matters. Words matter. Writing can make a difference in the way it helps us make sense of the seemingly senseless. Soon after witnessing the events of that day, Peck coped in the only way he knew how: he wrote. "When life—history—makes us start over, some of us have to write verse, short verse, in an attempt to pull all the sprawling world upon a single page, if only to give ourselves someplace to stand. I had to." The resulting poem, "September 11," ends with the following reminder of history's persistent value:

> But history isn't a folded-up map,
> Or an unread textbook tome;
> Now we know history's a fireman's child,
> Waiting at home alone.[77]

NOTES

1. Jennifer M. Brown, "A Long Way from Decatur," *Publishers Weekly*, 21 July 2003, 169–70.

2. Matt Berman, "Peck's Peak," *Times-Picayune*, 7 April 2002, Living 1.

3. Berman, "Peck's Peak."

4. Holly Atkins, "An Interview with Richard Peck," *St. Petersburg Times*, 17 May 2004, 6E.

5. Richard Peck, *Invitations to the World: Teaching and Writing for the Young* (New York: Dial, 2002), 185.

6. Richard Peck, "Newbery Medal Acceptance," *Horn Book* (July 2001): 397.

7. "Meet the Author," *CBC Magazine*, www.cbcbooks.org/cbcmagazine/mee/richard_peck.html.

8. "Meet the Author," *CBC Magazine*.

9. *Kirkus Reviews*, 1998, http://clcd.odyssi.com.

10. "Richard Peck's Scholastic Interview Transcript," *Scholastic*, www.books.scholastic.com/teacher/authorsandbooks/authorstudies.

11. "Richard Peck's Scholastic Interview Transcript."

12. Sharon Salluzzo, *Children's Literature*, http://clcd.odyssi.com.

13. *Kirkus Reviews*, 1998, http://clcd.odyssi.com.

14. Hazel Rochman, *Booklist*, 1 September 1998, 113.

15. Shawn Brommer, *School Library Journal* (October 1998): 144.

16. *VOYA* (December 1998): 358.

17. Rochman, *Booklist*, 1 September, 113.

18. Kitty Flynn, *Horn Book* (November–December 1998): 738–39.

19. Mark Talbert, "Richard Peck: Young Adult Literature Author Appreciates Friend and Mentor," *Horn Book* (July 2001): 403–7.

20. Hazel Rochman, *Booklist*, 15 October 2000, 436.

21. Patty Campbell, on Amazon.com.

22. Douglas K. Dillon, *Book Report* (May/June 2001): 61.

23. Sheila Gullickson, *ALAN Review* (Spring–Summer 2001): 35.

24. Rochman, *Booklist*, 15 October, 436.

25. Kitty Flynn, *Horn Book* (November–December 2000): 761–62.

26. Deirdre Baker, "In the Face of Adversity," *Toronto Star*, 7 January 2001.

27. Gullickson, *ALAN Review*, 35.

28. Alleen Pace Nilsen, Ken Donelson, and James Blasingame Jr., "Young Adult Literature: 2000 Honor List: A Hopeful Bunch," *English Journal* (November 2001): 116–22.

29. Atkins, "An Interview with Richard Peck," 6E.

30. Richard Peck, in "A Conversation with Richard Peck," *Fair Weather* (New York: Puffin, 2001), 142–43.

31. Peck, "A Conversation with Richard Peck," 141.

32. Peck, "A Conversation with Richard Peck," 141.

33. Berman, "Peck's Peak."

34. Peck, "A Conversation with Richard Peck," 141.

35. Peck, "A Conversation with Richard Peck," 142–43.

36. Kit Vaughan, *School Library Journal* (September 2001): 230.

37. Catherine M. Andronik, *Book Report* (March–April 2002): 50.

38. Nancy Gilson, *Columbus Dispatch*, 20 September 2001, 21.

39. Peck, "A Conversation with Richard Peck," 143.

40. Berman, "Peck's Peak."

41. Nancy J. Johnson and Cyndi Giorgis, "2001 Newbery Medal Winner: A Conversation with Richard Peck," *Reading Teacher* (December 2001–January 2002): 392–97.

42. Berman, "Peck's Peak."

43. Vaughan, *School Library Journal*, 230.

44. Karin Snelson, on Amazon.com.

45. Andronik, *Book Report* , 50.

46. Elizabeth Chang, *Washington Post*, 7 July 2004, C16.

47. Ilene Cooper, *New York Times*, 18 November 2001, 45.

48. Richard Peck, "A Note on the Story," *The River between Us* (New York: Puffin, 2003), 161–63.

49. Peck, "A Note on the Story," 159.

50. Linda Castellitto, "Lessons Learned," *First Person Book Page*, www.bookpage.com/0310bp/richard_peck.html.

51. Elizabeth Ward, *Washington Post*, 7 December 2003, T7.

52. Peter D. Sieruta, *Horn Book* (September–October 2003): 616–17.

53. Hazel Rochman, *Booklist*, 15 September 2003, 239.

54. Lynne Perri, *USA Today*, 30 October 2003, 7D.

55. Matt Berman, *Times-Picayune*, 2 November 2003, 7.

56. *Washington Post*, 24 October 2004, T11.

57. *Publisher's Weekly*, 1 November 2004, 63.

58. Jennifer Galvin, *Boston Herald*, 19 September 2004, A22.

59. Janis Flint-Ferguson, *KLIATT* (September 2004), http://clcd.odyssi.com.

60. *Kirkus Reviews*, 1 October 2004, 966.

61. *Book Links* (January 2005): 13.

62. Deirdre Baker, *Toronto Star*, 24 October 2004.

63. Patrick Jones, *VOYA* (December 2004): 392.

64. *Washington Post*, T11.

65. Dean Schneider, "Richard Peck: 'The Past Is My Favorite Place,'" *Book Links* (September 2006): 54–57.

66. Connie Tyrrell Burns, *School Library Journal*, 1 April 2006, 146.

67. Stephanie Zvirin, *Booklist*, 1 March 2006, 91.

68. *Publisher's Weekly*, 30 January 2006, 70.

69. Zvirin, *Booklist*, 91.

70. Stephanie L. Petruso, *VOYA* (February 2006): 479.

71. Zvirin, *Booklist*, 91.

72. Richard Peck, dust jacket for *On the Wings of Heroes*, Dial Books, 2007.

73. *Kirkus Reviews*, 1 January 2007, http://clcd.odyssi.com.

74. Sheldon Fogelman, *Publishers Weekly*, 8 January 2007, 52.

75. Geri DiOrio, *VOYA* (April 2007): 54.

76. Michael Cart, *Booklist*, 1 December 2006, 48.

77. Peck, *Invitations to the World*, 191–92.

· 9 ·

Short Stories and Children's Books

"*There* are some writers who write one novel after another and for whom any interruption would be anathema. But I'm always looking for materials to use with kids, because I'm still a teacher."

And so Richard Peck often produces other forms of writing between novels. For him, short stories, given their length and variety, provide a natural alternative for teen readers. To date, he has published thirteen short stories for teenagers, eleven of which have been anthologized. All thirteen stories are included in Peck's *Past Perfect, Present Tense: New and Collected Stories*, a collection supplemented with discussions of his writing process and recommendations for young authors. Whether it be contemporary, supernatural, or drawn from the past, Peck knows how to craft an effective yarn in few words.

CONTEMPORARY STORIES

"Priscilla and the Wimps," included originally in Don Gallo's *Sixteen: Short Stories by Outstanding Writers for Young Adults*, has become one of the most popular short stories ever written for teenagers, praised highly by teens as well as by teachers and librarians. Using characters that appear in the King Kobra gang in Peck's *Secrets of the Shopping Mall*, this very brief story, as one high school reader put it, "is about how bullies get it stuck to them after they push some people too far."[1] In Monk Klutter's case, his comeuppance is provided by a girl, Priscilla Roseberry. Although some boys have not been too pleased that a girl gets the better of a boy, young readers in general appreciate not only the fact that Monk is overpowered but especially the manner in which he meets his end. Reviewer Patty Campbell called this story a "delicious anecdote . . . in which every word builds with exquisite skill to an explosively comical conclusion."[2]

In "I Go Along," part of *Connections*, edited by Don Gallo, the male narrator, Gene, and his peers in a regular eleventh-grade English class wonder why Mrs. Tibbetts is taking her Advanced English class to hear a poet read from his works at a local college but hasn't asked them. Eventually invited to accompany the group, Gene skates into unfamiliar territory, first with a girl who sits with him and then with the poet—who doesn't look like what Gene has imagined a poet to be and whose poems don't sound like those he has read in school. Both Gene and the reader learn something about poetry in this delightful story that includes two original poems that Peck wrote for the occasion.

"The Kiss on the Carryon Bag," published in Don Gallo's *Destination Unexpected*, was aptly described by Alison Ching as a "whimsically quirky"[3] tale. Seb and his two buddies plan a simple night on the town and end up hanging out at the local café. There, Seb meets and is strongly attracted to Ally, an American girl traveling through Europe with her classmates. Yet when Ally intimates that they should spend the next day together, attending a parade in honor of the queen's birthday, he is unable to commit. At the parade the following morning, Ally spots Seb riding in the coach with his grandmother—the queen.

"The Three-Century Woman" appears in *Second Sight* and represents what Peck calls his "favorite kind of story, one that hopes to erase distance between young and old, to narrow the generation gap."[4] Megan travels to the elder-care facility to visit her Great-Grandma Breckenridge, a feisty woman who has lived in three centuries and to whom television and newspaper reporters have flocked to interview. Great-Grandma outsmarts them all in the tales she tells and earns Megan's respect in the telling. This "hilarious"[5] and "poignant"[6] story achieves its effect through Peck's creation and sharing of a "devilish old woman."[7]

In "Fluffy the Gangbuster," a new story published in *Past Perfect, Present Tense*, Peck strays from his typical style by employing an animal narrator. Guthrie and three friends play a never-ending Monopoly game at the home of Guthrie's great-aunt, unaware that Taylor Trumble and his bully supporters are about to attack them. As the kids play, Fluffy the cat keeps watch over the yard from her perch on the windowsill. When Taylor and the gang begin to encroach, Fluffy devises a plan of attack and solicits help from the dog next door. Together, they foil the gang's assault and leave Taylor follower-less and thus powerless, heightening Peck's exploration of "the contrast between gang membership and real friendship."[8]

SUPERNATURAL STORIES

Don Gallo published another Peck short story in *Visions*. In "Shadows," a young woman explains how she has grown up with ghosts in a New Orleans house owned by two eccentric aunts who are her guardians. Rather than fearing them, she says, "Ghosts were the company I came to count on." And then a strange boy appears to her. This story, a *VOYA* reviewer concludes, reveals "a different Peck," one whose "haunting imagery is enveloped in a beautiful ethereal veil."[9]

"Girl at the Window," first published in *Night Terrors*, edited by Lois Duncan, is a supernatural story that Peck says "shifts the shape of time, blending the past with the present."[10] The narrator, a new boy in town, is awakened one night to the sound of scratching at his upstairs window. Terrified but intrigued, he opens the screen and discovers a girl smelling of alcohol. Several nights later, the narrator follows the girl as she climbs the metal ladder of the town's water tower and falls to her death. A newspaper headline published the next day reveals the truth; the tragedy occurred thirty years prior. The narrator concludes, "She hadn't been a dream, but she wasn't real either."

"The Most Important Night of Melanie's Life," contained in *From One Experience to Another*, edited by M. Jerry Weiss and Helen S. Weiss, follows in the same supernatural tradition. Big sister Melanie doesn't want to babysit her little brothers while her parents attend a party, so she heads to a friend's house instead. In her absence, the new sitter arrives, an attractive sixteen-year-old male who seems a bit distracted but effectively entertains the boys. When Melanie returns home early, she is pleasantly surprised to meet her replacement and accepts his offer to go out for a while. Soon after she and her date leave, the parents arrive home with some news: the sitter was victim to a hit-and-run accident on his way over; his body was found by the side of the road—well before he was due to arrive at the house to babysit.

"Waiting for Sebastian," in Lisa Rowe Fraustino's *Dirty Laundry*, draws on supernatural elements to explore the effects of a young person's death on the remaining family members. Young Charlotte, waiting patiently for her older brother, Sebastian, to return from boarding school, suddenly remembers the truth of her past: Sebastian never returned home alive, and she took her own life by wrapping the curtain cord around her neck and falling from the high windowseat, a behavior she has repeated in her ghostly state for over eighty years. A *Publishers Weekly* reviewer calls the piece a "flavorful"[11] ghost story, but, as a result of Peck's use of the fantastic to capture the psychological reality of loss, it is much more.

STORIES SET IN THE PAST

"The Special Powers of Blossom Culp," included in *Birthday Surprises*, edited by Johanna Hurwitz, allowed Peck to revisit one his most beloved and popular characters. Written as a prequel to *The Ghost Belonged to Me*, this story describes the lasting impression Blossom makes soon after she and her mother arrive in Bluff City. Immediately plagued by her rival, Letty Shambaugh, Blossom vows to give Letty a most memorable birthday gift, a seemingly empty box filled with the "Special Powers" she inherited from Mama. In response to Letty's skepticism and desire to play Blossom for a fool, Blossom reveals each and every gift contained in each and every fancy box, thus ruining the surprise for her foe.

For "Shotgun Cheatham's Last Night above Ground," published in *Twelve Shots*, edited by Harry Mazer, Peck thought of "a lot of male-dominated yarns about how I killed a bear and it made a man out of me" and opted instead to create a comedy about a female character, "just to give Harry's collection some balance."[12] His inspiration soon arrived; he looked up from his writing desk, he says, "and there stood Grandma Dowdel with a 12-gauge double-barreled Winchester shotgun loose in her trigger-happy hand."[13] Upon the death of Shotgun Cheatham, a newspaper reporter comes to town to learn more about the former inhabitant. While stories of Shotgun's life become increasingly exaggerated, Grandma steps in to set the record straight—and, in the process, gives the reporter the scare of his life. A reviewer for *Kirkus* reaffirmed Peck's decision to go the comedic route: "Richard Peck's re-creation of some sawed-off shotgun shenanigans around a backwoods burial packs a load of belly laughs."[14] Peck's editor loved the story, too, and demanded (lovingly) that the author cull his mind for more such stories. The result? The Newbery finalist novel, *A Long Way from Chicago*.

"The Electric Summer," Peck's contribution to Don Gallo's historical *Time Capsule* anthology, captures the span of history from 1900 to 1910 and is centered around what Peck calls "the signal event of that decade . . . the great Louisiana Purchase Exposition, the world's fair of 1904 in St. Louis."[15] In the story, fourteen-year-old Geneva and her mother travel from their small town on a train, witness the wonders of the fair (the Ferris Wheel providing the grandest adventure), and head home changed irrevocably by the experience. Always interested in the growth of his characters, Peck found that the fair setting provided the "ideal metaphor for finding your future," an idea he developed further in *Fair Weather*, a novel featuring a "farm family of kids who find their twentieth-century futures at another fair, the World's Columbian Exposition in the Chicago of 1893."[16]

"By Far the Worst Pupil at Long Point School" is another new story Peck published in *Past Perfect, Present Tense*. During a family meal, a young boy listens in as Uncle Billy and Grandma compete to tell the story of Charlie, a rabble-rouser they knew in school—Uncle Billy as his peer, and Grandma as his teacher. As their telling progresses, the narrator learns of Charlie's exploits and, in a surprise twist, learns, too, the identity of the infamous Charlie, finding him seated right there at the table—and married to Grandma. The story didn't end there for Peck; it served as the seedbed for his later novel, *The Teacher's Funeral*, in which teenage big sister, Tansy, assumes the role of teacher in the one-room schoolhouse her younger brothers attend.

THE STORIES, COLLECTIVELY ORGANIZED

As noted, most of these stories were compiled and published in *Past Perfect, Present Tense*. While reviewers appreciated the ease of access to Peck's short story writing in this single volume, they valued even more the organizational structure of the collection and Peck's commentary and suggestions for young writers. Betty Carter, in *Horn Book Magazine*, noted: "While each story stands alone and satisfies as entertaining reading, the accumulated stories create an arc that both defines and unites Peck's writing career."[17]

Hazel Rochman echoed this sentiment: "Relaxed in style, the notes never try to 'explain' anything. The voice is laconic and wry. But the advice is tough. Then, suddenly, there's literary discussion about a story's epiphany. The combination is wonderful for both writers and readers. Read the story and the commentary, then go back to see how Peck does what he does."[18] It should also be noted that because of their brevity, subject matter, and vivid imagery, all of these stories are excellent choices for oral reading by an accomplished reader or storyteller.

A STORY FOR ADULT READERS

Peck demonstrates a more sophisticated writing style in "The Size of the Universe," a short story included in a 1986 issue of the *Southwest Review*. Compared to Peck's young adult stories and novels, the going is heavier here, the images more densely packed. Although much of this story presents the perspective of a young girl, it is told in the voice of that girl grown into a woman as she tries to come to terms with a grandmother who dominated the lives of everyone around her. The delineation of character and details of time and place outshine an almost nonexistent plot.

CHILDREN'S BOOKS

Taking a break after completing one of his earlier novels for young adults, Peck thought he'd try writing a story for children, "just to see if I could do it." *Monster Night at Grandma's House*, illustrated by Don Freeman, is a charming story about a young boy who is sure there's a monster standing near his bed at his grandmother's house. Opening his eyes and finding no monster, but thinking he sees the end of a tail exiting his doorway, Toby figures the monster is scared of him. After following the tail down the stairs and out to the porch to make sure the monster does not return, Toby falls asleep in the porch swing. In the morning, he proudly assures his grandmother: "It's gone. I took care of it. There's not a thing in the world to worry about."

The mood of the old Victorian country house, with its shadowy hallways, squeaky floorboards, and pesky beetles tapping at the window screens, is darkly portrayed by Don Freeman's India ink illustrations on scratchboard with blue watercolor overlays. The book's value lies in the switch in Toby's perspective from understandable fearfulness to proud self-assuredness, illustrating once again Richard Peck's desire to leave readers hopeful and stronger at the end.

If his second book for children is ever published, it will probably be called *What Ever Happened to Thanksgiving?* It is about how people commercialize holidays and about a family that, according to Peck, "has to look harder to find Thanksgiving."

Although Richard Peck is known for his novels, these shorter pieces contain the same qualities and characteristics of his longer works and are just as enjoyable to read.

NOTES

1. Lloyd Cooper, Maple Valley High School, Michigan, May 1987.
2. Patty Campbell, *Wilson Library Bulletin* (January 1985): 341.
3. Alison Ching, *School Library Journal* (May 2003): 151.
4. Richard Peck, *Past Perfect, Present Tense: New and Collected Stories* (New York: Puffin, 2004), 113.
5. Barbara, Scotto, *Library Journal* (December 1999): 142.
6. Linda Perkins, *Booklist*, 15 September 1999, 252.
7. *Kirkus Reviews*, 1999, Amazon.com.
8. Peck, *Past Perfect, Present Tense*, 112.
9. Lola H. Teabert, *Voice of Youth Advocates* (February 1988): 284.
10. Peck, *Past Perfect, Present Tense*, 67.
11. *Publishers Weekly*, 8 June 1998, 61.
12. Richard Peck, "Newbery Medal Acceptance," *Horn Book* (July 2001): 397.
13. Peck, "Newbery Medal Acceptance," 397.
14. *Kirkus*, 1997, Amazon.com.
15. Peck, *Past Perfect, Present Tense*, 17–18.
16. Peck, *Past Perfect, Present Tense*, 18.
17. Betty Carter, *Horn Book* (March–April 2004): 187.
18. Hazel Rochman, *Booklist*, 1 April 2004, 1361.

Poems and Poetry Collections

*M*ost biographical sources on Richard Peck make no references to his poetry, and he neglects to mention it himself in his autobiography, *Anonymously Yours*. "Though I believe in poetry and I write poetry, I am not a poet," he asserts. Maybe. Consider his accomplishments:

- Although the bulk of his writing is fiction, and he has never published enough poetry to comprise even one collection, some poets would covet being published in the magazines in which his poems have appeared, most notably *Saturday Review* and the *Chicago Tribune Magazine*.
- He has compiled and edited three anthologies of poems for teenagers; the first became one of the most widely used collections of contemporary poetry in the 1970s.
- He has included a poem or verse in almost every novel he has published.

Whether or not he is a poet, Richard Peck has made great efforts to bring the genre to teenagers.

INDIVIDUAL POEMS

Saturday Review published "Nancy," one of Peck's first poems, in 1969, following it with others, including "Street Trio." In "Street Trio," Peck wryly observes the dress and decorations of a then contemporary couple with their baby on a city street: "She of the electric hair" and "Vampira eyelids," wearing "floral-embroidered Levis" and "Marxist work shirt," and "He of the tie-dyed tank-top," "beaded headband," "rimless glasses," and "bandito mustachio." Their baby he describes as "Swinging low beneath her liberated bosom / In a denim sling." You can almost see the author smiling as he writes those descriptions, then ends with a twist, as lugging the baby along with "a bag of macrobiotic groceries," the woman staggers behind the man into the subway.[1]

"Nancy" exemplifies much of what the author was concerned with then and is today: spoiled teenagers vying with adults for power they have not yet earned. Nancy is the sullen, defiant student of the 1960s, wearing an expensive skirt over leather boots, "Trying hard to look hard," threatening anarchy, "burning / With borrowed fire," explaining to the teacher how irrelevant he has been.[2] Beneath the teacher's emotions lie a deep concern for the youth behind the façade.

Those characteristics are reflected in "Early Admission," an unpublished poem Peck wrote in 1971, in which a teacher, responding to a student's request for a college recommendation, drafts a "letter" to Mercedes. Playfully recounting Mercedes's qualities—her "peer-group leadership potential," her dazzling smile—the poet never mentions her ability as a *student*! Richard Peck says that both of these poems very much reflect the mood he was in during his last semester of teaching. "In fact," he adds, "they are more literal portraits of real students than I would allow myself (or be able to see) today. . . . I loved both those girls; otherwise I could have let them go without poems."

Not all his poems on serious subjects are so wry. "Jump Shot," first published in *Mindscapes: Poems for the Real World*, vividly details the movements of a basketball player on a city street.[3] And in "TKO," the poet describes the state of the once-grand Stillman's gym that is now "mostly on the ropes"—no Kid going twenty-eight rounds, no Irene Dunne watching at ringside—because "They pretty much threw in the towel."[4] Both of those poems are included in the anthology *Sports Poems* edited by R. R. Knudson and P. K. Ebert.

As part of a speech presented at the 1990 ALAN Breakfast and later published in the *ALAN Review*, Richard Peck wrote several poetic lines entitled "Notes for the Refrigerator Door." In them, the parent narrator lays down the law for her/his teenage child, each verse beginning with "No" and ending with "No, my darling child, / You CAN'T charge it."[5]

Although all of the aforementioned poems are written in free verse, not all of Peck's poems are. "The Geese," a twelve-line rhyming poem in iambic tetrameter, appeared in print for the first time in Peck's first poetry anthology, *Sounds and Silences* (1970). The poem reflects Peck's longing for travel as well as his attachment to the plains of his native Illinois and his love for his father. The poem begins: "My father was the first to hear / The passage of the geese each fall, / Passing above the house so near / He'd hear within his heart their call." Not a great piece of poetry: some lines feel forced; some images are clichéd. But the poem portrays a sensitive male image and leaves the reader with a pensive, even melancholy, feeling.

The saddest poem he has ever published—perhaps the saddest thing he has ever written—is a reaction to the effects of violence in Northern Ireland. Entitled "Irish Child," the piece describes a place "Where children learn to walk again on stumps," and one child envisions a heaven of "froth-cloud seas, / . . . Where whole-limbed children run, / . . . to the very ramparts / Of heaven," where they gaze through unshattered windows "Out upon blue and more blue." Its message is as appropriate today as it was when it was first published in the *Chicago Tribune Magazine* in 1972.[6]

Echoing these sentiments of loss are the lines Peck penned immediately following the 2001 attacks on the World Trade Center. Published in *Invitations to the World: Teaching and Writing for the Young*, Peck wrote "September 11" to inspire "a whole new system of history study: sequential, victimless history and how it repeats—how people who have forgotten the past are condemned to repeat it."[7]

In *Invitations to the World*, Peck includes additional poems regarding the education of the young, including "Twenty Minutes a Day."[8] Here, he advises parents to spend just twenty minutes each day reading to their children—while doing the laundry, making dinner, or preparing for bedtime. The power of language is celebrated in another of Peck's poems that begins "A story is a doorway."[9] And Peck expresses his frustration with parents and other adults who attempt to deny young people access to books in his piece that begins "What are you trying to tell me?"[10] Told from the perspective of an adult censor questioning why controversial texts have a place in school classrooms and libraries, the poem exposes the speaker's flawed logic and resulting hypocrisy.

EDITED COLLECTIONS OF POEMS

Sounds and Silences: Poetry for Now was the second major work of poetry that Peck published. As a teacher at Hunter College High School, Peck supplemented the traditional classroom fare by duplicating contemporary poems to involve his disinterested students. Peck recalls, "I wanted to introduce my students to poets living in their own time and using their own language." Half seriously, he reveals that he compiled this collection "because I was illegally mimeographing contemporary poetry and handing it out to my kids." "Besides," he adds, "I was tired of having purple fingers."

Sounds and Silences, consisting of 104 poems, is divided into twelve sections on topics that dominated the concerns of the youth of those Vietnam years (e.g., Illusion, Dissent, War) as well as topics that have concerned all people throughout time (e.g., Identity, Isolation, and the Family). "Here's a glimpse of the feel, a touch of the smell, an echo of the thought of this age," wrote a reviewer in the *Christian Science Monitor*.[11] "The tempo is definitely now," stated the *Saturday Review*.[12]

In this anthology are song lyrics by John Lennon and Paul McCartney, Malvina Reynolds, and Pete Seeger, along with some traditional poems often included in school anthologies by poets such as Robert Frost, Langston Hughes, and Theodore Roethke. There are also names that were likely new to both students and teachers then, among them Donald Hall and Philip Larkin, mixed in with poets whose works are now frequently anthologized: Gwendolyn Brooks, James Dickey, LeRoi Jones, and Denise Levertov. And there was one poem by Peck himself, "The Geese," described earlier in this chapter.

Although this anthology did not have the visual appeal of *Reflections on a Gift of Watermelon Pickle*, the most popular poetry anthology of the 1970s, *Kirkus* found it to be comparable in quality. And John W. Conner, writing in the *English Journal*, declared it to be "the most exciting collection of verse" he had read that year.[13] One of the most important characteristics that Conner noted was the brevity of the poems, which makes them easier for readers to study and enables teachers to introduce several poems on the same theme in one class period.

Encouraged by the extensive and enthusiastic reviews of *Sounds and Silences*, Dell Publishing approved a second anthology, which was published the following year. *Mindscapes: Poems for the Real World* consists of eighty-six poems, most of them first published in the 1960s, grouped into eleven categories and titled with lines taken from poems in those sections. These poems, Peck intimates in the introduction, stress reality over a more idealized view of the world, striving to encourage compassion without sentimentality, while enabling readers to explore the varied landscapes of the mind and venture beyond into undiscovered territories.

Although there are a few familiar poems in this book—A. E. Housman's "To an Athlete Dying Young" and Edward Arlington Robinson's "Mr. Flood's Party," for example—there are also poems that were unfamiliar to most people at the time: poems about astronauts and cowboys, bums and lovers, sharks and movie monsters, with new interpretations—sometimes jarring ones—of the "old time-honored themes of love, death, and nature." As Peck intended, these are poems through which readers can encounter "a real, hectic, un-pretty, and recognizable world."

Among such well-known older poets as Walt Whitman and A. E. Housman, and popular modern poets such as John Ciardi and William Carlos Williams, are the 1960s poets, Lawrence Ferlinghetti and Rod McKuen, and newer poets of note today, including May Swenson, William Stafford, Galway Kinnell, and Mari Evans. In addition, Peck includes two of his own previously unpublished poems: "Jump Shot" and "Mission Uncontrolled."

Although Walter Clemons concluded that this collection contains "too many easy, sentimental messages" presented "in open forms and plain language that dogs and cats can read,"[14] other reviewers found it "absorbing," "fresh and uncompromising,"[15] and "a good addition to high school poetry shelves."[16]

Pictures That Storm inside My Head, published in 1976 only in paperback, follows the successful pattern Peck established in his previous anthologies—except that the poems in this collection are a bit more sophisticated than those in the earlier collections. Was that intentional? Peck says, "No, I think it just worked out that way. It was probably that old schoolteacher in me who was saying: 'Now that you've been at one level, let's move on to the next.'"

As the book's title indicates, all of the poems illustrate storms of some kind: some vicious, some unexpected, and some, no matter what their form, that help clear the air. This is a collection, the anthologist points out, that is about thinking young, remembering "how grim it was to be imprisoned in childhood, how wonderful it was to know you were in love, how awful it was not to be able to say it, how good and terrible first things were."[17] Surprisingly, though, only a few selections are from a young person's perspective.

Divided into nine sections and a single end piece, this anthology mirrors its predecessors in its types of poems and its scope. There is a mixture of the famous—Nikki Giovanni, e. e. cummings, and Anne Sexton—and the not so famous—Lou Lipsitz, Sandra Hochman, Kalungano, and Peck (represented by his own "Nancy"). A few titles are familiar to most teachers—such as "Birches" by Robert Frost—but most were not widely known at the time of publication and are not especially familiar to the average person even today.

Reviews were scarcer on this collection, due probably to its not being first published in hardcover. Nevertheless, *Booklist* gave it a starred review and expected it to have "wide appeal for teenage poetry lovers."[18] And Tucson librarian Sarajean Marks concluded her *School Library Journal* review with the kind of comment made often about Richard Peck's novels: "Peck has an uncanny knack for knowing the tastes of teenagers."[19]

VERSE AND POEMS IN PECK'S FICTION

In addition to publishing anthologies of poetry, Peck includes a poem or verse in almost every one of his young adult novels, subtly educating readers to the pleasures and uses of poetry. "Poetry points out that we aren't as alone as we thought we were," Peck says.[20] "Whatever you do for a living, poetry comes in handy because it's a shortcut to the truth."[21] Three types of poetic forms are evident in those works: lines by famous poets, doggerel, and serious poems. Peck writes both of the latter two types.

Lines by Famous Poets

Peck referenced lines from famous poets in his first novel for young adults. Early in *Don't Look and It Won't Hurt*, Carol, the narrator, recalls a poem she and her younger sister had memorized years earlier when life was simpler, "Little Donkey, Close Your Eyes," by Margaret Wise Brown. Later, when her pregnant older sister leaves for Chicago, "going off alone to have a baby she'd have to give away to strangers," Carol recalls some lines from the Beatles' song "She's Leaving Home."

Lines about death from Tennyson's "Crossing the Bar" and John Donne's "Death Be Not Proud" are quoted in *Dreamland Lake*, along with two entire poems: Maurice Sagoff's "Frankenstein by Mary W. Shelley" (a poem that Peck reprinted three years later in *Pictures That Storm inside My Head*) and Reed Whittemore's "The High School Band" (which Peck included in *Mindscapes* two years before). Also on the topic of death, at the funeral of Byron and Jim Atwater's mother in *Father Figure*, the minister quotes four lines from Milton's *Samson Agonistes* that begin "Nothing is here for tears."

"All that was once so beautiful is dead," the ending lines from Conrad Aiken's "Music I Heard with You," appear in *Representing Super Doll*. In *Are You in the House Alone?*, Gail is unnerved by the Wordsworth poem her English class is studying: "Strange Fits of Passion I Have Known." Gerard Manley Hopkins's poem that begins "Margaret are you grieving / Over Goldengrove unleaving" plays a symbolic role in *Close Enough to Touch*. And a cub newspaper reporter in *The Ghost Belonged to Me* quotes two Longfellow lines to Alexander Armsworth: "A town that boasts inhabitants like me / Can have no lack of good society."

Peck continues the tradition of weaving poems written by other authors into the narrative in his more recent novels. Emily Dickinson's "Fame is a bee" makes a classroom appearance in *Strays like Us*, as do Adelaide Crapsey's "November Night" and Ralph Waldo Emerson's "Concord Hymn," each posted on the board and unnoticed by students. Some poems have a more lasting effect on Peck's characters. When Tilly of *The River between Us* hears the last lines of Oliver Wendell Holmes's "Brother Jonathan's Lament for Sister Caroline," read as part of a play featuring Abe Lincoln, she can't get the words out of her head, realizing the connection between the "rash sister" and her own war-torn nation.

William Shakespeare has served Richard Peck's purposes in several instances. Peck uses two lines from *Antony and Cleopatra* in *Through a Brief Darkness* to portend forthcoming unpleasantness: "The bright day is done, / And we are for the dark." In *Are You in the House Alone?*, Gail's boyfriend Steve gives her a copy of several lines from *Othello*, beginning with "My heart is turn'd to stone." And in *A Year Down Yonder*, Mary Alice is saddened to learn that, even in Grandma's small town, Shakespeare study in school is alive and well. Peck uses Shakespeare most extensively in *The Dreadful Future of Blossom Culp*, where Blossom frequently quotes lines from *Hamlet* to illustrate a point or explore an issue, including the expected "To be or not to be" as well as "There is nothing either good or bad, but thinking makes it so."

Doggerel

Given Peck's quick wit, it is not surprising to find instances of verse being used to make readers smile. The proper term for much of that verse is "doggerel," since the term "poetry" gives it too much status. On the cover of a student's notebook in *The Dreadful Future of Blossom Culp*, for example, are these immortal words: "If you love me as I love you, / No knife can cut our love in two." And in *Strays like Us*, philosophical lines on a stall door in the girls' restroom read: "I'm here and not here / Will I be here next year?"

Peck, seemingly enamored—or at least entertained—by poems of love, includes references to Valentine verses in several of his doggerel compositions. Blossom's teacher, Miss Fuller, obviously love struck, reads a pair of couplets that aren't much better than the notebook or stall scribblings referenced above. Blossom is convinced that Miss Fuller "had no doubt cribbed it off a two-cent valentine," which Peck really had done! In *A Long Way from Chicago*, Mary Alice and Joey find similar evidence of love when they discover wooing words preserved on paper in Grandma's trunk in the attic: "WHEN CUPID SENDS HIS ARROW HOME, / I HOPE IT MRS. YOU" and "WHEN YOU'RE OLD AND THINK YOU'RE SWEET, / TAKE OFF YOUR SHOES AND SMELL YOUR FEET." And, in *A Year Down Yonder*, Ina-Rae is the proud recipient of romantic sentiments from a secret admirer who writes: "I send this sentiment in haste / But at least I didn't eat the paste."

Peck finds poetic inspiration beyond matters of the heart and in the soul instead, as evidenced in his use of language reminiscent of tent revivalist preachers. As a representative example, he gives voice to the ever-devout Mrs. Effie Wilcox (*A Long Way from Chicago*) through a church song she intones with pure devotion. A pair of memorable lines are "Wash me clean of all I've been / And hang me out to dry." Later in the same novel, temperance-group members attending the fair belt out musical warnings to the sinners passing by.

Additional doggerel that appears in Peck's novels captures the everyday (and often outlandish) realities of high school life. In *Princess Ashley, Remembering the Good Times, Lost in Cyberspace,* and *The Great Interactive Dream Machine,* there are school cheers from the pep squad and cheerleaders—Peck's paraphrases of real cheers—as well as several hilariously outlandish cheers yelled by Hickory Fork students in *Bel-Air Bambi and the Mall Rats,* among which are these eternal lines: "In yo' face, / Pinetree Trace!" And, surely, readers will be inspired to ponder the nature of education upon reading the thought-provoking graduation motto noted in *A Year Down Yonder:* "WE FINISH—ONLY TO BEGIN."

Peck has a penchant for places, too, and works hard to make the most of setting. On the signs, billboards, or blank walls and fences that surround his characters, he includes examples of doggerel to set the stage for those who inhabit a particular location and time—often making readers laugh in the process. In *Here Lies the Librarian,* a sign above the door of the university library establishes ground rules for patrons: "Sit here and read, and read again / Until you have been rested; / But kindly don't forget to note / That SILENCE IS REQUESTED." Another suggested behavior is scrawled all over the door of the schoolhouse in *A Year Down Yonder:* "Ashes to ashes, / Dust to dust, / Oil them brains / Before they rust."

In *Father Figure,* Jim and Byron rent bicycles from a store with a sign in the window, a sign Peck observed in a real store window in Coconut Grove, Florida, when he was writing the novel: "Buy a car nevermore / Remember: Ten on the sprocket / Not four on the floor." Other ads appear in *The Teacher's Funeral.* The Overland Automobile Company encourages buyers to "SELL YOUR STEED, IT'S SPEED YOU'LL NEED." Cadillac gets in on the act with Peck's inclusion of the company motto, "Crank from your seat, / Not from the street," included in *Here Lies the Librarian.* And in *A Long Way from Chicago,* the Broshear Funeral Home reminds potential patrons, "When you come to the end, / You'll find a friend."

Cemeteries also provide fodder for surprising fun with verse. The tombstone for Electra Dietz, former town librarian in *Here Lies the Librarian,* reads: "AFTER YEARS OF SERVICE, / TRIED AND TRUE / HEAVEN STAMPED HER—/ OVERDUE.

Some of the most enjoyable lines of poetry in Peck's fiction are made (courtesy of Peck) by Pod, the lovable oddball in *Princess Ashley.*

The novel contains several of Pod's poetic efforts, such as "Gimme my red-eye gravy, my Coors, and my grits / And a day in the saddle till it hurts where I sits." Chelsea sympathetically calls this Pod's "Nashville period." Another humorously memorable verse comes from the recitation of a fifth-grade boy during the town Centennial Celebration in *A Long Way from Chicago*. The young interlocutor expresses his joy at being a boy. He explains that, according to Grandpa, all children begin by wearing dresses. Only those who "kicks and makes a noise / Gets promoted into boys. / Them that sits and twists their curls, / They just leaves them, calls them 'girls.'"

Serious Poems

Other poems by Peck are not intended to be funny. Gail receives a poem from her boyfriend, Steve, in *Are You in the House Alone?* that begins, "I'll be so gentle you won't know I'm there." In *Remembering the Good Times*, during tryouts for a part in *The Glass Menagerie*, Kate reads a poem that Travis had written, foreshadowing his suicide. In *Representing Super Doll*, the school newspaper prints a hurtful couplet about Darlene. Even more hurtful is the verse scrawled on the mirror of the sixth-grade girls' washroom in *Through a Brief Darkness* that ends with the line "But Karen's old man is a CROOK."

Still other poems in his historical novels educate readers by taking them back in time and exposing them to the research Peck accumulated. In *Fair Weather*, readers hear a railroad jingle describing Buffalo Bill Cody, the song that lent him the notable namesake. In the same novel, they read a verse on the wall of the Model Farm Kitchen at the fair, entitled "The Hymn of the Farm Wife," and are encouraged to imagine life without grocery stores, shopping malls, and alarm clocks. In *The River between Us*, readers are invited to a square dance where they hear the caller reference Jefferson Davis and Abraham Lincoln, thus providing historical context that enhances the fictional events described. In *A Year Down Yonder*, they hear Grandma chant a popular recipe under her breath while she prepares pumpkin pie. In the same novel, they listen in as Grandma reads an ad for Sweetheart soap featuring Kate Smith, a plus-sized beauty of the era.

Peck draws increasingly on American folk songs in his historical fiction, with similar intention and effect. Sometimes the inclusion is solemn, as seen in Peck's reference to the traditional Cajun song "Calinda" and to the Civil War ballad "Brother, Tell Me of the Battle," in *The River between Us*. At other times, the songs Peck selects hearken back to a more playful past, as evidenced by the raucous wailing of Granddad and his pals who, while roaming the streets, break into choruses of "Did ye ever hear tell of McGarry?" and generate their own rendition of "Dry Whiskey" in *Fair Weather*. Although the comic versions of "Mary Had a Little Lamb" in *The River between Us* bring forth a chuckle when readers imagine the little lamb, now dead, going to school with Mary "Between two hunks of bread," the fact that these tunes are presented as part of a minstrel show featuring singers in blackface reminds readers, too, of the less humorous, racially weighty elements in the tale.

Perhaps the poems that most challenged Richard Peck occur in *Princess Ashley*. Not only did Peck have to come up with several instances of doggerel that could be realistically attributable to Pod, but he also had to construct poems that an "angry, introverted fifteen-year-old girl" was supposed to have written. The most revealing of those poems is "Girl in the Mirror," which includes these lines: "I'd like to read her mind and look her in the eye, / I'd like to know her better but I'm shy." Reading those lines early in the novel, the reader, just like Chelsea, is convinced they belong to Ashley.

Peck's most ambitious effort to use poetry in a fictional work can be found in a story published in *Connections*. In "I Go Along," nonacademically oriented Gene explains how he was invited along with a gifted junior class to attend a poetry reading at a local college. Seeing a living poet for the first time, Gene is surprised: "He's not dressed like a poet. In fact, he's dressed like me: Levi's and Levi jacket. Big heavy-duty belt buckle. Boots, even. . . . It's weird, like there could be poets around and you wouldn't realize they were there." For the poetry that the speaker reads, Peck wrote two poems, one about a man watching his wife sleep, and another called "High School," in which a student dreams his worst fears, including forgetting his locker combination, being cut from the team, and being trapped in the building when someone tampers with the bell on the last period on Friday so it won't ring. Gene concludes that the others were poems, but not the last one. "You can't write poems about zits and your locker combination." His seatmate responds: "Maybe nobody told the poet that."[22]

At least nobody told Richard Peck that. Of course, Richard Peck insists, "I am not a poet."

NOTES

1. Richard Peck, in "Phoenix Nest," ed. Martin Levin, *Saturday Review*, 4 September 1971, 6.

2. Richard Peck, in "Phoenix Nest," ed. Martin Levin, *Saturday Review*, 21 June 1969, 6.

3. Richard Peck, *Mindscapes: Poems for the Real World* (New York: Delacorte, 1971), 8.

4. Richard Peck, in *Sports Poems*, ed. R. R. Knudson and P. K. Ebert (New York: Dell, 1971), 142.

5. Richard Peck, "Notes for the Refrigerator Door," *ALAN Review* (Winter 1992): 5.

6. Richard Peck, *Chicago Tribune Magazine*, 17 September 1972.

7. Richard Peck, *Invitations to the World: Teaching and Writing for the Young* (New York: Dial, 2002), 192.

8. Peck, *Invitations to the World*, 13–14.

9. Peck, *Invitations to the World*, 195.

10. Peck, *Invitations to the World*, 157–58.

11. *Christian Science Monitor*, 27 January 1971.

12. *Saturday Review*, 19 September 1970, 35.

13. John W. Conner, *English Journal* (September 1971): 830.

14. Walter Clemons, *New York Times Book Review*, 27 June 1971, 8.

15. *Kirkus Reviews*, 1 March 1971, 244.

16. Margaret A. Dorsey, *Library Journal*, 15 June 1971, 2140.

17. Richard Peck, *Pictures That Storm inside My Head: Poems for the Inner You* (New York: Avon, 1976), 23.

18. *Booklist*, 1 December 1976, 532.

19. Sarajean Marks, *School Library Journal* (May 1977): 71.

20. Richard Peck, *Sounds and Silences: Poetry for Now* (New York: Dell, 1970), xiii.

21. Peck, *Sounds and Silences*, xii.

22. Richard Peck, "I Go Along," in *Connections: Short Stories by Outstanding Writers for Young Adults*, ed. Donald R. Gallo (New York: Delacorte, 1989), 184–91.

· 11 ·

Essays and Other Nonfiction

$\mathcal{A}$lthough he is best known as a young adult novelist, Richard Peck began his writing career by publishing nonfiction. His essays have appeared in professional journals such as *School Library Journal, Horn Book Magazine, Booklist*, and the *ALAN Review*, in popular magazines such as *Parents' Magazine* and *Better Family Living*, and in newspapers such as the *New York Times*. His published book reviews have appeared in the *Los Angeles Times* and *American Libraries*. While articles in these periodicals focus primarily on books and writing for teenagers, several describe antiques, architecture, and travel. Peck has also written educational materials for textbooks, compiled and edited two collections of essays for high school students, and authored two biographical-sociological-pedagogical book-length texts for teachers and librarians.

EARLY ECLECTIC SUCCESSES

Peck's first piece was the self-published *Old Town: A Complete Guide*. Then his work as a fellow with the Council for Basic Education provided him additional opportunities to see his words in print in monthly newsletters and publications such as *A Consumer's Guide to Educational Innovations*. But the work that Peck sees as his initiation into the world of major commercial publishing resulted from his association with the late Ned Hoopes at Hunter College High School. As Peck tells it: "Here I was, new in New York, and he came up to me at the first faculty meeting and said 'Let's do a book.'" This was the mid-1960s, and Peck knew he had to do more than lecture and assign readings from traditional anthologies to reach his New York City students. When asked what kind of book he wanted to do, the young teacher replied: "Well, I will need a collection of nonfiction, contemporary readings for my students that they cannot reject as irrelevant." The result was *Edge of Awareness: Twenty-Five Contemporary Essays*. The title page says, "Edited by Ned E. Hoopes and Richard Peck," but it was Peck who did most of the legwork to put the book together. Hoopes knew what would sell, and he had the contacts with publishers. In November 1966, Dell published the collection in paperback. "It sold millions of copies," says Peck. "What a way to start!"

Divided into five sections, the twenty-five essays in *Edge of Awareness* provide mature and thought-provoking perspectives on contemporary society. Ranging from the thoughts of twentieth-century historians, scientists, anthropologists, and leaders such as Arnold Toynbee, Margaret Mead, and Adlai E. Stevenson to the writings of poets and other creative artists, the collection features texts reprinted from prestigious publications such as the *New Yorker*, *Saturday Review*, and the *New York Times*.

Seven years later, just as Richard Peck was publishing his first novels for teenagers, Dell released Peck's second collection of contemporary essays. Entitled *Leap into Reality: Essays for Now*, this anthology contains thirty pieces, most of which first appeared in the late 1960s in such magazines as *Harper's*, the *American Scholar*, *Smithsonian*, *Esquire*, and *Newsweek*, as well as the *New York Times*. Contributing authorities, such as historian Barbara Tuchman, anthropologist Loren Eiseley, composer Leonard Bernstein, and writer James Baldwin, provide a veritable *Who's Who* of cultural literacy of the 1960s.

Although these two collections are noteworthy for what they contain, they have two weaknesses. In spite of efforts to reflect the spirit and the key issues of the times, all but a few of the essays in each of the collections are written by white males. The adult perspectives and the highly sophisticated quality of the writing also make these collections difficult reading fare for all but the most advanced high school students. In fact, the majority of their sales are now to college classes, Peck reports.

In the early 1970s, after he had left teaching, Peck wrote several articles on antiques, architecture, history, and travel. For the *New York Times*, he produced occasional pieces about the buildings and design of historic neighborhoods in New York City. In both *Saturday Review* and *House Beautiful*, he wrote about the fine art of Art Deco. Nostalgia, a trademark feature of many of Peck's novels for both teenagers and adults, is evident in these pieces—see, for example, his description of the mix of past and present on Governors Island[1] or the last trolley running in New Orleans, the St. Charles.[2]

In the early 1970s, Peck's acquaintance with the growing field of young adult books and their publishers gave him entrance into the publishing world, and he was asked to write a quarterly series of book reviews for the "Current" column in *American Libraries* starting in February 1974, that publication's first column on young adult books. In the five columns he wrote, Peck reviewed books with the intent of making "inveterate, habitual, chronic readers out of the citizens of the 21st century."[3] In one review, he introduced readers to the most controversial book of 1974: Robert Cormier's *The Chocolate War,* calling it "the most uncompromising novel ever directed to the '12 and up reader'—and very likely the most necessary."[4] His reviews are fair, insightful, and lively.

CRITIQUES OF SCHOOLS AND THOSE WHO INHABIT THEM

Peck's most incendiary writing occurs in his essays about teaching and the roles of adults versus young people. The issue of who's in control is the focus of two articles published in magazines for parents in 1971, the year Peck resigned from teaching at Hunter College High School. In "We Can Save Our Schools," Peck attacks "naive" educational reformers of the 1960s who advocated "a utopian freedom in the classroom where self-directed youngsters pursue their own interests and learn happily at their own pace." In "Can Students Evaluate Their Education?" Peck laments the loss of teacher control. He sees life in schools as bleak: with restless, unmotivated students who conform to the empty words of rebellious leaders, a haphazard curriculum, and crumbled standards. "Without adults around to set standards, and to put up a good fight for maintaining them," writes Peck, "young people fall prey to the confusion that arises when there is no yardstick by which to measure achievements and contributions."[5]

In *Invitations to the World: Teaching and Writing for the Young,* Peck contrasts his own schooling experiences with those he witnessed while working as a classroom teacher and argues that the permissiveness of schools has bestowed unearned authority upon students and placed them in situations they are ill prepared to handle. He describes how his former high school students self-segregated in their selection of seats: Puerto Ricans sat with Puerto Ricans, whites sat with whites, for example. In response to this flocking response, Peck says, "To expect the young to defy their own psychologies in order to enact our political theories disfigured them and their education."[6] We gave them too much authority—over seating charts and much more.

These themes—the need for adult authority and the inability of contemporary teenagers to form a community for each other—are repeated throughout many of Peck's other published essays and speeches to teachers and librarians. At their strongest, they are hyperbolic put-downs of kids. Witness these statements from "People of the World: A Look at Today's Young Adults and Their Needs," a speech Peck presented at the 1981 American Library Association Conference in San Francisco:

- When you speak to parents, all their children are gifted. When you speak to the children, they're all remedial.[7]
- Adolescents would prefer to communicate with one another, but they can't because they don't have the vocabulary. They are verbally anorexic and happy to be.[8]
- Most adolescents cannot read well enough today to understand and be entertained by printed matter.[9]

Or this paragraph about teenagers from a guest column Peck wrote in 1985 for *School Library Journal*:

> Wherever they live, they regularly confuse the word for the deed, preaching tolerance and practicing exclusion. They are devoted, undependable friends to one another. They believe group identity will solve personal problems. They refuse to accept the consequences of their own actions, and they can project blame any distance.[10]

Yet, even amid these painful realities, Peck maintains his characteristic humor, demonstrating perspective and giving us some semblance of hope. Indeed, as Peck argues, "Puberty is the darkest time of life, for while it is the death of childhood, it isn't the birth of reason. You wake up one terrible morning, and nothing works, and everything's the wrong size."[11] But all is not lost; puberty is difficult, awkward, and confusing but a stage from which young people might emerge only slightly scathed, especially if they are fortunate to have a good book as a guide.

STORIES AND THE PROMISE OF THE POSSIBLE

Those are some of the same key factors that inspire and drive Richard Peck to write novels for teenagers. Peck wants his readers "to explore that gap between word and deed; to move beyond blame shifting; to search for the self in a landscape without the old landmarks; to see the book as a source of alternatives, the protagonist as role model."[12] If young people are misdirected, his novels might set a few of them straight. If his teenaged readers have a confused view of the world, his novels can provide at least one clear alternative view. If kids are, as Peck believes, essentially humorless, he will work extra hard to infuse his novels with comedic moments. If students are attracted so much to television because it is entertaining, he will attract them to books with what is entertaining to students. If adults in the real world do not provide adequate, authoritative guidance for young people, then adults in his novels—grandparent figures as well as supportive parents—can.

Similarly, Peck strives to create characters that choose independence over conformity in books that "invite them to champion themselves."[13] Like Huck Finn, Peck's ideal literary protagonist, these characters "have to be imperfect enough for improvement and willing to stand up for who they are." In the celebration of these "rebels and rebels-to-be, Huck Finns looking for themselves and the way out of town," Peck hopes to reach those "young people who are beginning to run for their lives."[14] By equipping them with motive and a map, Peck just might help his readers find a greater likelihood for success when they venture beyond the world they know, giving them stories that "end at new beginnings with a sense of more challenges lying yet ahead, rather like life."[15]

In most of his articles, Peck describes how he attempts to meet these perceived needs through his novels or how others have done so in their books, placing great emphasis on the young adult literary genre as a particularly powerful force in the attainment of this goal. For Peck, young adult titles have the capacity to provide companionship for young readers, provide a structure to balance the adolescent deconstruction of their homes and schools, dramatize life's chief lesson—that you will eventually be held accountable for your actions—and provide role models who question readers about their own lives.[16] Among young adult novels he has praised are S. E. Hinton's *The Outsiders*, M. E. Kerr's *Dinky Hocker Shoots Smack!*, and Chris Crutcher's *Running Loose*.[17] In "Walking in a Straight Line," Peck describes and celebrates Sharon Creech's *Walk Two Moons*, Patrice Kindl's *The Woman in the Wall*, and Rob Thomas's *Rats Saw God* for the way the authors of these texts locate "the shortest distance between reader and story" and capture the complexity of adolescence without "overburdening the plot."[18]

In "Love Is Not Enough," a speech delivered at the Author Achievement Award Luncheon at the 1990 conference of the ALA, Peck describes the inherent tension he experiences when writing for adolescents—the push and pull on his emotions, the frustration and joy of trying to reach an increasingly unresponsive crowd: "From Mark Twain we learn the Sacred Secret, to write in love and anger. Love for the world and anger at a world made wrong, at the callowness of the young before us and of the young we were."[19] For Peck, however, the fight is worth the effort. He self-mocks his staying power: "The years and books roll on. Vintage clothing shops fill up with the antique finery of the early 1990s, and it occurs to me that I have neckties older than my readers." But he keeps on writing.

To remain inspired, Peck imagines the teen who picks up a book—his or another's—and finds meaning and value in the words and worlds on the page. He imagines the voice of this young reader: "I read not for happy endings but for new beginnings: I'm just beginning myself, . . . and I wouldn't mind a map. I read because one of these days I'm going to get out of this town, and I'm going to go everywhere and meet everybody—and I want to be ready."[20]

LESSONS IN WRITING

Not all of Peck's essays focus on the failures of today's educational system or the inadequacies of today's young people—and his hopes for them in a world of stories. Some pieces describe pedagogical practices he recommends for teachers of writing and tips for writers themselves. In his piece "In the Beginning Was The . . . ," Peck poses questions related to the larger question of what to teach and why with respect to writing. In his wonderings, he intimates his frustration with teachers who fail to inspire young people to care about language and engage in a genuine writing process, asking,

> Do we tell them in the creative writing class that to be a writer you have to be a collector of words, and love them for themselves? . . . Do we point out that to a writer words are not mechanical parts but living things with beating hearts? Do we share with them the sensual satisfaction of finding just the right word and erasing the so-so? In student compositions, do we circle the repeated word, the lazy word, the boring word? Do we suggest better ones and encourage a search for more? Or do we give them grades on rough drafts, grateful for what we can get?[21]

In "Nobody but a Reader Ever Became a Writer," he argues against overly personal writing, claiming that "urging the young to express the self and nothing else well before they know anything about the self can lead in downward directions."[22] For writers of all ages, Peck offers an alternative to the "write about what you know" approach. In "How to Write a Short Story," the final chapter of his short-story collection *Past Perfect, Present Tense*, Peck says: "Fiction isn't what is; it's what if?" He encourages the potential writer in all of us to pay attention; when "something in the real world jogs or jars, you tuck it away."[23]

Several of Peck's articles focus on an analysis of the elements of good young adult fiction, modeling techniques young (and old) writers might wish to emulate. "Some Thoughts on Adolescent Literature," for example, analyzes three key characteristics of the young adult novel,[24] while "Ten Questions to Ask about a Novel" presents exactly that.[25] The title of "The Care and Feeding of the Visiting Author" is also self-explanatory.[26] And in "The Genteel Unshelving of a Book," Peck recounts a censorship effort that banned his *Father Figure* from a junior high school library because one mother feared that the book would undermine the standards of behavior she established for her daughter[27]—an ironic twist on Peck's preoccupation with the lack of parental authority in contemporary society.

A CENSURE OF THE CENSORS

While that attack in the mid-1980s was Richard Peck's first encounter with censors, it was not his last. Attacks on his novels have attained the dubious status of nationwide attention from organized religious groups, likely begun, Peck believes, by Phyllis Schlafly who, in her column, condemned both *The Ghost Belonged to Me* and *Ghosts I Have Been*. Schlafly and other religious fundamentalists express concerns over any book about ghosts or witches, associating them with devil worship. Peck readily identifies what he perceives to be misplaced blame on behalf of censors. In "Battered by Left and by Right: Censorship in the '90s as Viewed by a Novelist from Illinois Whose Books Have Wound Up on Forbidden Lists," he argues that censorship is a reflection of the larger societal fabric, not the result of authors trying to incite parents through their textual choices. He says, "Authors aren't nearly as uninhibited as their detractors aver. In books I write for the young, I don't use their language or the words written on the walls of the schools I visit, the words very young children hear from television—if not in their own homes, then elsewhere."[28]

In an effort to counter such attacks and rally librarians, educators, and other people in the book business, Peck wrote one of his most effective essays for *Booklist*, "The Great Library-Shelf Witch Hunt." In it, he posits that parents attack books because they can't control their children's television addiction, or their children. They fear the loss of control and therefore attack what they can control, but "books aren't that powerful," Peck believes, "and their children aren't that innocent." "Only the non-reader fears books," he proclaims.[29] He echoes this sentiment in "From Strawberry Statements to Censorship," citing, in particular, his concerns regarding the current generation of parents:

> Parents who in their youth marched against authority have today joined the ranks of those who censor what young people read. . . . This generation of censorious parents finds it easier to get a teacher fired, to demean the professionalism of a librarian, to burn a book than to challenge the mounting power of their own children, who demand more freedoms in the 1990s than they themselves demanded a quarter century ago.[30]

Similarly, in his essay "The Last Safe Place on Earth," Peck warns that generations beget generations, and "the inmates of our present-day remedial classes are the book-burning parents of the century lying dead ahead.''[31]

"Discussing the content of books with people who don't read them'' is futile, Peck says. So he urges librarians, teachers, and writers to "encourage parents to ventilate their real concerns rather than dignifying their search for scapegoats,'' and to bring the attacks on books into the open. Trying to keep the challenge to a book quiet in the name of damage control is itself a kind of censorship.[32] And it's time to be increasingly unified in response to such attacks. "We have to use aggressive, public new ways to point out to people hungry for power that we aren't powerless,'' Peck states. "Those with sectarian motivation attend churches where they're in an absolute majority because all dissent is silenced. This can give them a distorted view of a world where they are still a minority. As a result, when we meet, it shouldn't be one-on-one. They need to see librarians and teachers and administrators grouped, united, and ready.''[33]

NOTES

1. Richard Peck, "It's a World Away and Yet So Close,'' *New York Times*, 8 October 1972, 4.

2. Richard Peck, "St. Charles Is the Last Trolley Left,'' *New York Times*, 28 January 1973, 3, 17.

3. Richard Peck, "Consciousness-Raising,'' *American Libraries* (February 1974): 75.

4. Richard Peck, "Delivering the Goods,'' *American Libraries* (October 1974): 492.

5. Richard Peck, "We Can Save Our Schools,'' *Parents' Magazine and Better Family Living* (September 1971): 51.

6. Richard Peck, *Invitations to the World: Teaching and Writing for the Young* (New York: Dial, 2002), 129.

7. Richard Peck, "People of the World: A Look at Today's Young Adults and Their Needs,'' *School Library Media Quarterly* (Fall 1981): 17.

8. Peck, "People of the World,'' 18.

9. Peck, "People of the World,'' 19.

10. Richard Peck, "Growing Up Suburban: 'We Don't Use Slang, We're Gifted,''' in "In the YA Corner,'' *School Library Journal* (October 1985): 119.

11. Richard Peck, "Communicating with the Pubescent,'' *Booklist*, 1 June 1994, 1819.

12. Peck, *Invitations to the World*, 76.

13. Peck, "Growing Up Suburban," 119.

14. Richard Peck, "Huck Finns of Both Sexes: Protagonists and Peer Leaders in Young Adult Books," *Horn Book* (September–October 1993): 554–58.

15. Richard Peck, "Sharing the Truth with the First Citizens of the 21st Century," Speech presented at the 1996 Highlights Foundation Writing for Children Workshop. Also printed in *Highlights Foundation Newsletter* (1996), 4.

16. Richard Peck, "Books for the Readers of the 21st Century," Ezra Jack Keats Lecture delivered at the University of Southern Mississippi, 24 March 2000, www.lib.usm.edu/~degrum/html/aboutus/au-fall2000keatslecture.shtml.

17. Richard Peck, "YA Books in the Decade of the Vanishing Adult," *Dell Carousel* (Fall–Winter 1985–1986): 1–2.

18. Richard Peck, "Writing in a Straight Line," *Horn Book* (September–October 1997): 529–33.

19. Richard Peck, "Love Is Not Enough," *School Library Journal* (September 1990): 153.

20. Peck, "Love Is Not Enough," 153–54.

21. Richard Peck, "In the Beginning Was The . . . ," *ALAN Review* (Spring 1997): 2–4.

22. Richard Peck, "Nobody but a Reader Ever Became a Writer," in *Authors' Insights: Turning Teenagers into Readers and Writers*, ed. Donald R. Gallo (Portsmouth, N.H.: Boynton/Cook, 1992), 79–80.

23. Richard Peck, *Past Perfect, Present Tense: New and Collected Stories* (New York: Puffin, 2004), 168.

24. Richard Peck, "Some Thoughts on Adolescent Lit," *News from ALAN* (September–October 1975): 5–6.

25. Richard Peck, "Ten Questions to Ask about a Novel," *ALAN Newsletter* (Spring 1978):1, 7.

26. Richard Peck, "Care and Feeding of the Visiting Author," *Top of the News* (Spring 1982): 251–55.

27. Richard Peck, "The Genteel Unshelving of a Book," *School Library Journal* (May 1986): 37–39.

28. Richard Peck, "Battered by Left and Right: Censorship in the '90s as Viewed by a Novelist from Illinois Whose Books Have Wound Up on Forbidden Lists," *Illinois Issues* (July 1993): 25.

29. Richard Peck, "The Great Library-Shelf Witch Hunt," *Booklist*, 1 January 1992, 816.

30. Richard Peck, "From Strawberry Statements to Censorship," *School Library Journal* (January 1997).

31. Richard Peck, "The Last Safe Place on Earth," *Book Links* (September 1995): 26.

32. Peck, "The Great Library-Shelf Witch Hunt," 817.

33. Peck, *Invitations to the World*, 155.

· 12 ·

Adult Novels

"*Y*ou could write a historical novel like Rosemary Rogers," Richard Peck's editor at Avon said one day.

Claiming to know little about the adults who would be the audience for the kind of book his editor was suggesting, Peck replied, "No, I couldn't."

Switching tactics, the editor said, "*If* you were going to, where would you set it?"

Peck's answer came rather quickly: "I'd set it in the Edwardian era, which is accessible, and around everybody's favorite disaster, the sinking of the *Titanic.*"

She said, "Fine, I'll draw up a contract. Get going." And the rest, to twist a common expression, is historical fiction.

AMANDA/MIRANDA

Because Peck enjoys nonfiction and doing historical research, and because England is one of his favorite places, the setting for his first adult novel, the Isle of Wight where he once vacationed, was ideally suited to him. The island, he says, represents "England in microcosm. It has one castle, one royal palace, one this, one that." To further prepare to write, Peck joined the Titanic Historical Society of America, studied the histories of families who were on the ship, and, he says, "lived for two years with the deck plan of the *Titanic* around my room." Because so many people are well versed in *Titanic* lore, Peck felt he needed to be absolutely accurate about the locations of everything on board, to the point of knowing which way his characters would turn when they left their staterooms.

Because he was working on other projects, his first book for adults took him more than four years to complete, and he was not comfortable writing it. But *Amanda/Miranda* attained phenomenal success. As Peck told interviewer Jean Ross, "everything you could hope would happen to a book happened to *Amanda/Miranda*."[1] It was translated into nine languages and printed in special editions by the Literary Guild and Reader's Digest, as well as in Braille. And Peck received a hefty array of letters about the book—this time from adult readers.

Amanda/Miranda is a tale of romance, intrigue, deception, and adventure with numerous plot twists and surprises. Although a reviewer for the *Washington Post* thought the book a "jumbled hand-me-down from Mishmasterpiece Theatre,"[2] another found it to be "a gorgeously romantic, implausible affair comfy as eiderdown."[3]

The tale focuses on Amanda—the selfish, overindulged, devious daughter of the owners of Whitwell Hall—and her new, innocent servant, Mary, renamed Miranda by Amanda, after the heroine in Shakespeare's *The Tempest*. Among the cast in the manor are John Thorne, the estate's maintenance man and chauffeur, who is also Amanda's secret lover; Gregory Forrest, the handsome, idealistic American son of a German beer baron who is courting Amanda; Amanda's black-sheep brother, Gordon; and various other rich folks and their servants. Coincidentally, Amanda and Miranda are look-alikes, thus establishing the possibilities for mistaken identities and intermixed romances.

Amanda sums up her own character: "I am meant to have what I want." And she sets elaborate schemes to do just that. Poor Miranda is victimized by Amanda and John Thorne and by life in general in this high society. But Miranda is not stupid, and she learns from each painful episode. "I had been raised to expect nothing for myself," she explains, but little by little, she nurtures small sparks of self-worth and independence.

Her chance for independence comes late in the novel, during her crossing to America on board the *Titanic* with Amanda. Amanda—secretly pregnant with Thorne's baby, though Thorne is conveniently now married to Miranda and Amanda is on her way to marry Gregory—drowns in the sinking, while Miranda, dressed like Amanda and wearing Amanda's jewelry, is rescued from the icy waters. In love with Gregory since she first met him, Miranda, masquerading now as Amanda, becomes a bigamist by marrying Gregory and finds happiness in America.

Much more than a stereotypical historical romance, this novel clearly delineates the manners of the times and elucidates the attitudes of the upper class toward servants and of servants toward their masters and mistresses. It is also the story of strong women, especially of a woman who gains strength in herself as she loses her innocence. It was Peck's intent to reverse the usual role of women in romance novels. "I have presented the heroine as the ingenious one in adversity, winner of the male prize, for a change," he told a *Publishers Weekly* interviewer.[4]

The novel is also chock full of vivid details about clothing, architecture, transportation, and daily life of the Edwardian age. From the "Flemished tapestries" and "thousand curving silversides of teapots and urns" to "great glittering chandeliers," the sense of place remains with the reader long after the details of the story have faded.

Readers in their seventies and eighties and some related to passengers on the *Titanic* shared their responses to the story. One woman from Altadena, California, wrote to Peck weekly. As part of the correspondence, she sent Peck documents her mother had recorded at her job in a Pasadena library, among them a young woman's account of traveling west in a covered wagon in the mid-1800s. That account inspired Peck's third adult novel, *This Family of Women*, which he dedicated to his faithful correspondent: Isabelle Daniels Griffis.

Although Peck wrote *Amanda/Miranda* for an adult audience, some reviewers believed the book appropriate for teenagers as well. Joni Bodart argued that *Amanda/Miranda* should have been included on the ALA Best Books for Young Adults list for 1980.[5] Dial publishers, too, saw the book's appeal, so Richard Peck agreed to abridge the novel—from 460 pages to 169—and the young adult version was published in 1999.

Peck wryly observes about his two audiences: "It's wonderful, but it makes you realize that you are in two fields in which you are just about to lose your readers: teenagers grow up very quickly and the very old die."[6] To deal with that problem, Richard Peck wrote a novel for people his own age who are going through midlife crises.

NEW YORK TIME

New York Time grew out of a comment from one of Richard Peck's friends—"a woman younger than I by a generation"—who, Peck recalls, complained: " 'There are no novels about me.' She had gone to college, joined a sorority, and married the guy most likely to succeed. She then lived in a dream house in Winnetka and came to the time in her life when she says, 'So is this it?' "

"Marriages are funny things," thirty-eight-year-old Barbara Renfrew says in the opening line of *New York Time*. "Let me tell you about mine." What she reveals in this witty, satirical novel is that she's "quietly confused." She not only misses the romance of her college sorority days but also faces disruption in her once secure life with husband Tom when he is transferred to New York City and she must leave suburban Chicago.

New York is not good for Barbara. Apartment hunting in Manhattan is horrifying (a dead body recently decorated the floor of the apartment they eventually lease). And then Tom leaves her, wants a divorce, and returns to the North Shore of Chicago to an old flame, Marlene Milisap (the name tells it all). Barbara falls apart, leading an empty, aimless life sustained by soap operas, until she meets Ed, an urban horticulturalist. He's twenty-three, tall, handsome, sexy, and gentle with her. Twenty-three! Their passion triumphs over everything else. He makes her very happy. Then he makes her pregnant, which makes her even happier. Unhappy with Marlene, Tom returns to beg Barbara to take him back. But she's found herself and her love and her place in the world, so she sends Tom away. She marries Ed. Tom marries Marlene. And Ed's great-grandmother dies and leaves him and Barbara her enormous, gorgeous apartment. The end.

A reviewer from the Boston Public Library was right on target in drawing a comparison between Erma Bombeck's style and Barbara's skewed views of life's vagaries.[7] But not everyone appreciates Erma Bombeck's kind of humor. Thus Peck came in for his share of negative comments on this book. One reviewer did not like the abundance of "aphorisms and digressions" but found them "undeniably witty" and the ending "moving."[8] *Kirkus* found the ending "saccharine" and the book as a whole without sufficient impact, even though it contains "lots of fine witchy humor."[9] The reviewer for *Booklist*, focusing on what others had minimized, praised the "memorable eccentricities and abundant zesty barbs, well and liberally planted."[10] But the reviewer for *Mademoiselle* seems to have understood the novel best, saying that *New York Time* "is not profound and doesn't pretend to be." She labeled it "amusing" and "urbane," "a shrewd and witty modern version of a 1940s movie."[11]

Although it's clearly a book for women, Peck has received a lot of letters from men, who write about the crazy experiences they have had in New York: "But it's also a very warm response that 'We've been through this together, haven't we?' " That's the kind of response Peck values most.

THIS FAMILY OF WOMEN

Richard Peck's third adult novel, *This Family of Women*, is awash with interesting characters, mostly female, but the stories of the real women behind the fictional characters are just as fascinating. Peck explains the theory behind his lengthy saga: "The American West was not won by men with guns but by women without them. When you learn the local histories of towns like Reno and Virginia City, you find that the men were shooting everything in sight, and the women were trying to found the schools and the church and finally the country club."[12]

Among the documents sent to Peck by Isabelle Griffis, mentioned earlier, were notes from Susan Thompson's diary. Her family, traveling to California in 1851, came upon a tragedy: Indians had killed the adults in the Oatman family, which had been traveling just ahead of them, had abducted the teenage daughters, and had scalped and left the son, Lorenzo, to die. Lorenzo survived, and he and the Thompsons eventually reached California and settled in El Monte. Years later, Lorenzo located his sister, Olive, who had been living with Mohave Indians in Arizona, and brought her to El Monte. But, according to the diary, Olive was unable to adjust to living among whites. To fill in the gaps in Susan Thompson's account and to imagine what might have happened to her, Richard Peck began *This Family of Women*.[13]

From over two years of research, primarily in Carson City, Nevada, and San Francisco, Richard Peck shaped an epic novel about five generations of women, all related by blood or friendship, starting with fourteen-year-old Lena Wheatley (based on Susan Thompson) and Sarah Ann Ransom (based on Olive Oatman). Book one recounts the horrifying wagon trip to California, Lena's marriage to Evan Freeman, Sarah Ann's repatriation from the Indians, Lorenzo's leaving to fight in the Civil War, and the birth of Lena and Evan's daughter, Opal, as well as Sarah Ann's mixed-race baby, Effie. Book two is Effie's story. Raised to believe Lena is her mother, Effie, with her family, moves to Virginia City, where Evan dies searching for gold, and the women struggle to survive by working in a boarding house and later borrowing money to build a brothel. Effie falls in love with Lorenzo, who happens to visit the brothel, but later learns he is her uncle and Sarah Ann is her mother. Meanwhile, Opal has married and moved to San Francisco.

In book three, the story follows Effie—now renamed Eve—to London as a famous actress, where the reader is introduced to numerous historical characters, including Lillie Langtry, George Bernard Shaw, a young Winston Churchill, and the Prince of Wales, who becomes Eve's lover. Eve's daughter, Constance, returns to America and becomes one of the country's first female architects.

Books four and five explore the lives of Constance's childhood friend, Rose, who becomes a prosperous businesswoman in San Francisco, and Rose's daughter, June, who works as a nurse in London during World War I, where she falls in love with Andy, a pilot who happens to be Connie's son. Before book five is over, these characters are involved in various ways in the great San Francisco earthquake and fire of 1906.

Unlike the previous books, the final one is told from a male's point of view. June's husband, Andy, recounts Connie's architectural successes, Rose's business accomplishments, June's death, and Eve's final revelations about her life. With a second world war on the horizon, Andy whisks his daughter, Claire, from London to the safety of America, becoming the first man in the story to be a nurturer and keep the family together. But in the end, it is the self-assured Claire who leads her father "into the future." In contrast to the grim beginning, the novel's ending suggests hope for the future of this family of women, as well as for female readers. While the women in this novel have been strengthened through grief and adversity, most of the men in their lives have abandoned them, abused them horribly, or died. The book, in fact, is replete with negative comments about the behavior of men, such as "I knew he'd leave us behind because that's what men do," and "Men are slow to see."

Not that the women come off looking saintly. They often reject others to protect themselves. Effie receives none of the love and closeness she needs from either Lena or Sarah Ann. Effie, as Eve, in turn, is unable to give Constance much warmth until her later years, when she admits: "I'd been deprived of love, and so I deprived Constance." The novel thus addresses a contemporary problem of communication between mothers and daughters in a historical setting.

In addition to beginning the novel from a sketch of real people in a real event, Peck modeled several of the main characters on real women. Vivacious Eve was based largely on the American actress Maxine Elliott, whom Peck describes as "the most beautiful woman who *ever* lived." The Virginia City portion of the novel was inspired by the real-life Isobel Field as described in her autobiography, *This Life I've Loved* (circa 1936). Isobel's stepfather was the famous writer Robert Louis Stevenson. And the real-life Julia Morgan, the first female to receive an architectural degree from the University of California at Berkeley, who designed nearly 800 buildings in a variety of styles over the span of her career, and who planned San Simeon, William Randolph Hearst's magnificent California mansion, provided the background for the character Constance.

After his novel was published, Peck discovered what happened to the real Olive Oatman. While speaking to a group of librarians in Los Angeles, he learned that the Oatmans were a prominent family in the area and that Olive, whom he supposed had never readjusted to "civilized" life, had, to his embarrassment, become a public speaker, telling people about her life in captivity, and had written a best-selling book!

This Family of Women became a best seller and was named a Literary Guild and Doubleday Book Club alternate selection. Reviewers rightly praised its dramatic impact, its "narrative sweep rich in historic detail,"[14] and its focus on individual women with pasts as well as presents. But several reviewers also justifiably found parts of the book contrived; one found the dialogue and narration in book one jarring, though she also thought those elements improved as the book progressed and the narrators became better educated.[15] The most balanced assessment of the novel came from Stephanie Zvirin, who contended that, even though Peck sometimes leaves the lives of the characters "maddeningly unsettled, rushing on too quickly from one generation or narrator to the next," the novel is nevertheless filled with "historical richness and craftsmanship, and it rises well above the sweltering passions and cardboard conventions of so many multigenerational family sagas."[16]

Although this novel, like *Amanda/Miranda*, was intended for an adult audience, there is much in it for older teenagers. The rich historical details—from the character of young Winston Churchill to the architecture of the Fairmont Hotel, from the actions of Buffalo Bill's Wild West show to the destruction of San Francisco—provide more lasting impressions than do school history texts. Further, almost all of the major characters are teenage girls at the start of their story, and each tale is essentially a coming-of-age story developed over a longer time period than the typical young adult novel manages. And the shifting of narrators and the abundance of action keep the 414-page novel moving. The novel was praised for just those characteristics when it was rated one of the best books of the year by high school students in the 1984 Iowa Books for Young Adults poll.[17]

LONDON HOLIDAY

While Peck's fourth novel for adults, *London Holiday*, references life in school, teen angst, friendship, romance, even ghosts, it is less likely to be appreciated by teen readers than might *Amanda/Miranda* or *This Family of Women*. The novel demands life experience from readers as it explores the periods of adolescent-like behavior that recur in several stages of our lives. As Peck puts it, "maybe life is just one adolescence after another—if we keep growing."[18]

The primary characters in this story, three women in their forties, face what Peck calls "the uncertainties of change"[19] common to adolescents as a part of their growing-up processes. Les, Julia, and Margo initially grow up together in their small Missouri community. As young women, however, they part ways. Les gets pregnant to trap the eligible and wealthy Harry and moves with him to St. Louis. Julia attends school in New York City to flee the overbearing grandmother who raised her. Margo marries the first man to show an interest and settles in Chicago as an elementary school teacher. None is happy. Years later, as middle-age adults, the distant friends grow up together again when they, at Les's urging, travel to London for a vacation. Les, restless and discontent in her role as a society woman, desires distraction. Julia, extremely talented in her work but equally lonely, justifies the trip as a business opportunity. Margo, recently divorced, burdened with an ungrateful teen daughter, and injured by a gunshot fired by a deranged parent of one of her students, just needs a break.

The three arrive at a bed and breakfast run by Mrs. Smith-Porter, the consummate English lady—at least on the surface; she, too, has a past she is escaping. A survivor of World War II and former mistress to Mr. Smith-Porter, "a husband, though not hers," she runs her home with pride and efficiency, personalizing the stay of each and every guest. Mrs. Smith-Porter knows just what to say and do as she helps guide these women through their necessary transformations.[20] As a result of their travels, and Mrs. Smith-Porter's nudging, each woman has the opportunity to reinvent herself.

As is true in his other novels for adults, Peck writes about women and for women, for reasons that are both psychological ("Women are more accessible than men because they speak more openly about relationships and their emotional lives"[21]) and pragmatic ("Women read more fiction than men"[22]). His ability to empathize with and capture the voices of those unlike him attests to his keen observation skills. Critics agree. A *Publishers Weekly* reviewer claimed, "The epiphanies experienced by the three women pour over readers with the light, dry sparkle of good champagne."[23]

Peck's passion for England resurfaces in *London Holiday*. "The English got to me at an impressionable age," Peck says, "and so England remains my other country and perhaps a symbol of escape."[24] Away from what they know, Les, Julia, and Margo are allowed to engage in this escapism, to rethink the people they want to be. Readers, too, learn not only about themselves but about antiques, London history, and finding the perfect place for tea on their next visit. Peck paints vivid images of place and time, wanting the novel to "serve in part as a guide to enjoying this city." To that end, he "wrote much of the novel there, checking details carefully."[25] When the three women visit the orangery and sit "between marble sculptures in a room that soared above them like frozen seventeenth-century court music," readers feel they are right there with them.

Reviewer response to *London Holiday* was overall positive, with complimentary critics describing the novel as "effervescent"[26] and "cozy, charming, and marvelously entertaining."[27] And a *Publishers Weekly* reviewer claimed that Peck conveys the adventures of the travelers "with stylish brio that eschews cliché and sentimentality."[28] A *Kirkus* reviewer disagreed, on all counts, however, calling the story "a thoroughly silly, predictable tale from a prolific YA author."[29] The truth, expressed well by Jill Marquis of Amazon.com, might be somewhere in the middle: "This is not a very profound book but it is rather fun."[30]

Not even the distinguished, impeccable Richard Peck would aim for profound. But fun, entertaining, informative, enjoyable? Absolutely.

NOTES

1. Richard Peck, quoted by Jean W. Ross in *Contemporary Authors*, New Revision Series, vol. 19, ed. Linda Metzger (Detroit: Gale Research, 1987), 368.

2. *Kirkus Reviews*, 1 January 1980, 32.

3. *Publishers Weekly*, 18 January 1980, 130.

4. Richard Peck, Interview by Jean F. Mercier, in "PW Interviews Richard Peck," *Publishers Weekly*, 14 March 1980.

5. Joni Bodart, "The Also-Rans; or 'What Happened to the Ones That Didn't Get Eight Votes?'" *Top of the News* (Fall 1981): 72.

6. Peck, quoted by Ross, 368.

7. Kate Waters, *School Library Journal* (March 1981): 161–62.

8. *Publishers Weekly*, 23 January 1981, 120.

9. *Kirkus Reviews*, 1 January 1981, 35.

10. Stephanie Zvirin, *Booklist*, 1 July 1981, 1388.

11. Jane Howard, *Mademoiselle*, March 1981, 70.

12. Richard Peck, Interview at Montclair, New Jersey, Public Library, 9 December 1987.

13. Cathie Lou Porrelli, "El Monte Pioneers' Tale Told in New Novel," *San Gabriel Valley Tribune*, 16 June 1983.

14. Mary Sucher, *ALAN Review* (Spring 1984): 33.

15. Sarah McGowan, *Best Seller* (May 1983): 44–45.

16. Stephanie Zvirin, *Booklist*, 1 February 1983, 698.

17. John W. Connor et al., "1984 Books for Young Adults Poll," *English Journal* (December 1984): 64.

18. Richard Peck, "A Conversation with the Author," *Penguin Readers Guide to London Holiday*, 1998, 4.

19. Peck, "A Conversation with the Author," 4.

20. Peck, "A Conversation with the Author," 5.

21. Peck, "A Conversation with the Author," 4.

22. Peck, "A Conversation with the Author," 5.

23. *Publishers Weekly*, 11 May 1998, 50.

24. Peck, "A Conversation with the Author," 6.

25. Peck, "A Conversation with the Author," 6.

26. *Publishers Weekly*, 11 May 1998, 50.

27. Elizabeth Bryant Mellett, *Library Journal*, 1 May 1998, 140.

28. *Publishers Weekly*, 11 May 1998, 50.

29. *Kirkus Reviews*, 1998.

30. Jill Marquis, Amazon.com.

· 13 ·

Theme, Characters, and Style

"$\mathscr{F}$ew novelists perceive their audience as clearly as does Richard Peck," writes Janice Tovey in a scholarly analysis of Peck's young adult novels published through 1988.

> His novels address the subjects and events, which concern his audience and focus on problems to which they want answers. He writes to adolescents about themselves, their friends and peers and gets their attention by creating characters whom they recognize. He describes the families, the lifestyles, the towns, the societies and the cultures in which his audience lives. He mirrors adolescent fads in language and clothing. . . . By creating a community of discourse with his readers, Peck gains their trust and respect. He then confronts and challenges them to think about problems, which they prefer to ignore, but which are important to them as individuals.[1]

Although many of Peck's novels written since Tovey's analysis contain characters that live in times distant to today's readers and are set in communities bearing little resemblance to their own, Peck challenges his audience in much the same way. He knows what his readers need and provides it, helping them learn how their lives have been and might be shaped by events and people of an earlier era. He gives them the gift of perspective as they strive to determine their place in the twenty-first-century world.

THEME

Whether the topic is suicide or shopping malls, rape or romance, death or divorce, World's Fair or World War, and whether events unfold in

147

1861 or the present, one theme prevails in all of Peck's novels: the importance of acting independently. In addition, as previous examinations of his novels reveal, Peck also focuses on setting, social class differences, gender roles, parental roles, connections to the past, and teachers and teaching, employing characteristic structural and language techniques that point to his unique authorial style.

In a 1976 interview, Peck said: "In all of my novels, the main character takes a trip, a geographic trip. They all slip the bonds of peer group and family for an independent look at the world. Then they return, a bit more able to cope."[2] While this doesn't hold true for every novel published since then, it is certainly true of many. *Those Summer Girls I Never Met* contains the most extensive physical journey; most of the novel takes place on a cruise ship, with stops in major cities on the Baltic Sea. *Fair Weather*, too, embodies well this physical journey, with the protagonist venturing from her small town to the big city fair and returning a changed person. Peck says his teenage characters "have to be removed a great distance much against their wills in order to take a step nearer their futures and their roots. Nobody grows up until he has to. In young adult novels somebody always has to."[3] He adds, "I want [readers] to leave their peer group. I want them to go somewhere in the book the peer group cannot dictate. I express it in geographical terms."[4] Thus, the physical journey enables the protagonist to make an intellectual and emotional journey toward independence and understanding.

The journey is even more extreme where Peck's characters travel through time and space. For example, in *Blossom Culp and the Sleep of Death*, Blossom and Alexander are transported back 4,000 years to ancient Egypt; in *Voices after Midnight*, three young characters exist in present-day New York City during a hot summer and during the unprecedented winter of 1888; in *The Great Interactive Dream Machine*, two contemporary prep-school boys transport themselves to various dream locations, quite literally. Not only do these journeys help the teenage characters learn something about themselves, but they also allow the writer to teach a little bit of history to unsuspecting readers.

SETTINGS

A small town in the Midwest, patterned after Peck's hometown in Illinois, provides the setting for three of his first four young adult novels, along with all four of the Blossom Culp books (where the town is named Bluff City). Rural Missouri, Illinois, and Indiana provide the stage for his eight most recent titles for adolescent readers. By contrast, *Those Summer Girls I Never Met* takes the reader to London, Leningrad, and ports in Scandinavia, while *Unfinished Portrait of Jessica* takes place in Chicago, Illinois, and Acapulco, Mexico. *Bel-Air Bambi and the Mall Rats* begins and ends briefly in Hollywood, California, with most of the events occurring in a rural town somewhere in middle America.

Although Richard Peck has lived in New York City during all the years he has been a professional writer, only three of his young adult novels—*Voices after Midnight*, *Lost in Cyberspace*, and *The Great Interactive Dream Machine*—take place there. Three of his other young adult novels begin in New York but move the characters elsewhere for most of the story. Peck says he generally avoids New York City as a setting for his young adult books (though not for his adult novels) because, he says, almost none of his readers live there. Several of Peck's other novels are set in or around suburban areas. The suburban settings, based in part on his experience teaching in Northbrook, Illinois, provide Peck with ammunition for criticizing affluent parents for being too permissive, not maintaining control over their children, and failing to communicate with them, problems shown most forcefully in *Remembering the Good Times* and *The Last Safe Place on Earth*. In Peck's stories, it is often the less affluent parents who are more supportive of their children, as evidenced by Buck's father in *Remembering the Good Times* and by Verna's farm family in *Representing Super Doll*.

Increasingly, Peck favors a midwestern setting for his stories because "editors and publishers are in Boston or New York, and they are not very familiar with real American life."[5] Peck claims, "I think the Middle West is underrepresented. I like the folkways, the names, the language of the [region]—the rustic, self-reliant American humor."[6] "The older I get," he says, "the more midwestern I become. A day never passes here in New York without my saying, under my breath, 'You couldn't get away with that where I come from!' "[7]

Older places not only have more character for Richard Peck, but they provide significant links to the past. One especially valuable aspect of the Blossom Culp novels is that they picture a place and time where life seems to be safer and more fun. At the same time, the emotions and basic problems of Blossom and Alexander are contemporary ones, like being accepted by the group and dealing with school boredom. Similarly, Mary Alice of *A Year Down Yonder* might live with her feisty grandmother in 1937, Tilly Pruitt of *The River between Us* might witness the atrocities of the Civil War, and Russell Culver of *The Teacher's Funeral* might experience farm life in rural Indiana in 1904, but all, regardless of the time and place in which they live, experience the timeless adolescent condition. They dream of freedom, question their identity and their place in the larger community, and want to be loved and paid attention to.

Probably the two most important elements that establish time and place in Richard Peck's contemporary novels are the teenagers' clothing and language. By carefully dressing his characters in fashions of the time and having them use current expressions, Peck helps readers identify more easily with them. In *Close Enough to Touch*, for example, readers find characters dressed in Jordache jeans, Nike and Puma sneakers, and other "preppie" clothing. And Drew, in *Those Summer Girls*, checks his Swatch and wears a CB Windbreaker. In *Remembering the Good Times*, readers find familiar expressions such as "gross," "macho," and "far out," while in *Voices after Midnight*, a disliked character is called a "dweeb." And in *Bel-Air Bambi*, Justin, a California character, speaks a rarefied slang: "Do you want to take your stick down to the beach and get tubed, or would you rather stay home and pouch-grovel?"

The places characters frequent are also familiar landmarks to contemporary teenagers: Friendly's, Sizzler, Marshalls, Planet Hollywood, the Hard Rock Cafe, and naturally, McDonald's. (In *Those Summer Girls*, Drew and Steph, while in London, unexpectedly see "a couple of mini-golden arches laminated onto a three-hundred-year-old wall.") And the names of products the characters use in their daily lives ring familiar: Eggo waffles, Coke, and Jell-O, to name a few. The names of movie idols and music stars pop up occasionally, too—Emilio Estevez and Molly Ringwald, Cher, Tom Cruise, and Madonna—as well as the titles of popular television programs of the time—*M*A*S*H*, *The Wonder Years*, and *Beverly Hills 90210*.

Some argue that these elements of contemporary teenage society date Peck's books. But Peck has been wise—and possibly a little lucky—in selecting products and personalities that don't fade from the teen scene quickly. Or perhaps readers of the future will view those merely as historical elements in Peck's older books.

In his historical fiction, Peck creates a convincing sense of time and place by drawing on period details and language that render the setting believable. Grandma Dowdel (*A Long Way from Chicago* and *A Year Down Yonder*) teaches readers how to use a twelve-gauge double-barreled Winchester Model 21, make gooseberry pie from scratch, and set winter traps for foxes in hopes of selling their pelts for extra cash. On her journey to Cairo, Illinois, Tilly (*The River between Us*) paints a grim and educative picture of the inadequate sanitation services and medical facilities in place at the time. Russell (*The Teacher's Funeral*) describes his experiences in a one-room schoolhouse, replete with privies, slates, rostrum, and stoves. Peewee McGrath (*Here Lies the Librarian*) provides readers rich instruction into the various automobiles of the time. And young Davy Bowman (*On the Wings of Heroes*) takes readers along with him into dusty, musty attics as he and his buddy search for rationed items to donate to the war effort.

Each of these characters speaks with conviction, modeling the language patterns and content reflective of the time and place each represents. Grandma Dowdel tells of kittens recently born: "There's a new litter living down in the cobhouse now, and I let 'em. They keep down the vermin." Tilly describes her family's food supply and dependence upon the natural world: "We thought we et pretty good. Noah was right smart to kill game: squirrel and prairie chickens and in the fall before it wintered up, possum. Quail, pheasant, ducks. We baked corn dodgers and fried meat in the fireplace. But white beans, gristle, and cornmeal mush got us through the darkest part of winter." And Peewee reveals her attitude toward expected gender roles: "I'm sure as shoot not going to wear a durn dress to patch a tire or take a cylinder head apart."

SOCIAL CLASS DIFFERENCES

The academic and social levels of Peck's narrators also provide significant reference points. In his contemporary titles, Peck usually focuses on a teenager on the edge of the action, not from an upper-middle-class suburban home, or not among the academically talented group in school. For example, in *Don't Look and It Won't Hurt*, Carol remarks, "Anybody's house looks good to me compared to my own." In *Remembering the Good Times*, Buck comes from a blue-collar family and is not an especially good student, providing a strong contrast to his wealthy friend,

Tray, who is academically outstanding. Although Todd, in *The Last Safe Place on Earth*, lives in suburbia, he doesn't aspire to much, wanting only to have some fun and meet a girl. And there is the unforgettable Blossom Culp, who lives on the other side of the (trolley) tracks and whose mother represents the lowest level of Bluff City society. All of these characters, however, are especially good observers, even if, like Buck in *Remembering the Good Times* or Chelsea in *Princess Ashley*, they cannot instantly figure out what's going on. These characters are thus easier for the "average" student to identify with.

In each of Peck's historical titles, money is tight due to the economic realities of life in the rural Midwest at the time. Consequently, characters are thrifty and resourceful and recognize the value of seemingly simple things modern-day readers might take for granted. A new dress or hat or scarf, a train ticket, oil lamps, indoor plumbing, automobiles—these are luxuries rather than necessities for them. Peck's country characters depend on their crops, animals, and hard work for survival. They are also more likely to depend on one another, further minimizing class distinction. "The Middle West," he argues, "is a wonderful place for stories because there's a much stronger sense of community than the East knows anything about. There's a social contract in the towns. It's not always pleasant, but it's there."[8]

GENDER ROLES

In their analysis of the best books written for young adults prior to 1980, Donelson and Nilsen point out that, although nearly half the young adult novels written by women have a male narrator or lead character, Richard Peck is one of the few male writers who writes from the perspective of female characters.[9] In fact, more than half of Peck's novels have a female narrator or are from a female's point of view. With the exception of Chelsea in *Princess Ashley*, the female protagonists in Peck's young adult novels tend to be intellectually adept, insightful, and very independent. Kate in *Remembering the Good Times* and Margaret in *Close Enough to Touch* are prime examples. Blossom Culp's spunk and resilience—not to mention her Second Sight—put her in a class by herself. And Mary Alice in *A Year Down Yonder*, Tilly in *The River between Us*, and Peewee McGrath in *Here Lies the Librarian* demonstrate the capacity of girls to do whatever work is necessary—man's or otherwise—in the pursuit of what they want in life.

The male protagonists, on the other hand, are not stereotypical macho heroes. In fact, Jim in *Father Figure*, Matt in *Close Enough to Touch*, Buck in *Remembering the Good Times*, Joey in *A Long Way from Chicago*, and Davy in *On the Wings of Heroes* are some of the most sensitive male characters in all of young adult literature. They tend to be average guys instead of leaders. Peck is critical of traditional "maleness," often revealing the inadequacies of men through the words of the strong women who populate his stories. In *The Teacher's Funeral*, Tansy realizes Mrs. Tarbox is expecting another child. Russell doesn't believe it. Tansy explains: "I'm a woman. Women know these things." Russell asks: "Tansy, how come the female sex think they know more than the male sex?" Tansy replies, "Because we do." And when Grandma Dowdel, Joey, and Mary Alice witness Rod and Gun Club members singing bawdy songs and drinking in their underwear, Mary Alice says, "They're not acting right." Grandma responds, "Men in a bunch never do."

Relationships between males and females in Peck's young adult novels are usually platonic, never sexual—with, of course, the exception of *Are You in the House Alone?*, where Gail reportedly has had sex with her boyfriend and is later raped by another boy, and *Don't Look and It Won't Hurt*, in which the narrator's older sister gets pregnant. In *Through a Brief Darkness*, Karen is attracted to Jay, who helps rescue her; in *Secrets of the Shopping Mall*, Teresa and Barnie spend most of their days and nights together, but platonically. And in *Strays like Us*, Will climbs the slant of the roof to sneak into Molly's room in the middle of the night to do nothing more than talk. There is no more than hand-holding and a very chaste exchange of kisses, if that, in those stories. Although Matt in *Close Enough to Touch* was on the verge of having a sexual relationship with Dory, she died before they got that far, and at the end of the novel, he and Margaret are just beginning to become physically close. Drew in *Those Summer Girls* has lustful thoughts about women, but he is somewhat inept, as well as immature, in his dealings with the female dancers on the cruise ship and so gets little more than sisterly hugs and kisses from them. Similarly, in *The Last Safe Place on Earth*, although Todd's fantasies about females comprise the bulk of his daily thoughts, he never engages sexually with a real girl.

In his books set in the past, Peck respects the virtues of the time.

Mary Alice (*A Year Down Yonder*) flirts innocently with Royce by asking him to be her tutor. Tansy (*The Teacher's Funeral*) receives gifts and favors from potential suitors who compete for her attention. Delphine (*The River between Us*) withholds any obvious gestures of love toward Noah out of fear she might lose him in battle. And Jake (*Here Lies the Librarian*), Peewee's older brother, blushes red at the revelation of ankles peeking out from under the young librarians' skirts. In short, friendships are more important than sexual relationships in Peck's young adult novels.

That is not the case in his adult novels, as one might predict. There is a fair amount of sexual activity in those four stories, though none of it very explicit. The female characters are stronger and more admirable than the males, though Amanda is a despicable manipulator. Interestingly, Peck has not yet written an adult novel with a male protagonist. "I keep starting it," he reports. "I've got this guy driving down the Hutchinson River Parkway"—which leads into and out of New York City—"in the middle of his life." But that's as far as he's gone.

PARENTAL ROLES

As the earlier discussion of individual novels demonstrates, parents play significant roles in many of Peck's young adult books. Some parents are supportive—like Matt's father in *Close Enough to Touch*, Buck's father in *Remembering the Good Times*, Beth and Bill Babcock in *Bel-Air Bambi*, Verna's parents in *Representing Super Doll*, Todd's parents in *The Last Safe Place on Earth*, Rosie's parents, especially her mother, in *Fair Weather*, and Davy's father in *On the Wings of Heroes*. Other parents are too permissive, out of touch with their children, or just never around—like the absent father and the harried mother in *Don't Look*, Jessica's immature and often absent father in *Unfinished Portrait*, Blossom Culp's bizarre gypsy mother, Tray's wealthy parents in *Remembering the Good Times*, and Molly's drug-addicted mother in *Strays like Us*. Still others are absent in ways that don't reflect poor parenting at all—like Mary Alice's parents in *A Year Down Yonder*, who send her to Grandma's house out of financial necessity, and the mothers in *The Teacher's Funeral* and *Here Lies the Librarian*, who are deceased as the result of childbirth. Some other parents are too domineering—like Darlene's mother in *Super Doll* and Dory's socialite mother in *Close Enough to Touch*. A few parents try to help but struggle as much as their children do—like Jim and Byron's father in *Father Figure*, Chelsea's mother in *Princess Ashley*, and Tilly's mother in *The River between Us*.

A preponderance of the parents of the main characters in Peck's novels are divorced or otherwise living without a partner. In only eleven of Peck's thirty young adult novels do the main characters live with both biological parents, and in several of those, the parents of other characters are divorced. There are three extreme cases: neither lead character in *Secrets of the Shopping Mall* has biological parents; Drew's grandfather in *Those Summer Girls* is unaware that he even sired a daughter; and in *Here Lies the Librarian*, Peewee and her brother are fully responsible for raising themselves once their father runs off, unable to deal with his wife's death.

Some of Peck's fathers—Matt's, Buck's, Russell's, and Davy's, in particular—are unusually understanding, sharing their feelings and helping their respective sons deal with their own emotions. Such male roles are especially welcome in Peck's novels, since they are in such contrast to Gail's ineffectual father in *Are You in the House Alone?*, Chelsea's psychologically damaged father in *Princess Ashley*, Jessica's absent father in *Unfinished Portrait*, and Tilly's irresponsible and negligent father in *The River between Us*. Davy's father (*On the Wings of Heroes*) is especially notable, given Peck's decision to build the character around his own father, a man whose gentle humor and strong values are celebrated in fictional form.

Three mother figures—two of whom are not biological mothers—are worth singling out for their supportive roles. Marietta, Mr. Atwater's girlfriend in *Father Figure*, is not only important for the self-concept she projects, but, in her own way, she also mothers both Jim and his younger brother, deflecting Jim's Oedipal advances and helping him deal with his relationship with his previously estranged father. In *Close Enough to Touch*, Beth Moran is one of the most admirable stepmothers in young adult literature, giving "love and support to her stepson without forcing herself into the role of mother."[10] And, in *Fair Weather*, Rosie's mother sends her to the fair, knowing the journey will allow Rosie to gain access to ideas and experiences she herself cannot provide.

CONNECTIONS TO THE PAST

An old person is a prominent figure in twenty of Peck's young adult novels, all but Jim Atwater's grandmother in *Father Figure* having a positive influence. Some are the main character's grandmother or grand-father; some are someone else's grandmother or grandfather; some are members of the character's extended family, great-aunts and great-uncles; some are teachers; others are residents of the town in which the main characters live. All of them are spunky, eccentric, and wise, providing a nostalgic link to the past when life seemed simpler. Among the women, top honors in this category go to the balding, gold-toothed, wheelchair-bound Polly Prior, Kate's great-grandmother in *Remembering the Good Times*, to Drew and Stephanie's grandmother, Connie Carlson, the ter-minally ill jazz singer from the 1940s in *Those Summer Girls*, to Molly's hardworking and tough-talking Great-Aunt Fay in *Strays like Us*, to Grandma Dowdel, mentor and muse to Joey and Mary Alice in *A Long Way from Chicago* and *A Year Down Yonder*, and to Miss Eulalia Titus, Davy's wonderfully talented and forthright teacher in *On the Wings of Heroes*. Among the men, the nosy, crotchety, free-spirited Great-Uncle Miles in *The Ghost Belonged to Me*, the larger-than-life Great-Uncle Lucius Pine in *Unfinished Portrait*, Josh's exacting and inspiring history teacher in *Lost in Cyberspace*, Rosie's lively Granddad Fuller in *Fair Weather*, quietly passionate Noah in *The River between Us*, the seemingly mad Colonel in *Here Lies the Librarian*, and Davy's neighborly neighbor, Mr. Hiser, in *On the Wings of Heroes* deserve high honors.

Whatever the gender, these characters provide positive images of significant old people for contemporary readers who often have little or no contact with their own grandparents. Peck says: "These ambulatory ancient monuments are there to offer wisdom and balance to a self-referential youth culture."[11]

TEACHERS AND TEACHING

There is at least one teacher in most of Richard Peck's novels, except for *Those Summer Girls I Never Met*, *Voices after Midnight*, *Unfinished Portrait of Jessica*, *A Long Way from Chicago*, *Fair Weather*, and *The River between Us*, because those novels take place mostly during vacation times. The images that these teachers project as a collective are not positive, though there are some effective educators among the group. The majority of teachers described in the novels, understandably, are English teachers, though a few are teachers of social studies, physical education, and—Peck's least favorite—contemporary social issues. Educators who choose to analyze the teaching techniques of ex-teacher Peck's fictional faculty will find a variety of approaches, most of them unproductive.

The most evident technique used by Mrs. DeFalco to teach social studies in an inner-city junior high school in *Secrets of the Shopping Mall* is to scream for quiet. Mrs. Tolliver, teaching British literature in *Close Enough to Touch*, uses photocopied worksheets continually. The least prepared teacher is Ms. Sherrie Slater in *Remembering the Good Times*, a first-year teacher who cannot control her junior high school students and so is transferred to the high school, where she does no better. Probably the worst educators of all are the English teacher in *Bel-Air Bambi*, Jean Poole, whose own grammar is atrocious, and the guidance counselor, Miss Venable, in *Are You in the House Alone?*, who is completely unable to help Gail.

School administrators fare no better. In *Father Figure*, the headmaster from Byron's school is concerned more about his school's reputation than the condition of one of his students who has been mugged on the way home from school. In *Remembering the Good Times*, no administrator is visible when Skeeter explodes. When one of the school's best students commits suicide, administrators call a community meeting to discuss the problem but take no responsibility for helping students cope. In *Princess Ashley*, when a disturbed student physically attacks Mrs. Olinger, the school's administration does nothing about it. No one from the school even visits Mrs. Olinger in the hospital; only the secretary phones to see how she is. The entire school system is out of control in *Bel-Air Bambi*. Probably the most complimentary portrayal of a school administrator comes in the form of Principal Ericson in *The Last Safe Place on Earth*. In response to attempts by a citizens' group to remove *The Diary of Anne Frank* and Robert Cormier's *The Chocolate War* from the junior high curriculum and library, Ericson says, "Parents have a right to decide what their children read. Any student can be assigned an alternate reading. But parents have no right to decide what other students will or will not read."

The most positive teachers in Peck's novels are demanding but fair and concerned. Miss Klimer (*Dreamland Lake*) "believed strongly in Written Expression." Miss Augusta Fairweather (*Blossom Culp and the Sleep of Death*), a former suffragette, puts her students through their paces in studying Egypt. And Mr. Mallory (*Princess Ashley*), an exchange teacher from Great Britain, sets high standards in his creative writing class but is also a caring person. These effective contemporary teachers seem to find their models in the past. Tansy (*The Teacher's Funeral*) expects much from her students but maintains a sense of compassion and sensitivity, too. Similarly, Miss Eulalia Titus (*On the Wings of Heroes*) is both tough and kind. Davy describes an instance in which he incorrectly uses the word "laying" in a composition. He reports, "She graded me down for that. Way down. Down, down, down. But it cured me." Given his views on classroom methods, these strict but nurturing exemplars perhaps embody the kind of teachers Peck had—and was.

STRUCTURE

Several structural qualities are worth noting in Peck's novels. In many, a key crisis or turning point occurs at nearly the exact middle of the novel. At the central point of *Father Figure*, for example, Jim and Byron arrive in Florida to begin a new life with their father. The middle of *Remembering the Good Times* finds Kate, Tray, and Buck at the start of their freshman year; only a few pages later, Tray yells at Ms. Slater for not teaching them anything, and she reveals that she is being harassed by Skeeter. Rosie (*Fair Weather*) arrives at the fair just halfway through her novel. Tilly (*The River between Us*), at the center point of the narrative, learns the real identity of Delphine and Calinda and begins to understand the complexity of their flight from New Orleans.

That midpoint crisis is often tied in with Peck's method of revealing tantalizing fragments of information that create mystery and keep readers turning pages to find out what will happen. Peck notes that he likes to keep his readers guessing: "Everybody likes secrets. My stories often concern family secrets or a secret I'm keeping [from readers] until I can spring it on them. They like scandals, mysteries—things suddenly coming to light and surprises in the end."[12] Throughout *Dreamland Lake*, for example, the reader learns only bits and pieces about pitiable Elvan Helligrew and his preoccupation with Nazi memorabilia and what that has to do with the dead man in the amusement park. Even though Brian is telling the story two years later, he keeps readers in suspense until the sudden tragic ending. In *Those Summer Girls*, Drew (and the reader) doesn't learn until nearly the end of the cruise—and the end of the novel—why his grandmother has suddenly wanted to spend time with him and his sister after years of not seeing them. And in *The River between Us*, young Howard, narrator of the novel's opening and closing chapters, is surprised to learn in the final pages that the family story he has believed true for so long is not.

Peck frequently uses foreshadowing to help readers anticipate future events and encourage reading on. That's especially easy in the Blossom Culp novels, of course, because Blossom or her mother can see into the future and make cryptic predictions. The reader is compelled to read on to see what it means when Blossom is told, for instance, that she will take two trips over water, one of them in the past that has been "interrupted . . . by death." In other novels, the narrator sometimes gives a hint of future complications. In *Are You in the House Alone?*, Gail, finding her mother sitting alone in a darkened house with a drink in her hand, says, "Neither the darkness nor the drink seemed odd at the time." Joey, in *A Long Way from Chicago*, utters this teaser: "You wouldn't think we'd have to leave Chicago to see a dead body." And Peewee, in *Here Lies the Librarian*, keeps readers guessing when she says, "The tornado that touched down on that spring day in 1914 blew Jake and me an entirely new fortune." Peck employs this technique most extensively in his first adult novel, *Amanda/Miranda*. Miranda says at one point, "we had seemed to skirt a small lovers' quarrel. I had no premonition of a greater crisis ahead."

In addition, most of Peck's novels end without a solution. That is not to suggest that the reader is left hanging, only that there are no pat answers to some of the problems raised. As Peck insists, "A novel is never an answer; it's always a question," and "a novel worth reading is one that the readers continue writing in their minds."[13] For example, at the end of *Don't Look and It Won't Hurt*, Carol returns home from visiting her pregnant sister in Chicago, still unsure if Ellen will be coming back to join the family. Gail, in *Are You in the House Alone?*, knows her rapist remains unpunished, even though she has done one small thing to get back at him. At the conclusion of *The Last Safe Place on Earth*, Laurel's attempt to brainwash Todd's little sister is thwarted, but Laurel remains committed to her limited vision of the world. Readers are left wondering the identity of her next victim. And although *On the Wings of Heroes* concludes with Davy's relief that his brother will return safely from war, it also suggests that the road back will not be easy. Like his father, Davy's brother will carry both emotional and physical scars from the experience.

The endings, while not necessarily happy, are credible and appropriate. Peck says of his 1991 novel: "It's called *Unfinished Portrait* because all our novels are unfinished portraits. The truth is that life involves dealing with one set of problems so that you can go on to the next set. That throughout life, you have to start over every morning."[14]

HUMOR AND LANGUAGE

Another distinctive mark of Richard Peck's style is his ability to include comedy even in novels about the most serious subjects. For instance, while *Those Summer Girls I Never Met* deals in part with the fatal illness of the teenagers' grandmother, the novel is one of Peck's most humorous. The humor, of course, is not about death, but the comic incidents keep the novel from becoming bleak. Similarly, the grisly realities of the Civil War in *The River between Us* are interrupted by the frenetic music and inspired dancing of the mesmerizing Calinda during a riverboat party. Peck's employment of humor works in reverse, too. Even *A Long Way from Chicago* and *A Year Down Yonder*, often hailed for their humor, contain serious threads. As Peck says, "These books are about people living on the edge of survival during the Depression. That's just not the way I tell the story. That's not the way Mark Twain—my god—wrote of racial intolerance and slavery. He told about those things through the great comic character of Huck Finn."[15]

Humor in Peck's books is evidenced in events themselves—the commotion caused by Blossom's accidentally setting fire to Old Man Leverette's outhouse or the panic aroused in Tansy's conjuring up the spirit of dead Miss Myrt Arbuckle to terrify Russell—as well as in characters and language. The character of Daisy-Rae in *The Dreadful Future of Blossom Culp* is worth a laugh nearly every time she appears. Most of the time, she is found hiding in one of the stalls of the girls' room at school, determined never to enter a classroom. Her brother, Roderick, a "medium simple," "apathetic little gnome" of a kid, never speaks a word throughout the entire novel, though he does drool at appropriate times. And Granddad Fuller of *Fair Weather* arouses chuckles each time he opens his mouth. Whether warning his young charges about ordering bratwurst at the fair ("Chicago's a meat-packin' town, and once in a while a workin' man will fall into the grinder and come out as links of prime smoked sausage") or defending Lillian Russell, the woman of his dreams, from Aunt Euterpe's attacks regarding her multiple marriages, Granddad imbues the narrative with energy and wit.

Peck's use of language to convey humor is evidenced regularly. In *Here Lies the Librarian*, when potential librarian Grace Stutz explains that her desire to work in the field stems from her interest in children, Old Man Unrath yells out, "Then why don't you get married and have you some?" When Grandma Dowdel, in *A Long Way from Chicago*, uses explosives to catch the Cowgill boys in the act of trying to tip her privy, Joey reports, "The cherry bomb had scared them witless, except for Ernie, who was witless anyway." And in *On the Wings of Heroes*, Davy goes to the home of Old Lady Graves to check her attic for newspapers. While there, he finds her dress dummy and says that it "looked like her, but better. It had no head." Peck enjoys the challenge of writing humor for young people, noting, "Comedy is a higher calling than realism or tragedy. It's uphill work because kids don't always get it—the young are not used to laughing unless it is at one another."[16]

Peck pays close attention to language in every scene he writes, whether it's spoken by punkers, Valley Girls, preppies, or farm kids. One of Blossom's more characteristic uses of language—in addition to her less-than-standard English—is clichés. Her narration abounds with such chestnuts as "always darkest before the dawn," "took the bull by the horns," and "no use cryin' over spilt milk." Russell Culver (*The Teacher's Funeral*), too, has a style all his own, drawing imaginative comparisons in his descriptions of the world around him. Describing Miss Myrt Arbuckle laid out in her coffin, he says, "She had the longest nose in North America. . . . She had a snout on her long enough to drink water down a crawdad hole."

There are, intentionally, no vulgarities in Peck's novels. "I am very careful of the language—much more careful than I want to be," Peck says. "I work pretty hard to keep the language cleaner in my books than the language of my readers. . . . I don't want my books to be kept out of the hands of readers for the wrong reasons." He comes closest to taboo words in *Bel-Air Bambi and the Mall Rats* but always has another character interrupt the speaker, as in the following description given by Buffie: "And the back of the truck . . . was full of heads. People in the back of the truck, a whole gang of them, silent, holding on. It was like a hayride from h—'Bambi!' Dad said. 'Get off my head.' "

Peck's concern with language is also evident in the abundance of wordplay in his novels, especially in the Blossom Culp books. For example, Alexander says in *The Ghost Belonged to Me*, "I knew she hadn't eaten anything since Friday noon in order to get into her coming out dress." In *Bel-Air Bambi and the Mall Rats*, Bambi reports: " 'That does it,' she muttered, and there was murder in her mutter." Describing the impact of the tornado on the community, Peewee of *Here Lies the Librarian* reports, "The twister created another tempest."

It is evident that Richard Peck enjoys himself as he writes. "I like the uses of humor in writing," he says. "I like satire. I like wordplay. I like whole comic scenes. I like humor to serious intent." He even has fun with characters' names. There's Bertha Small, the huge security guard in the department store in *Secrets of the Shopping Mall*. And if Fairweather isn't an appropriate enough name for a supportive teacher (in *Blossom Culp and the Sleep of Death*), then Mallory is as good a name as you'll find for a British English teacher (in *Princess Ashley*). Speaking of Ashley herself, with a last name of Packard, how can she (ironically) be anything else but classy? Almost every character in *Bel-Air Bambi* has a punny name, from Justin Thyme to Tanya Hyde. Lug of *Here Lies the Librarian* lumbers around carrying "a behind the size of a sagging settee." And more seriously, Cass of *The River between Us* conjures images of ancient Cassandra in her ability to see the future.

One final characteristic of Peck's use of language as a stylistic benchmark is his employment of aphorisms. Although they are sometimes a bit more erudite than the maturity of the teenager speaking them would warrant, they allow Peck to make comments on people, school, society—all his favorite targets—throughout his novels. For example, in *Remembering the Good Times*, Buck says, "It's funny how much you want to work before you're old enough to hold a job." In *Princess Ashley*, Chelsea says, "in tenth grade you like rumors better than the truth anyway." And when Tansy (*The Teacher's Funeral*) expresses disinterest in the latest steam engines and threshing machines passing through town on the train, Russell reflects, "It occurred to me even that early in life that there's not much romance in a woman's soul."

Peck's writings are awash in such stylistic elements. Any reader who has heard this author speak in a classroom, a library, a bookstore, or at a professional conference can hear Peck's distinctive voice in everything he writes—his witty, insightful, charmingly critical one-liners. And Richard

Peck continues to teach in every novel he writes. He says, however, "I don't really believe my books are going to change people's lives." But some books obviously do hit home: "I get letters from young people who say, 'I'm the character in your book' or 'It happens here.' I want that to happen, because I want young people to think that what's in a book is just as real and important as what is in their lives and a whole lot more important than television. . . . But I can't preach it; I've got to write something entertaining about it."[17]

No matter what Richard Peck's next book is about, it undoubtedly will be entertaining—and it will undoubtedly sneak in a lesson with the fun.

NOTES

1. Janice K. Tovey, *Writing for the Young Adult Reader: An Analysis of Audience in the Novels of Richard Peck*, master's thesis, Illinois State University, 1988, 77.

2. Paul Janeczko, "An Interview with Richard Peck," *English Journal* (February 1976): 97.

3. Richard Peck, "Traveling in Time," *ALAN Review* (Winter 1990): 2.

4. Donna Marie Pocius, "In Search of Perfection," *Reading Today* (October–November 2005): 27.

5. Duane Meyer, "A Morning with the 2001 Newbery Medal Winner, Richard W. Peck, DePauw '56," *Delta Chi Quarterly* (Fall–Winter 2001): 20.

6. Doug Pokorski, "Decatur Native a Finalist for National Book Award," *State Journal Register* (Springfield, Ill.), 15 November 1998, 51.

7. Meyer, "A Morning with the 2001 Newbery Medal Winner," 20.

8. Meyer, "A Morning with the 2001 Newbery Medal Winner," 20.

9. Kenneth L. Donelson and Alleen Pace Nilsen, *Literature for Today's Young Adults* (Glenview, Ill.: Scott, Foresman, 1980), 19.

10. Tovey, *Writing for the Young Adult Reader*, 22.

11. Richard Peck, "Newbery Medal Acceptance," *Horn Book* (July 2001): 397.

12. Pocius, "In Search of Perfection," 27.

13. Richard Peck, in Bantam Doubleday Dell publicity brochure, n.d.

14. Richard Peck, *Anonymously Yours* (New York: Julian Messner, 1991), 50.

15. Karen MacPherson, "Since Winning Newbery, Author Peck Is Busier Talking than Writing," *Pittsburgh-Post Gazette*, 8 May 2001, E2.

16. Linda Castellitto, "Lessons Learned," *First Person Book Page*, www.book page.com/0310bp/richard_peck.html.

17. Richard Peck, Interview at Montclair, New Jersey, Public Library, 9 December 1987.

Appendix A: Honors and Prizes

AMANDA/MIRANDA

Literary Guild Selection
Reader's Digest Condensed Book

ARE YOU IN THE HOUSE ALONE?

Best Books for Young Adults, 1976, American Library Association
Best Books of the Year, 1976, *School Library Journal*
Best of the Best Books, 1970–1983, American Library Association
Best of the Best Books for Young Adults, 1966–1986, American Library Association
Books for Young Adults Poll, 1977, University of Iowa
California Young Reader Medal Nominee, 1979
Colorado Blue Spruce Young Adult Book Award Nominee, 1986
Edgar Allan Poe Mystery Award, 1977

BEL-AIR BAMBI AND THE MALL RATS

Best Books of the Year, 1993, *School Library Journal*

BLOSSOM CULP AND THE SLEEP OF DEATH

Notable Books for Children, 1986, American Library Association

CLOSE ENOUGH TO TOUCH

Best Books for Young Adults, 1981, American Library Association
Colorado Blue Spruce Young Adult Book Award Nominee, 1987

DREAMLAND LAKE

Edgar Allan Poe Special Mystery Award, 1973

FAIR WEATHER

Best Books for Young Adults, 2002, American Library Association
Best Books of the Year, 2001, *Publishers Weekly*
Books for the Teen Age, 2002, 2003, 2004, 2005, 2006, New York Public Library
Editors' Choice, 2001, *Booklist*
Editors' Choice, 2001, *New York Times*
Great Lakes Book Award Children's Medal, 2002, Great Lakes Booksellers Association
Maryland Black-Eyed Susan Book Award Nominee, 2002–2003
Pacific Northwest Young Reader's Choice Award Nominee, 2004
Rebecca Caudill Young Readers' Book Award Nominee, 2004
Young Adult Fiction Prize, 2001, *Chicago Tribune*

FATHER FIGURE

Best Books for Young Adults, 1978, American Library Association
Best of the Best Books, 1970–1983, American Library Association
Colorado Blue Spruce Young Adult Book Award Nominee, 1985

THE GHOST BELONGED TO ME

Friends of American Writers Award, 1976
Maud Hart Lovelace Book Award Nominee, 1985
Notable Books for Children, 1975, American Library Association

GHOSTS I HAVE BEEN

Best Books for Young Adults, 1977, American Library Association
Best Books of the Year, 1977, *School Library Journal*
Best of the Best Books, 1970–1982, American Library Association

Best of the Best Books for Young Adults, 1966–1986, American Library Association
Michigan Young Readers Award Nominee, 1980
Outstanding Books of the Year, 1977, *New York Times*

THE GREAT INTERACTIVE DREAM MACHINE

Best Science Fiction, Fantasy, and Horror Selection, 1996, *Voice of Youth Advocates*

HERE LIES THE LIBRARIAN

Battle of the Books Finalist, 2007–2008, Wisconsin Educational Media Association
Books for the Teen Age, 2006, New York Public Library
Parents' Choice Award, 2006

THE LAST SAFE PLACE ON EARTH

Best Books for Young Adults, 1996, American Library Association
Popular Paperbacks for Young Adults (Books for the Soul), 1997, Young Adult Library Services Association
Quick Picks for Reluctant Young Adult Readers, 1996, American Library Association

A LONG WAY FROM CHICAGO

Best Books for Young Adults, 1999, American Library Association
Dorothy Canfield Fisher Children's Book Award Nominee, 1999–2000
Flicker Tale Children's Book Award Nominee, 2000–2001
Kentucky Blue Grass Award Master List, 2002
Maryland Black-Eyed Susan Book Award Nominee, 2000–2001
National Book Award Finalist, 1998, National Book Foundation
Newbery Honor Book, 1999, American Library Association
Nutmeg Book Award Nominee, 2002

Pacific Northwest Young Reader's Choice Award Nominee, 2001
Popular Paperbacks for Young Adults (Humor), 2001, Young Adult Library Services Association
Rebecca Caudill Young Readers' Book Award Nominee, 2001
Utah Beehive Award, 2001, Children's Literature Association of Utah
Wyoming Soaring Eagle Book Award Nominee, 2001
Young Hoosier Book Award Nominee, 2001–2002

LOST IN CYBERSPACE

Sunshine State Young Readers Award Nominee, 1999–2000

ON THE WINGS OF HEROES

Flicker Tale Children's Book Award Nominee, 2007–2008
Summer Reading Title for the Hennepin County, Minn., Library System

PAST PERFECT, PRESENT TENSE

Books for the Teen Age, 2005, New York Public Library

PRINCESS ASHLEY

Best Books for Young Adults, 1987, American Library Association
Best Books of the Year, 1987, *School Library Journal*
Colorado Blue Spruce Young Adult Book Award Nominee, 1988
Nevada Young Readers Award, 1990–1991
Notable Books for Children, 1987, American Library Association
Wyoming Soaring Eagle Book Award, 1991

REMEMBERING THE GOOD TIMES

Best Books for Young Adults, 1985, American Library Association
Best Books of the Year, 1985, *School Library Journal*
Books for Young Adults Poll, 1986, University of Iowa

California Young Reader Medal Nominee, 1988
Colorado Blue Spruce Young Adult Book Award Nominee, 1989
Dorothy Canfield Fisher Children's Book Award Nominee, 1986–1987
Notable Children's Book, 1985, American Library Association
Rebecca Caudill Young Readers' Book Award Nominee, 1988

REPRESENTING SUPER DOLL

Best Books for Young Adults, 1975, American Library Association
Books for Young Adults Poll, 1975, University of Iowa

THE RIVER BETWEEN US

Best Books for Young Adults, 2004, American Library Association
Books for the Teen Age, 2004, 2005, 2006, New York Public Library
Dorothy Canfield Fisher Children's Book Award Nominee, 2004–2005
Indian Paintbrush Award Nominee (Wyoming), 2007
Kentucky Blue Grass Award Master List, 2005
National Book Award Finalist, 2003, National Book Foundation
Notable Books for Children, 2003, American Library Association
Nutmeg Book Award Nominee, 2002
Pacific Northwest Young Reader's Choice Award Nominee, 2006
Rebecca Caudill Young Readers' Book Award Nominee, 2006
Scott O'Dell Award for Historical Fiction, 2003

SECRETS OF THE SHOPPING MALL

Maud Hart Lovelace Book Award Nominee, 1986

STRAYS LIKE US

Best Book, 1998, *Parents Magazine*
Best Books for Young Adults, 1999, American Library Association

THE TEACHER'S FUNERAL:
A COMEDY IN THREE PARTS

Best Books for Young Adults, 2005, American Library Association
Best Books of the Year, 2004, *Kirkus Reviews*
Best Books of the Year, 2004, *Washington Post*
Best Historical Fiction Book for Children, *Disney Adventures Magazine*, 2004
Christopher Medal, 2004
Dorothy Canfield Fisher Children's Book Award Nominee, 2005–2006
Kentucky Blue Grass Award Master List, 2006
Land of Enchantment Book Award Nominee, 2006–2007
Notable Books for Children, 2004, American Library Association
Pacific Northwest Young Reader's Choice Award Nominee, 2007
Top Shelf Fiction for Middle Schools, 2005, Voice of Youth Advocates
Young Hoosier Book Award Nominee, 2006–2007

THIS FAMILY OF WOMEN

Books for Young Adults Poll, 1984, University of Iowa
Doubleday Book Club Alternate
Literary Guild Alternate

THOSE SUMMER GIRLS I NEVER MET

Colorado Blue Spruce Young Adult Book Award Nominee, 1990

VOICES AFTER MIDNIGHT

Maryland Black-Eyed Susan Book Award Nominee, 1992–1993
Maud Hart Lovelace Book Award Nominee, 1993
Quick Picks for Reluctant Young Adult Readers, 1990, American Library Association
Rebecca Caudill Young Readers' Book Award Nominee, 1994
Sunshine State Young Readers Award Nominee, 1993–1994
Utah Children's Book Award Nominee, 1993, Children's Literature Association of Utah

A YEAR DOWN YONDER

Best Books for Young Adults, 2001, American Library Association
Books for the Teen Age, 2001, 2003, New York Public Library
Colorado Blue Spruce Young Adult Book Award Nominee, 2003
Dorothy Canfield Fisher Children's Book Award Nominee, 2001–2002
Flicker Tale Children's Book Award Nominee, 2002–2003
Kentucky Blue Grass Award Master List, 2002
Newbery Medal Winner, 2001, American Library Association
Notable Books for Children, 2000, American Library Association
Rebecca Caudill Young Readers' Book Award Nominee, 2003

GENERAL AWARDS

1991 Medallion, University of Southern Mississippi
ALAN Award, 1990
Anne V. Zarrow Award for Young Readers' Literature, 2002, Tulsa Library Trust
    and Tulsa City-County Library
Illinois Writer of the Year, 1977, Illinois Association of Teachers of English
Jeremiah Ludington Award, 2004, Educational Paperback Association
Margaret A. Edwards Award, 1990, American Library Association
National Council for the Advancement of Education Writing Award, 1971
National Humanities Medal, 2001, National Endowment for the Humanities
Society of Children's Book Writers and Illustrators Member of the Year, 2004

Appendix B: Film Adaptations

THE GHOST BELONGED TO ME

Richard Peck's first novel in the Blossom Culp series was filmed by Walt Disney Productions as a television movie and appeared in 1977 on what is now called the "Wonderful World of Disney" under the title *Child of Glass*. It stars Barbara Barrie and Biff McGuire.

Peck is not pleased with the film. He had no access to the script and little contact with the people who made the movie. (The same was true for the films of his other novels.) About specifics, Peck says: "They promised to keep the name of the book—and they changed it within two weeks of airing. They turned the great-uncle in my novel, who is a portrait of my own great-uncle, Uncle Miles—who is the kind of old man the young boy [Alexander] would like to be one day—they turned him into an alcoholic murderer. And they set the novel in the present [instead of the original 1913], perhaps to save money on period sets and costumes."

"The movie usually reappears each year on television around Halloween," Peck says with a sigh.

This ninety-four-minute film is available from Walt Disney Films.

ARE YOU IN THE HOUSE ALONE?

Peck's sixth novel for young adults was adapted for a two-hour television movie by CBS-TV and had its first run during prime time in 1978. Capitalizing on the topical rape issue, the film begins with Gail being taken to the hospital after the rape and then flashes back to the start of Gail's story. She says, "I can't tell anybody. They won't believe me." And so the film shows how her attacker, a son in the wealthiest family in town, pursued her. The movie then goes on to reveal the resulting aftermath.

Richard Peck was pleased with the casting of this film, which stars Kathleen Beller as Gail, Dennis Quaid as the rapist, and Blythe Danner as Gail's mother. Probably for the sake of convenience, the setting was changed from suburban Connecticut to Marin County, California, a change that reflected some of the social differences, though not the small-town attitudes that are an important basis of the novel. Other changes in Judith Parker's script transform the mother for whom Gail babysits into a lawyer, allow Gail's boyfriend to know who the attacker is, and reshape the unsympathetic male police chief into a slightly less offensive female officer. The change that most disturbs Richard Peck, however, is the ending of the film: Gail sets a trap for Phil that leads to his being tried and convicted of the lesser charge of assault. Peck's purpose in writing the book was to show that there is no justice in our society when it comes to a case like Gail's and to raise the question of how the victim will respond when she knows that. As Peck explains it: "How are you going to arrange your life now that you've found out that life is not a party, that the crooks aren't caught? But in the film the crook is caught! Which invalidates the book as far as I'm concerned."

Leonard Maltin calls the film an "unsatisfactory adaptation" of Peck's novel,[1] and Steven Scheuer says, "This clanky TV movie thriller was not worthy of the neat suspense novel on which it was based."[2] But it could have been worse, and it does provide some insight into the feelings of a courageous teenager who has little support from friends, parents, and society.

The ninety-six-minute video of this film, made by Stonehenge Productions, is available from Worldvision Home Video, Inc.

FATHER FIGURE

Leonard Maltin calls this made-for-television movie an "affecting drama,"[3] and indeed, it is the best of the three television dramatizations of Peck's novels. Although the William Hanley screenplay, which first aired on CBS-TV in October 1980, holds together quite well, the story's perspective is shifted from the seventeen-year-old son, played by Timothy Hutton, to the middle-aged father, played by Hal Linden. Janet Seigel, in "From Page to Screen: Where the Author Fits In," explains that film producers and directors, although they like the stories that young adult novels contain, "rarely let the books speak for themselves." In almost every case, Seigel maintains, the role of the adult in the story is "magnified in order to attract an established adult star, ensuring adequate financing for production."[4] That is true of the mother's role that Blythe Danner played in *Are You in the House Alone?*, and it is especially true of Hal Linden's role in *Father Figure*.

In the novel, the father is "a low-key figure," Peck says, a dropout from life who is "quite in love with a young woman but he has no way to get her—not as a wife, not as a mistress." But in the scene in the film where the father is introduced, he's lying in bed with his mistress, who is pleading with him to marry her. Some of the other differences between the film and the book are significant, while others are not. But Richard Peck is pleased that the film at least ends in the same way his novel does. "That's an achievement," he says. "And it's the right ending."

The video of this ninety-five-minute film, made by Time-Life Productions, is available from Lightning Video International.

DON'T LOOK AND IT WON'T HURT

Twenty years after this novel was published, its story provided the background for a low-budget, highly praised feature film called *Gas Food Lodging*, written and directed by Allison Anders. The R-rated film's story is similar to Peck's novel in that it's about an unmarried, pregnant teenager (played with an empty sexiness by Ione Skye); her younger sister, who is the story's narrator (played effectively by Fairuza Balk); their mother (realistically portrayed by Brooke Adams), a waitress whose life is a shambles and whose control of her daughters' lives is minimal; and an absent father. But the similarities end there. Anders has eliminated a third daughter, changed the setting from Illinois to New Mexico, contemporized the issues, and given new names to all the characters. For example, Carol, the sixteen-year-old narrator of the novel, becomes Shade, a much younger girl in the film. Ellen becomes Trudi. And the world-weary mother, named Nora, is as much the focus of the film as are her two daughters.

Unlike Peck's novel, this film is, in the words of an *Entertainment Weekly* reporter, "a sort of working-class ode to single motherhood."[5] It's also a search for love and romance, with each of the female characters in the film seeking to connect with a male who will care about her in return. Each finds it in a way at the end, though each is betrayed in a different way by men along the way. This is an "ebullient comic drama with a tinge of pain at its center," says one reviewer.[6] And George Schickel declared it "smart, tough and compassionate."[7]

Regardless of the movie's departures from the novel on which it is based, it is an excellent film, which *Time* singled out as one of the best movies of 1992.[8] And Richard Peck, whose name appears prominently on the silver screen, concludes: "Reflected glory is better than no glory at all."

This movie was released on DVD by Sony Pictures in September 2003.

OTHER NOVELS

In 1975, Peck announced that Walt Disney Productions had purchased the rights to *Through a Brief Darkness* and was about to start filming it with Linda Blair in the starring role.[9] But the film was never made. And at the 1981 ALA annual conference in San Francisco, Peck announced that *Close Enough to Touch* was soon to be filmed for television by MGM.[10] That was followed by an article in the *Boston Herald American* in 1982 stating that *Close Enough to Touch* had been "filmed for television."[11] But no film was ever made of that novel. Richard Peck indicates that, while most of his novels have been optioned for films, only the four noted above have yet been made.

NOTES

1. Leonard Maltin, ed., *Leonard Maltin's TV Movies and Video Guide* (New York: American Library, 1988), 40.

2. Steven H. Scheuer, *The Complete Guide to Videocassette Movies* (New York: Holt, Rinehart and Winston, 1987), 26.

3. Maltin, *Leonard Maltin's TV Movies and Video Guide*, 308.

4. Janet Seigel, "From Page to Screen: Where the Author Fits In," *Top of the News* (Spring 1984): 282.

5. Kelli Pryor, "Allison Anders—Working-Class Heroine," *Entertainment Weekly*, 21 August 1992, 39.

6. "Desert Hearts," *Entertainment Weekly*, 21 August 1992, 39.

7. Richard Schickel, "Family Values Get Real," *Time*, 17 August 1992, 63.

8. "The Best Movies of 1992," *Time*, 4 January 1993, 54.

9. Richard Peck, Speech at Central Connecticut State University, 9 April 1975.

10. Richard Peck, "People of the Word: A Look at Today's Young Adults and Their Needs," *School Library Media Quarterly* (Fall 1981): 21.

11. M. D. Kramer, "A Bushel of Peck for Teens," *Boston Herald American*, 5 September 1982.

Selected Bibliography

PRIMARY WORKS

Young Adult Novels

Are You in the House Alone? New York: Viking, 1976; Dell, 1977; Puffin, 2000.

Bel-Air Bambi and the Mall Rats. New York: Delacorte, 1993; Dell, 1995.

Blossom Culp and the Sleep of Death. New York: Delacorte, 1986; Dell, 1987, 1994.

Close Enough to Touch. New York: Delacorte, 1981; Dell, 1982, 1986.

Don't Look and It Won't Hurt. New York: Holt, Rinehart and Winston, 1972; Avon, 1973, 1979, 1983.

The Dreadful Future of Blossom Culp. New York: Delacorte, 1983; Dell, 1984, 1986, 1987; Puffin, 2001.

Dreamland Lake. New York: Holt, Rinehart and Winston, 1973; Avon, 1974; Dell, 1982, 1986; Puffin, 2000.

Fair Weather. New York: Dial, 2001; Puffin, 2003.

Father Figure. New York: Viking, 1978; New American Library, 1979; Dell, 1988; Puffin, 1996.

The Ghost Belonged to Me. New York: Viking, 1975; Dell, 1976, 1986, 1987; Puffin, 1997.

Ghosts I Have Been. New York: Viking, 1977; Dell, 1979, 1986, 1987; Puffin, 2001.

The Great Interactive Dream Machine. New York: Dial, 1996; Puffin, 1998.

Here Lies the Librarian. New York: Dial, 2006; Puffin, 2007.

The Last Safe Place on Earth. New York: Delacorte, 1995; Dell, 1996, 2005.

A Long Way from Chicago. New York: Dial, 1998; Puffin, 2000, 2004.

Lost in Cyberspace. New York: Dial, 1995; Puffin, 1997.

On the Wings of Heroes. New York: Dial, 2007; Puffin, 2008.

Princess Ashley. New York: Delacorte, 1987; Dell, 1988.

Remembering the Good Times. New York: Delacorte, 1985; Dell, 1986.

Representing Super Doll. New York: Viking, 1974; Avon, 1975, 1980; Dell, 1982, 1986; Puffin, 1997.

The River between Us. New York: Dial, 2003; Puffin, 2005.

Secrets of the Shopping Mall. New York: Delacorte, 1979; Dell 1980, 1986, 1989.

Strays like Us. New York: Dial, 1998; Puffin, 2000.

The Teacher's Funeral: A Comedy in Three Parts. New York: Dial, 2004; Puffin, 2006.

Those Summer Girls I Never Met. New York: Delacorte, 1988; Dell, 1989.

Through a Brief Darkness. New York: Viking, 1973; Avon, 1974, 1981; Dell, 1982, 1986; Puffin, 1997.

Unfinished Portrait of Jessica. New York: Delacorte, 1991; Dell, 1993.

Voices after Midnight. New York: Delacorte, 1989; Dell, 1990.

A Year Down Yonder. New York: Dial, 2000; Puffin, 2002.

Adult Novels

Amanda/Miranda. New York: Viking, 1980; Avon, 1981; (Abridged) Dial, 1999; Puffin, 2001.

London Holiday. New York: Viking Penguin, 1998; Penguin, 1999.

New York Time. New York: Delacorte, 1981; Dell, 1982.

This Family of Women. New York: Delacorte, 1983; Dell, 1984.

Children's Picture Books

Monster Night at Grandma's House. Illustrated by Don Freeman. New York: Viking, 1977; Dial, 2003.

What Ever Happened to Thanksgiving? Unpublished manuscript.

Edited Essay Collections

Edge of Awareness: Twenty-Five Contemporary Essays. With Ned E. Hoopes. New York: Dell, 1966.

Leap into Reality: Essays for Now. New York: Dell, 1973.

Edited Poetry Collections

Mindscapes: Poems for the Real World. New York: Delacorte, 1971; Dell, 1972, 1990.

Pictures That Storm inside My Head: Poems for the Inner You. New York: Avon, 1976, 1983.

Sounds and Silences: Poetry for Now. New York: Delacorte, 1970; Dell, 1970; Avon, 1976; Dell, 1990.

Educational Books

A Consumer's Guide to Educational Innovations. With Mortimer Smith and George Weber. Washington, D.C.: Council for Basic Education, 1972.

The Creative Word. Vol. 2. With Stephen N. Judy. New York: Random House, 1973.

Invitations to the World: Teaching and Writing for the Young. New York: Dial, 2002.

Love and Death at the Mall: Teaching and Writing for the Literate Young. New York: Delacorte, 1994.

Open Court Correlated Language Arts Program. LaSalle, Ill.: Open Court, 1967.

Transitions: A Literary Paper Casebook. (Compiled). New York: Random House, 1974.

Urban Studies: A Research Paper Casebook. (Compiled). New York: Random House, 1973.

Self-published Book

Old Town, A Complete Guide: Strolling, Shopping, Supping, Sipping. 2nd ed. With Norman Strasma. Chicago, 1965.

Autobiography

Anonymously Yours. New York: Julian Messner, 1991.

Short Stories

"By Far the Worst Pupil at Long Point School." In *Past Perfect, Present Tense: New and Collected Stories*, ed. Richard Peck, 60–65. New York: Dial, 2004; Puffin, 2006.

"The Electric Summer." In *Time Capsule*, ed. Donald R. Gallo, 3–18. New York: Delacorte, 1999; Dell, 2001.

"Fluffy the Gangbuster." In *Past Perfect, Present Tense: New and Collected Stories*, ed. Richard Peck, 116–31. New York: Dial, 2004; Puffin, 2006.

"Girl at the Window." In *Night Terrors: Stories of Shadow and Substance*, ed. Lois Duncan, 30–43. New York: Simon and Schuster, 1996; Simon Pulse, 1997.

"I Go Along." In *Connections: Short Stories by Outstanding Writers for Young Adults*, ed. Donald R. Gallo, 184–91. New York: Delacorte, 1989; Dell, 1990.

"The Kiss in the Carryon Bag." In *Destination Unexpected*, ed. Donald R. Gallo, 147–63. Cambridge, Mass.: Candlewick, 2003, 2006.

"The Most Important Night of Melanie's Life." In *From One Experience to Another*, ed. M. Jerry Weiss and Helen S. Weiss, 105–11. New York: Forge Books, 1997, 1999.

"Priscilla and the Wimps." In *Sixteen: Short Stories by Outstanding Writers for Young Adults*, ed. Donald R. Gallo, 42–45. New York: Delacorte, 1984; Dell, 1985.

"Shadows." In *Visions: Nineteen Short Stories by Outstanding Writers for Young Adults*, ed. Donald R. Gallo, 2–9. New York: Delacorte, 1987; Dell, 1988.

"Shotgun Cheatham's Last Night above Ground." In *Twelve Shots*, ed. Harry Mazer, 122–37. New York: Delacorte, 1997; Dell, 1998.

"The Size of the Universe." *Southwest Review* (Autumn 1986): 493–509.

"The Special Powers of Blossom Culp." In *Birthday Surprises*, ed. Johanna Hurwitz, 1–13. New York: HarperCollins, 1995, 1997.

"The Three-Century Woman." In *Second Sight: Stories for a New Millennium*, 109–19. New York: Philomel, 1999.

"Waiting for Sebastian." In *Dirty Laundry*, ed. Lisa Rowe Fraustino, 80–87. New York: Viking, 1998.

Short Story Collection

Past Perfect, Present Tense: New and Collected Stories. New York: Dial, 2004; Puffin, 2006.

Poems

"Early Admission." Unprinted. Written 1971.

"The Geese." In *Sounds and Silences: Poetry for Now*, ed. Richard Peck, 9. New York: Delacorte, 1970.

"Irish Child." *Chicago Tribune Magazine*, 17 September 1972.

"Jump Shot." In *Mindscapes: Poems for the Real World*, ed. Richard Peck, 8. New York: Delacorte, 1971.

"Lesson in History." *Chicago Tribune Magazine*, 7 July 1974.

"Mission Uncontrolled." In *Mindscapes: Poems for the Real World*, ed. Richard Peck, 86–87. New York: Delacorte, 1971.

"Nancy." In "Phoenix Nest," ed. Martin Levin, 6. *Saturday Review*, 21 June 1969.

"Notes for the Refrigerator Door." *ALAN Review* (Winter 1992): 5.

"Street Trio." In "Phoenix Nest," ed. Martin Levin, 6. *Saturday Review*, 4 September 1971.

"TKO." In *Sports Poems*, ed. R. R. Knudson and P. K. Ebert, 142. New York: Dell, 1971.

Chapters in Books

"Nobody but a Reader Ever Became a Writer." In *Authors Insights: Turning Teenagers into Readers and Writers*, ed. Donald R Gallo, 77–89. Portsmouth, N.H.: Boynton/ Cook-Heinemann, 1992.

"A Note on the Story." In *The River between Us*, 159–64. New York: Puffin, 2003.

"Problem Novels for Readers without Any." In *Reading Their World: The Young Adult Novel in the English Classroom*, ed. Virginia R Monseau and Gary M. Salvner, 71–76. Portsmouth, N.H.: Boynton/Cook-Heinemann, 1992.

Essays

"Art Deco: The Newest 'Antique.' " *House Beautiful* (August 1973): 61–83.

Bantam Doubleday Dell publicity brochure, n.d.

"Battered by Left and Right: Censorship in the '90s as Viewed by a Novelist from Illinois Whose Books Have Wound Up on Forbidden Lists." *Illinois Issues* (July 1993): 24–26.

"The Book That Changed My Life." *National Book Foundation.* www.nationalbook .org/bookchanged_rpeck_nbm.html.

"Can Students Evaluate Their Education?" *PTA Magazine* (February 1971): 4–7.

"Care and Feeding of the Visiting Author." *Top of the News* (Spring 1982): 251–55.

"Coming Full Circle: From Lesson Plans to Young Adult Novels." *Horn Book* (April 1985): 208–15.

"Communicating with the Pubescent." *Booklist*, 1 June 1994, 1818–19.

"Consciousness-Raising." *American Libraries* (February 1974): 75–76.

"A Conversation with Richard Peck." Dell publicity brochure, n.d.

"Delivering the Goods." *American Libraries* (October 1974): 492–94.

Dell publicity brochure, November 1988, 6.

"An Exclusive Interview with Blossom Culp." Dell publicity brochure, 1987.

"From Realism to Melodrama." *American Libraries* (February 1975): 106–8.

"From Strawberry Statements to Censorship." *School Library Journal* (January 1997).

"Future-Laugh." In "Phoenix Nest," ed. Martin Levin, 69–70. *Saturday Review*, 26 August 1972.

"The Genteel Unshelving of a Book." *School Library Journal* (May 1986): 37–39.

"The Great Library-Shelf Witch Hunt" *Booklist*, 1 January 1992, 816–17.

"Growing Up Suburban: 'We Don't Use Slang, We're Gifted.' " *School Library Journal* (October 1985): 118–19.

"Huck Finns of Both Sexes: Protagonists and Peer Leaders in Young Adult Books." *Horn Book* (September–October 1993): 554–58.

"In the Beginning Was The . . ." *ALAN Review* (Spring 1997): 2–4.

"In the Country of Teenage Fiction." *American Libraries* (April 1973): 204–7.

"The Invention of Adolescence and Other Thoughts on Youth." *Top of the News* (Winter 1983): 182–90.

"It's a World Away and Yet So Close." *New York Times*, 8 October 1972, 4, 12.

"I Was the First Writer I Ever Met." *Voice of Youth Advocates* (October 1981).

"The Last Safe Place on Earth." *Book Links* (September 1995): 25–26.

"Love Is Not Enough." *School Library Journal* (September 1990): 153–54. Printed also in *Journal of Youth Services in Libraries* (Fall 1990): 35–39.

"Of Rabbits and Roadsters." *American Libraries* (July–August 1974): 360–61.

"People of the Word: A Look at Today's Young Adults and Their Needs." *School Library Media Quarterly* (Fall 1981): 16–21.

"A Personal Letter from: Blossom Culp to: Whom It May Concern." Dell publicity brochure, n.d.

"Rape and the Teenage Victim." *Top of the News* (Winter 1978): 175–76.

"Richard Peck Discusses Adolescent Rape." Dell publicity release, n.d.

"Richard Peck Responds to National Book Week with 7 Do's and 7 Don'ts for Parents." Avon Books publicity release.

"Some Thoughts on Adolescent Lit." *News from ALAN* (September–October 1975): 4–7.

"St. Charles Is the Last Trolley Left." *New York Times*, 28 January 1973, 3, 17.

"Suicide as a Solution?" Dell publicity brochure, n.d.

"Teenagers' Tastes." *American Libraries* (May 1974): 235–36.

"Ten Questions to Ask about a Novel." *ALAN Newsletter* (Spring 1978): 1, 7.

"Traveling in Time." *ALAN Review* (Winter 1990): 1–3.

Viking publicity brochure, n.d.

"We Can Save Our Schools." *Parents' Magazine and Better Family Living* (September 1971): 51–52, 98–101.

"A Writer from Illinois." *Illinois Libraries* (June 1986): 392–94.

"Writing in a Straight Line." *Horn Book* (September–October 1997): 529–33.

"YA Books in the Decade of the Vanishing Adult." *Dell Carousel* (Fall–Winter 1985–1986): 1–2.

"Young Adult Books." *Horn Book* (September–October 1986): 619.

Prayers and Credos

"The Fervent Prayer of a Teenager's Parent." *ALAN Review* (Winter 1987): 51.

"I Read." From Acceptance Speech for the Margaret A. Edwards Award, American Library Association Conference, Chicago, June 1990. Published in *School Library Journal* (September 1990): 154; and *Journal of Youth Services to Libraries* (Fall 1990): 38–39.

"A Teacher's Prayer." *News from Dell Books*, n.d. Reprinted in *ALAN Review* (Winter 1989): 35.

"A Teenager's Prayer." *Horn Book* (September–October 1968): 621.

Speeches

"Books for the Readers of the 21st Century." Ezra Jack Keats Lecture delivered at the University of Southern Mississippi, 24 March 2000. www.lib.usm.edu/~degrum/html/aboutus/au-fall2000keatslecture.shtml.

"Newbery Medal Acceptance." *Horn Book* (July 2001): 397.

"Sharing the Truth with the First Citizens of the 21st Century." Speech delivered at the 1996 Highlights Foundation Writing for Children Workshop. Also printed in *Highlights Foundation Newsletter* (1996), 2–5.

Speech at Central Connecticut State University, 9 April 1975. Unpublished.

Speech at the Children's Book Council/American Booksellers Association, New Orleans, 24 May 1986. Unpublished.

Speech at the Children's Literature Festival, University of Southern Mississippi, Hattiesburg, 19 March 1981. Unpublished.

Speech delivered at the Florida Association for Media in Education Conference, Orlando, Florida, 20 October 2005. Also printed in *Florida Media Quarterly* (Winter 2005).

SECONDARY WORKS

Books and Parts of Books

Cart, Michael. *From Romance to Realism: 50 Years of Growth and Change in Young Adult Literature*. New York: HarperCollins, 1996.

Commire, Anne, ed. *Something about the Author*, vol. 18, 242–44. Detroit: Gale Research, 1980.

Contemporary Authors Online. Detroit: Thomson Gale, 2006. http://galenet.gale group.com.

Crew, Hilary. "Richard Peck." In *Twentieth-Century Young Adult Writers*, ed. Laura Standley Berger, 523–26. Detroit: St. James, 1994.

Donelson, Kenneth L., and Alleen Pace Nilsen. *Literature for Today's Young Adults*. Glenview, Ill.: Scott, Foresman, 1980.

Dust Jacket for *On the Wings of Heroes*. New York: Dial, 2007.

Dust Jacket for *Princess Ashley*. New York: Delacorte, 1987.

Gallo, Donald R., ed. *Speaking for Ourselves*, 165–67. Urbana, Ill.: National Council of Teachers of English, 1990.

Gunton, Sharon R., ed. *Contemporary Literary Criticism*, vol. 21, 295–301. Detroit: Gale Research, 1982.

Kovacs, Deborah. *Meet the Authors*, 76–79. New York: Scholastic, 1995.

Locher, Frances Carol, ed. *Contemporary Authors*, vol. 85–88, 458–59. Detroit: Gale Research, 1980.

Maltin, Leonard, ed. *Leonard Maltin's TV Movies and Video Guide*. New York: New American Library, 1988.

Nilsen, Alleen Pace, and Kenneth L. Donelson. *Literature for Today's Young Adults*, 2nd ed. Glenview, Ill.: Scott, Foresman, 1985.

Reed, Arthea J. S. *Reaching Adolescents: The Young Adult Book and the School*, 6–7, 50–51, 184. New York: Merrill, 1994.

Sarkissian, Adele, ed. *Something about the Author Autobiography Series*, vol. 2, 175–86. Detroit: Gale Research, 1985.

Scheuer, Steven H. *The Complete Guide to Videocassette Movies*. New York: Holt, Rinehart and Winston, 1987.

Schwartz, Sheila. *Teaching Adolescent Literature: A Humanistic Approach*. Rochelle Park, N.J.: Hayden, 1979.

Tovey, Janice K. "Writing for the Young Adult Reader. An Analysis of Audience in the Novels of Richard Peck." Master's thesis, Illinois State University, 1988.

Yunghans, Penelope. *Prize Winners: Ten Writers for Young Readers*, 108–22. Greensboro, N.C.: Morgan Reynolds, 1995. 118.

Articles

Baker, Deirdre. "In the Face of Adversity." *Toronto Star*, 7 January 2001, Entertainment.

———. "On the Road to Find Out." *Toronto Star*, 24 October 2004, D14.

Berman, Matt. "Peck's Peak." *Times-Picayune*, 7 April 2002, Living 1.

"Best of the Best Books 1970–1982." *Booklist*, 15 October 1983, 351–54.

"The Best Movies of 1992." *Time*, 4 January 1993, 54.

Bodart, Joni. "The Also-Rans; or 'What Happened to the Ones That Didn't Get Eight Votes?' " *Top of the News* (Fall 1981): 70–72.

Brown, Jennifer M. "A Long Way from Decatur." *Publishers Weekly*, 21 July 2003, 169–70.

Campbell, Patty. "Funny Girls." *Horn Book* (May–June 1999): 359–63.

Carlsen, G. Robert, Connie Bennett, and Anne Harker. "1977 Books for Young Adults Book Poll." *English Journal* (January 1978): 90–95.

Carlsen, G. Robert, Tony Manna, and Jan Yoder. "1975 BYA Book Poll." *English Journal* (January 1976): 95–99.

Carter, Betty. "Best of the Best: Twenty-Five Years of Best Books for Young Adults." *ALAN Review* (Fall 1994): 67–69.

Castellitto, Linda. "Lessons Learned." *First Person Book Page*. www.bookpage.com/ 0310bp/richard_peck.html.

Connor, John W., et al. "1984 Books for Young Adults Poll." *English Journal* (December 1984): 64–68.

Connor, John W., and Kathleen Tessmer. "1986 Books for Young Adults Poll." *English Journal* (December 1986): 58–61.

Crew, Hillary. "Blossom Culp and Her Ilk: The Independent Female in Richard Peck's YA Fiction." *Top of the News* (Spring 1987): 297–301.

Cuniberti, Betty. "Author's Book Explores What Teen-Age Boys Are Made Of." *Los Angeles Times*, 14 November 1982, part 6.

"Desert Hearts." *Entertainment Weekly*, 21 August 1992, 39–40.

Elleman, Barbara. "50 Books Too Good to Be Missed." *Learning* (April–May 1985): 24–28.

Gallo, Donald R. "Who Are the Most Important YA Authors?" *ALAN Review* (Spring 1989): 18–20.

Gilson, Nancy. "Seeding the Suburban Desert: Author's Books Tug at the Blinders Worn by American Teen-Agers." *Columbus Dispatch*, 20 September 2001, 08G.

Gourley, Catherine. "Richard Peck: Researching Fiction." *Writing!* (November–December 2001): 26.

Green, Judy. "Richard Peck Looks Back in a Changing World." *Sacramento Bee*, 13 January 2002, E1.

Harmanci, Reyhan. "Blossom Culp Never Loses Her Spirit, Appeal." *San Francisco Chronicle*, 28 August 2005, C6.

Hartvigsen, M. Kip, and Christen Brog Hartvigsen. "The Divine Miss Blossom Culp." *ALAN Review* (Winter 1989): 33–35.

Henke, James T. "The Death of the Mother, the Rebirth of the Son: *Millie's Boy* and *Father Figure*." *Children's Literature in Education* (Spring 1983): 21–34.

Hipple, Ted. " 'Have You Read . . . ?' (part 4)." *English Journal* (November 1992): 91.

Jankowski, Jane. "Books Spur Complaints." *Decatur Herald and Review*, 11 March 1986.

Kerby, Mona. "Richard Peck." *The Author Corner*. www.carr.org/mae/peck.

Ketcham, Diana. "Rediscovering San Simeon's Architect." *New York Times*, 28 April 1988.

Kramer, M. D. "A Bushel of Peck for Teens." *Boston Herald American*, 5 September 1982.

Loer, Stephanie. "Novel Sequel Wins Newbery." *Boston Globe*, 21 January 2001, F5.

MacPherson, Karen. "Since Winning Newbery, Author Peck Is Busier Talking than Writing." *Pittsburgh-Post Gazette*, 8 May 2001, E2.

"Meet the Author." *CBC Magazine*. www.cbcbooks.org/cbcmagazine/mee/richard_peck.html.

Meyer, Duane. "A Morning with the 2001 Newbery Medal Winner, Richard W. Peck, DePauw '56." *Delta Chi Quarterly* (Fall–Winter 2001): 6–7, 20.

Nilsen, Alleen Pace, Ken Donelson, and James Blasingame Jr., "Young Adult Literature: 2000 Honor List: A Hopeful Bunch." *English Journal* (November 2001): 116–22.

"Nothin' but the Best: Best of the Best Books for Young Adults 1986–1986." *Booklist*, 15 October 1988, 401–4.

Pocius, Donna Marie. "In Search of Perfection." *Reading Today* (October–November 2005): 27.

Pokorski, Doug. "Decatur Native a Finalist for National Book Award." *State Journal Register*, 15 November 1998, 51.

Porrelli, Cathie Lou. "El Monte Pioneers' Tale Told in New Novel." *San Gabriel Valley Tribune*, 16 June 1983.

Pryor, Kelli. "Allison Anders—Working-Class Heroine." *Entertainment Weekly*, 21 August 1992, 39.

Reed, J. D. "Packaging the Facts of Life." *Time*, 23 August 1982, 65–66.

"Richard Peck." *Fifth Book of Junior Authors*. New York: H. W. Wilson, 1983. See also "EPA's Top 100 Authors." Educational Paperback Association. www.edupap erback.org.

"Richard Peck Author Page." Penguin Group. http://us.penguingroup.com/nf/ Author/AuthorPage.

"Richard Peck: Right for All Ages, Writing for All Ages." *Openers* (Summer 1982).

"Richard Peck's Biography." Scholastic. www.books.scholastic.com/teacher/ authorsandbooks/authorstudies.

Romano, Katherine. "Richard Peck: Listen and Learn." *Teaching PreK–8* (August–September 2002): 76–78.

Schickel, Richard. "Family Values Get Real." *Time*, 17 August 1992, 63–65.

Schleler, Curt. "Peck Is Author Whose Dreams Came True." *Grand Rapids Press*, 25 July 1982.

Schneider, Dean. "Richard Peck: 'The Past Is My Favorite Place.' " *Book Links* (September 2006): 54–57.

Seigel, Janet. "From Page to Screen: Where the Author Fits In." *Top of the News* (Spring 1984): 282–83.

Smith, Patrice. "Author Aims at Teen-Age Ideals." *Evansville Courier*, 1986.

Sulkin, Randi. "Richard Peck: Writing Is Communication." *Ketchikan Daily News*, 3–9 March 1984, 2.

Talbert, Mark. "Richard Peck: Young Adult Literature Author Appreciates Friend and Mentor." *Horn Book* (July 2001): 403–7.

"Tips That Get Kids Reading." *Ketchikan Daily News*, 3–9 March 1984, 3.

Interviews

Atkins, Holly. "An Interview with Richard Peck." *St. Petersburg Times*, 17 May 2004, 6E.

"A Conversation with Richard Peck." *Fair Weather*, 140–46. New York: Puffin, 2001.

"A Conversation with the Author." *Penguin Readers Guide to London Holiday*, 4–7, 1998.

Gallo, Donald R. Interview with Nancy Gallt (telephone). 22 July 1988.

————. Interview with Richard Peck (tape recording). Montclair, New Jersey, Public Library, 9 December 1987.

"An Interview with Richard Peck." *Scholastic Voice*, 6 September 1985, 12–13.

Janeczko, Paul. "An Interview with Richard Peck." *English Journal* (February 1976): 97– 99.

————. Interview with Richard Peck. *From Writers to Students: The Pleasures and Pains of Writing*, ed. M. Jerry Weiss, 79–83. Newark, Del.: International Reading Association, 1979.

Johnson, Nancy J., and Cyndi Giorgis. "2001 Newbery Medal Winner: A Conversation with Richard Peck." *Reading Teacher* (December 2001/January 2002): 392–97.

Mercier, Jean F. "PW Interviews Richard Peck." *Publishers Weekly*, 14 March 1980, 6–7.

"Richard Peck's Scholastic Interview Transcript." Scholastic www.books.scholastic.com/teacher/authorsandbooks/authorstudies.

Ross, Jean W. "CA Interview." *Contemporary Authors*, New Revision Series, vol. 19, ed. Linda Metzger, 367–70. Detroit: Gale Research, 1987.

Stanek, Lou Willett. "Just Listening: Interviews with Six Adolescent Novelists: Patricia McKillip, Robert Cormier, Norma Klein, Richard Peck, S. E. Hinton, Judy Blume." *Arizona English Bulletin* (April 1976): 23–38.

Sutton, Roger. "A Conversation with Richard Peck." *School Library Journal* (June 1990): 36–40.

Workshop

Workshop at Montclair, New Jersey, Public Library, 9 December 1987. Tape recording.

Letter

Cooper, Lloyd. Maple Valley High School, Michigan. Letter to Donald R. Gallo, May 1987.

Pamphlet

"Nothin' but the Best: The Best of the Best Books for Young Adults 1966–1986." Chicago: American Library Association, 1988.

SELECTED REVIEWS

Amanda/Miranda

Bill, Rise. *Best Sellers* (May 1980): 50.
Kirkus Reviews, 1 January 1980, 32.
Langten, Jane. *Washington Post*, 23 March 1980, 12.
Publishers Weekly, 18 January 1980, 130.

Are You in the House Alone?

Heins, Paul. *Horn Book* (February 1977): 60.
Kirkus Reviews, 1 September 1976, 982.
Leonberger, Janet. *Young Adult Cooperative Book Review Group of Massachusetts* (February 1977): 89–90.
Levy, J. W. *Journal of Reading* (April 1978): 655.
Nelson, Alix. *New York Times Book Review*, 14 November 1976, 29.
Sutherland, Zena. *Bulletin of the Center for Children's Books* (March 1977): 111–12.

Bel-Air Bambi and the Mall Rats

Bushman, John H. *ALAN Review* (Spring 1994). http://scholar.lib.vt.edu/ejournals/ALAN.
Cooper, Ilene. *Booklist*, 1 September 1993, 62.
The Horn Book Guide, 1993.
Kirkus Reviews, 1993. http://clcd.odyssi.com.
Lesene, Teri S., and Lois Buckman. *Journal of Reading* (March 1994): 521.
Publishers Weekly, 16 August 1993, 104.
Raasch, Bonnie L. *Book Report* (March/April 1994): 37.
Stevenson, Deborah. *Bulletin of the Center for Children's Books* (October 1993).
Toth, Luann. *School Library Journal* (July 1996): 331.
Whitehurst, Lucinda Snyder. *School Library Journal* (September 1993): 234.
Zynda, Barbara A. *KLIATT* (July 1995).

Blossom Culp and the Sleep of Death

Campbell, Patty. *Wilson Library Bulletin* (March 1986): 51.
Cart, Michael. *School Library Journal* (May 1986): 108.
Levine, Susan. *Voice of Youth Advocates* (June 1986): 82.
Publishers Weekly, 21 March 1986.

Close Enough to Touch

Bagnall, Norma. *ALAN Review* (Winter 1982): 21.
Best Sellers (January 1982): 403.
Bulletin of the Center for Children's Books (November 1981): 53.
Chelton, Mary K. *Voice of Youth Advocates* (October 1981): 36.
Davis, Paxton. *New York Times Book Review*, 15 November 1981, 56, 69.
O'Connell, Kay Webb. *School Library Journal* (September 1981): 140.
Publishers Weekly, 2 October 1981, 111.

Don't Look and It Won't Hurt

Booklist, 15 February 1973, 574.
Kirkus Reviews, 15 August 1972, 949.
Pogrebin, Letty Cottin. *New York Times Book Review*, 12 November 1972, 8, 10, 14.
Publishers Weekly, 25 September 1972, 60.
Sullivan, Peggy. *Library Journal*, 15 December 1972, 4080.

The Dreadful Future of Blossom Culp

Crompton, Anne Eliot. *Parents' Choice* (Spring–Summer 1984), 5.
Gauch, Patricia Lee. *New York Times Book Review*, 18 December 1983, 21.
Heins, Ethel L. *Horn Book* (February 1984): 64.
Ocala Star Banner, 25 December 1984.
Sorenson, Marilou. *Deseret News*, 29 January 1984.
Williamson, Susan H. *KLIATT* (October 1984): 4.

Dreamland Lake

Booklist, 15 November 1973, 342.
Kirkus Reviews, 15 June 1973, 648.
New York Times Book Review, 13 January 1974, 10.
Publishers Weekly, 6 August 1973, 65.
School Library Journal (December 1976): 69.
Sutherland, Zena. *Bulletin of the Center for Children's Books* (January 1974): 83–84.
Yucht, Alice H. *School Library Journal*, 15 November 1973, 53.

Fair Weather

Andronik, Catherine M. *Book Report* (March–April 2002): 50.
Carter, Leslie. *Voice of Youth Advocates* (October 2001): 282.

Chang, Elizabeth. *Washington Post*, 7 July 2004, C16.
Cooper, Ilene. *New York Times Book Review*, 18 November 2001, 45.
Gilson, Nancy. *Columbus Dispatch*, 20 September 2001, 21.
Green, Judy. *Sacramento Bee*, 13 January 2002, E4.
Ingram, Jenny. *Voice of Youth Advocates* (October 2002): 322.
Jemtegaard, Kristi Elle. *Horn Book* (May–June 2003): 377.
Phelan, Carolyn. *Booklist*, 1 September 2001.
Publishers Weekly, 23 July 2001, 77.
Snelson, Karin. Amazon.com.
Sutton, Roger. *Horn Book* (January–February 2003): 106.
Vaughan, Kit. *School Library Journal* (September 2001): 230.

Father Figure

Booklist, 15 July 1978, 1728.
Kirkus Reviews, 1 September 1978, 953.
Pollack, Pamela D. *School Library Journal* (October 1978): 158.
Publishers Weekly, 17 July 1978, 168.
Rosen, Winifred. *Washington Post Book World*, 12 November 1978, E4.
Top of the News (Fall 1980): 62.

The Ghost Belonged to Me

Atwater, Judith. *School Library Journal* (September 1975): 109.
Booklist, 1 July 1975, 1129.
Clements, Bruce. *Psychology Today* (September 1975): 11, 75.
Junior Bookshelf (June 1977): 182–83.
Kirkus Reviews, 15 April 1975, 456.
Levine, Joan Goldman. *New York Times*, 27 July 1975, 8.

Ghosts I Have Been

Heins, Ethel L. *Horn Book* (February 1978): 56.
Jackson, Jane B. *KLIATT* (Fall 1979): 10, 12.
Kirkus Reviews, 15 September 1977, 991.
Manna, Tony. *ALAN Review* (Fall 1979).
Milton, Joyce. *New York Times Book Review*, 30 October 1977, 34.
Publishers Weekly, 11 July 1977, 81.
Silver, Linda. *School Library Journal* (November 1977): 61.

The Great Interactive Dream Machine

Burns, Connie Tyrrell. *School Library Journal*. www.Amazon.com.
Kirkus Reviews, 1996. http://clcd.odyssi.com.
Litton, Joyce A. *ALAN Review* (Spring 1997): 34.
Phelan, Carolyn. *Booklist*, 1 September 1996, 131.
Publishers Weekly, 2 September 1996, 131.
Voice of Youth Advocates (April 1997): 46.

Here Lies the Librarian

Burns, Connie Tyrrell. *School Library Journal*, 1 April 2006, 146.
Kirkus Reviews, 1 March 2006, 237.
Leggett, Karen. *Children's Literature*. http://clcd.odyssi.com.
Lempke, Susan Dove. *Horn Book* (May–June 2006): 324.
Petruso, Stephanie L. *Voice of Youth Advocates* (February 2006): 479.
Publisher's Weekly, 30 January 2006, 70.
Zvirin, Stephanie. *Booklist*, 1 March 2006, 91.

"The Kiss in the Carryon Bag"

Ching, Alison. *School Library Journal* (May 2003): 151.

The Last Safe Place on Earth

Amazon.com.
Dishnow, Ruth E. *Voice of Youth Advocates* (February 1995): 340.
Edwards, Carol A. *School Library Journal* (April 1995): 154.
Miller, Donna Pool. *Book Report* (March/April 1995): 39.
Mollineaux, William R. *ALAN Review* (Winter 1996), 27.
Publisher's Weekly, 19 December 1994, 55.
Rochman, Hazel. *Booklist*, 15 January 1995, 913.

London Holiday

Connally, Molly. *School Library Journal* (August 1998): 197.
Kirkus Reviews, 1998. www.Amazon.com.
Marlowe, Kimberly B. *New York Times Book Review*, 16 August 1998, 17.
Marquis, Jill. Amazon.com.
Mellett, Elizabeth Bryant. *Library Journal*, 1 May 1998, 140.

Publishers Weekly, 11 May 1998, 50.
Truax, Sue Story. *Omaha World Herald*, 21 June 1998, 21.

A Long Way from Chicago

Brommer, Shawn. *School Library Journal* (October 1998): 144.
Flynn, Kitty. *Horn Book* (November–December 1998): 738–39.
Kirkus Reviews, 1998. http://clcd.odyssi.com.
Publishers Weekly, 6 July 1998, 61.
Rochman, Hazel. *Booklist*, 1 September 1998, 113.
Salluzzo, Sharon. *Children's Literature*. http://clcd.odyssi.com.
Voice of Youth Advocates (December 1998): 358.

Lost in Cyberspace

Appleby, Bruce C. *ALAN Review* (Spring 1996): 29.
Connor, Anne. *School Library Journal* (September 1995): 202.
Evans, Terri. *Voice of Youth Advocates* (April 1996): 43.
Lieberman, Jan. *Children's Literature*. http://clcd.odyssi.com.
Phelan, Carolyn. *Booklist*, 15 October 1995, 402.
Publishers Weekly, 2 September 1996, 131.

Love and Death at the Mall: Teaching and Writing for
the Literate Young

Gallo, Donald R. *ALAN Review* (Fall 1994). http://scholar.lib.vt.edu/ejournals/
    ALAN.
Regenbogen, Sally. *ALAN Review* (Spring 1995). http://scholar.lib.vt.edu/
    ejournals/ALAN.

Mindscapes: Poems for the Real World

Booklist, 15 July 1971, 952.
Clemons, Walter. *New York Times Book Review*, 27 June 1971, 8.
Dorsey, Margaret A. *Library Journal*, 15 June 1971, 2140.
Kirkus Reviews, 1 March 1971, 244.

Monster Night at Grandma's House

French, Janet. *School Library Journal* (September 1977): 113.
Kirkus Reviews, 1 March 1977, 485.

Publishers Weekly, 13 June 1977, 107.

Stein, Ruth M. *Language Arts* (January 1978): 45–46.

New York Time

Branch, Susan. *Library Journal*, 1 February 1981, 370.

Howard, Jane. *Mademoiselle*, March 1981, 70.

Kirkus Reviews, 1 January 1981, 35.

Martin, Stoddard. "Knights in Blue Denim," *Times Literary Supplement*, 21 August 1981, 966.

Publishers Weekly, 23 January 1981, 120.

Waters, Kate. *School Library Journal* (March 1981): 161–62.

Zvirin, Stephanie. *Booklist*, 1 July 1981, 1388.

On the Wings of Heroes

Bock, Lee. *School Library Journal* (April 2007): 146.

Bush, Elizabeth. *Washington Post*, 22 April 2007, BW11.

Cart, Michael. *Booklist*, 1 December 2006, 48.

DiOrio, Geri. *Voice of Youth Advocates* (April 2007): 54.

Fogelman, Sheldon. *Publishers Weekly*, 8 January 2007, 52.

Kirkus Reviews, 1 January 2007.

Past Perfect, Present Tense

Benson, Linda. *VOYA* (June 2004): 134.

Carter, Betty. *Horn Book* (March–April 2004): 187.

Dobson, Stephanie L. *Library Media Connection* (November–December 2004): 71.

Hoth, Karen. *School Library Journal* (April 2004): 160.

Hubert, Jennifer. Amazon.com.

Kirkus Reviews, 15 February 2004, 183.

Publishers Weekly, 27 March 2006, 81–82.

Rochman, Hazel. *Booklist*, 1 April 2004, 1361.

Pictures That Storm inside My Head: Poems for the Inner You

Booklist, 1 December 1976, 532–33.

Marks, Sarajean. *School Library Journal* (May 1977): 71.

Sorensen, Marilou. *Deseret News* (Fall 1981).

Princess Ashley

Anton, Denise A. *School Library Journal* (August 1987): 97.
Kirkus Reviews, 1 May 1987, 723–24.
Meyer, Carolyn. *Los Angeles Times*, 11 July 1987.
Publishers Weekly, 29 May 1987, 79.
School Library Journal (December 1987): 38.
Wilson, Evie. *Voice of Youth Advocates* (June 1987): 82.

"Priscilla and the Wimps"

Campbell, Patty. *Wilson Library Bulletin* (January 1985): 341.

Remembering the Good Times

Bodart, Joni. *Voice of Youth Advocates*, 15 June 1985, 134.
Brewbaker, Jim. *ALAN Review* (Winter 1987): 33.
Flowers, Ann A. *Horn Book* (July–August 1985): 457–58.
Gregory, Kristiana. *Los Angeles Times Book Review* 10 August 1986.
Leibold, Cynthia K. *School Library Journal* (April 1985): 99.
Oran, Mary R. *Book Report* (September–October 1985).
Publishers Weekly, 17 May 1985, 118.
Rochman, Hazel. *Booklist*, 1 March 1985, 945.
Skenazy, Lenore. *Advertising Age*, 18 April 1985, 13.

Representing Super Doll

Alexander, Jean. *Washington Post Book World*, 10 November 1974, 8.
Booklist, 1 October 1974, 158–59.
Publishers Weekly, 9 September 1974, 68.
Sutherland, Zena. *Bulletin of the Center for Children's Books* (November 1974): 51.
Wheatley, Bonnie R. *School Library Journal* (October 1974): 120.

The River between Us

Berman, Matt. *Times-Picayune*, 2 November 2003, 7.
Burns, Connie Tyrrell. *School Library Journal* (September 2003): 218.
Bush, Elizabeth. *The Bulletin of the Center for Children's Books* (November 2003).
Gilson, Nancy. *Columbus Dispatch*, 11 September 2003, 11.
Hawkes, Lynda. *Reading Teacher* (November 2004): 291.

Kirkus Reviews, 15 August 2003, 1077.
Perri, Lynne. *USA Today*, 30 October 2003, 7D.
Publishers Weekly, 9 May 2005, 73.
Publishers Weekly, 14 July 2003, 77.
Rochman, Hazel. *Booklist*, 15 September 2003, 239.
Sieruta, Peter D. *Horn Book* (September–October 2003): 616–17.
Sullivan, Ed. *Library Media Connection* (January 2004): 66.
Tilottson, Laura. *Book Links* (January 2004): 15.
Voice of Youth Advocates (October 2003): 317.
Ward, Elizabeth. *Washington Post*, 7 December 2003, T7.
Wilde, Susan. *Children's Literature.* http://clcd.odyssi.com.

Secrets of the Shopping Mall

Campbell, Patty. *Wilson Library Bulletin* (October 1979): 12–13.
Davidson, Dave, et al. *English Journal* (May 1980): 94–95.
Foster, Joan. *Danbury News-Times*, 3 February 1980.
Kay, Marilyn. *School Library Journal* (November 1979): 92.
Kirkus Reviews, 15 October 1979, 1213.
McBroom, Gerry. *ALAN Review* (Spring 1980): 19.
Sutherland, Zena. *Bulletin of the Center for Children's Books* (February 1980): 115.

"Shadows"

Teabert, Lola H. *Voice of Youth Advocates* (February 1988): 284–85.

"Shotgun Cheatham's Last Night above Ground"

Kirkus Reviews, 1997. Amazon.com.

Sounds and Silences: Poetry for Now

Booklist, 1 November 1970, 224.
Christian Science Monitor, 27 January 1971.
Conner, John W. *English Journal* (September 1971): 829–30.
Saturday Review, 19 September 1970, 35.
Seacord, Laura F. *Library Journal*, 15 November 1970, 4058.

"The Special Powers of Blossom Culp"

Rochman, Hazel. *Booklist*, 15 April 1995, 1497.

Strays like Us

Brabander, Jennifer M. *Horn Book* (May–June 1998): 348.
Budin, Miriam Lang. *School Library Journal* (May 1998): 147.
Davenport, Stephen. *Journal of Adolescent and Adult Literacy* (December 1999–January 2000): 387.
Foster, Hal. *ALAN Review* (Fall 2000). http://scholar.lib.vt.edu/ejournals/ALAN.
Ginsberg, Sherri Forgash. *KLIATT* (September 2000).
Kirkus Reviews, 1998. http://clcd.odyssi.com.
Petrini, Catherine. *Children's Literature*. http://clcd.odyssi.com.
Publishers Weekly, 13 April 1998, 76.
Rochman, Hazel. *Booklist*, 1 April 1998, 1325.
Voice of Youth Advocates (June 1998): 124.

The Teacher's Funeral: A Comedy in Three Parts

Baker, Deirdre. *Toronto Star*, 24 October 2004, Entertainment.
Book Links (January 2005): 13.
Flint-Ferguson, Janis. *KLIATT* (September 2004).
Galvin, Jennifer. *Boston Herald*, 19 September 2004, A22.
Gilson, Nancy. *Columbus Dispatch*, 28 October 2004, 13.
Green, Judy. *Sacramento Bee*, 19 December 2004, L3.
Jones, Patrick. *Voice of Youth Advocates* (December 2004): 392.
Kirkus Reviews, 1 October 2004, 966.
Phelan, Carolyn. *Booklist*, 1 October 2004, 326.
Publisher's Weekly, 1 November 2004, 63.
Richardson, David L. *Reading Today* (August–September 2005): 28.
Riley, Susan. *School Library Journal* (November 2004): 152.
Sieruta, Peter D. *Horn Book* (September–October 2004): 595
Washington Post, 24 October 2004, T11.

This Family of Women

Block. Marylaine. *Library Journal*, 15 February 1983, 413–14.
Clancy, Cathy. *School Library Journal* (May 1983): 97.
Kirkus Reviews, 1 February 1983, 142–43.
McGowan, Sarah. *Best Sellers* (May 1983): 44–45.

Sucher, Mary. *ALAN Review* (Spring 1984): 33.
Zvirin, Stephanie. *Booklist*, 1 February 1983, 698.

"The Three-Century Woman"

Kirkus Reviews, 1999. See Amazon.com
Perkins, Linda. *Booklist*, 15 September 1999, 252.
Scotto, Barbara. *Library Journal* (December 1999): 142.

Those Summer Girls I Never Met

Bradburn, Frances. *Wilson Library Bulletin* (February 1989): 5.
Bush, Margaret A. *Horn Book* (January–February 1989): 79.
Kirkus Reviews, 15 August 1988, 1246.
Publishers Weekly, 12 August 1988, 462.
Rochman, Hazel. *Booklist*, 1 October 1988, 259.
Sutton, Roger. *Bulletin of the Center for Children's Books* (September 1988): 17.

Through a Brief Darkness

Fisher, Margery. "Fashion in Adventure." *Growing Point* (April 1976): 2844–48. See
    298 in *Contemporary Literary Criticism*, vol. 21, ed. Sharon R. Gunton. Detroit:
    Gale Research, 1982.
Junior Bookshelf (October 1976): 183.
Kirkus Reviews, 1 December 1973, 1314.
Sullivan, Peggy. *School Library Journal* (February 1974): 72.

Unfinished Portrait of Jessica

Blubaugh, Penny. *Voice of Youth Advocates* (October 1991): 230.
Bushman, John H., and Kay Parks Bushman. *English Journal* (April 1992): 85.
Monseau, Virginia. *ALAN Review* (Spring 1992): 27.
Rochman, Hazel. *Booklist*, 15 September 1991, 137.
Sutherland, Zena, *Bulletin of the Center for Children's Books* (September 1991): 18.
Whitehurst, Lucinda Snyder. *School Library Journal* (August 1991): 195.

Voices after Midnight

Bush, Margaret A. *Horn Book* (November 1989): 776.
Cart, Michael. *School Library Journal* (September 1989): 276.

Elleman, Barbara. *Booklist*, 1 October 1989, 353.
Feicht, Sylvia. *Book Report* (November–December 1989): 46.
Hearne, Betsy. *Bulletin of the Center for Children's Books* (October 1989): 41.
MacRae, Cathi. *Wilson Library Bulletin* (November 1989): 96–97.
Publishers Weekly, 29 September 1989, 69.

"Waiting for Sebastian"

Publishers Weekly, 8 June 1998, 61.

A Year Down Yonder

Campbell, Patty. Amazon.com.
Dillon, Douglas K. *Book Report* (May–June 2001): 61.
Flynn, Kitty. *Horn Book* (November–December 2000): 761–62.
Gullickson, Sheila. *ALAN Review* (Spring–Summer 2001): 35.
Jones, Trevelyn E., Luann Toth, Barbara Auerbach, Darryl Grabarek, Jeanne Leiboff, and Gerry Larson. *School Library Journal* (September 2000): 236.
Lesesne, Teri. *Voice of Youth Advocates* (December 2000): 360.
Publisher's Weekly, 25 September 2000, 118.
Rochman, Hazel. *Booklist*, 15 October 2000, 436.
Williamson, Courtney. *Christian Science Monitor*, 25 January 2001, 21.

Index

About the Authors

Donald R. Gallo is professor of English, *emeritus*, at Central Connecticut State University and is the nation's foremost anthologist of short stories for young adults. Among his award-winning anthologies are *Sixteen*, *No Easy Answers*, *On the Fringe*, *Destination Unexpected*, *What Are You Afraid Of?* and *Owning It*. He is also the coauthor (with Sarah K. Herz) of *From Hinton to Hamlet: Building Bridges between Young Adult Literature and the Classics* (2005), a former columnist for the *English Journal*, author of numerous articles and book chapters, and the recipient of the ALAN Award for outstanding contributions to young adult literature. He has interviewed more than fifty notable authors for the Authors4Teens website.

Wendy J. Glenn is an associate professor in the Department of Curriculum and Instruction in the Neag School of Education at the University of Connecticut. In her role as coordinator of English education, she teaches undergraduate and graduate courses in the theories and methods of teaching language, literature, and composition. She is the author of *Sarah Dessen: From Burritos to Box Office* (Scarecrow, 2005) and coeditor of *Portrait of a Profession: Teachers and Teaching in the 21st Century* (2005). She has published articles in the *ALAN Review*, *English Journal*, *Journal of Adolescent and Adult Literacy*, *SIGNAL*, *Teacher Education Quarterly*, and *Peremena/Thinking Classroom*. Her authored book chapters appear in *Censored Books: Critical Viewpoints*, vol. 2 (Scarecrow, 2002), *Beyond the Boundaries: A Transdisciplinary Approach to Teaching and Learning* (2003), *Boys, Girls, and the Myths of Literacies/Learning* (in press), and *Interdisciplinary Assess-*

ment (2008). She currently serves on the editorial review boards of the *ALAN Review* and the *Journal of Literacy Research*, is an ALAN Executive Board member, and works as "Literature and Literary Analysis" section editor for the *Journal of Literacy Research*.